Mission-Oriented Innovation Policies for Net Zero

HOW CAN COUNTRIES IMPLEMENT MISSIONS TO ACHIEVE CLIMATE TARGETS?

OECD
BETTER POLICIES FOR BETTER LIVES

Please cite this publication as:
OECD (2024), *Mission-Oriented Innovation Policies for Net Zero: How Can Countries Implement Missions to Achieve Climate Targets?*, OECD Publishing, Paris, https://doi.org/10.1787/5efdbc5c-en.

ISBN 978-92-64-64045-0 (print)
ISBN 978-92-64-81498-1 (PDF)
ISBN 978-92-64-58249-1 (HTML)
ISBN 978-92-64-96231-6 (epub)

Photo credits: Cover design by Sylvain Fraccola, Directorate for Science, Technology and Innovation.

Corrigenda to OECD publications may be found at: https://www.oecd.org/en/publications/support/corrigenda.html.

Foreword

The OECD report on Mission-oriented policies for Net Zero arrives at a critical moment. As more countries adopt mission-oriented innovation policies (MOIPs) to address urgent challenges such as climate change, the need for clear evidence of their effectiveness has never been more pressing. While still in the early stages of implementation, MOIPs are already under scrutiny to demonstrate their impact and added value compared to traditional approaches. This report aims to address that gap, providing insights from 101 net-zero missions and 17 in-depth case studies to assess how well MOIPs support national greenhouse gas emissions reduction commitments.

MOIPs have introduced a new approach to tackling large-scale challenges by fostering the collective development of ambitious objectives, aligning their plans on these objectives and moving together towards their realisation. This report highlights the progress made by net-zero missions. Over the last five years of intense implementation of and learning on missions, the leadership of Science, Technology, and Innovation (STI) authorities has been crucial in these missions, convening diverse stakeholders to align efforts.

However, many of these missions still face obstacles, such as a lack of clear directions, persisting siloes, limited joint-action, and unfit evaluation. Furthermore, while missions tend to benefit from more stable, long-term funding than traditional STI initiatives, their resources are often fragmented. To fully unlock their potential, dedicated multi-annual funding is essential to incentivise partners, fill gaps, and enhance portfolio management. Furthermore, private sector engagement remains underdeveloped, requiring new funding mechanisms and financial models to raise the necessary capital for large-scale implementation.

These issues highlight the need for deeper change, not only of the missions themselves but also of the wider systems in which they are embedded, including for instance the structure of incentives, budgeting mechanisms, agencies capabilities and practices.

Going forward, a major challenge remains: securing stronger commitments from sectoral and financial partners to scale up and implement solutions. Missions must ensure they are connected to national climate and industrial policy funds and other large sustainability resources to bridge the final gap from innovation to large-scale deployment.

Overcoming obstacles will require a new generation of MOIPs – ones that are truly transformative and equipped with the necessary tools, resources, and collaborations to meet national and global targets.

Acknowledgements

This report was drafted by Philippe Larrue, lead for the work on mission-oriented innovation policy under the aegis of the OECD Committee for Scientific and Technological Policy (CSTP). Valuable fieldwork support was provided by Bora Kim, Rebecca Santos (both from the Directorate for Science, Technology and Innovation, OECD, at the time of their contribution) and Charles McIvor (Directorate for Science, Technology and Innovation, OECD).

This report complements and deepens Chapter 5 of the *OECD Science, Technology and Innovation Outlook 2023* on mission-oriented innovation policy. It includes numerous examples drawn from case studies of net zero missions. These examples have been reviewed by the authorities responsible for those specific initiatives. Detailed information on most of the mission-oriented innovation policy initiatives covered in this report are available on the MOIP online Toolkit (https://stip.oecd.org/moip).

The author would like to thank the Austrian Federal Ministry of Education, Science and Research (BMBWF) for its financial and technical support to this strand of work. Many thanks also to all the members of the project steering group (see Annex F) whose support, ideas and experience have been instrumental throughout the project and, for many of them, since the inception of CSTP work on mission-oriented innovation policies in 2019.

The authors are grateful to Kyriakos Vogiatzis (DSTI) for his secretarial assistance and to Sylvain Fraccola (DSTI) for his communications and publication support. Special thanks are given to Jennifer Allain for her editorial contributions.

Finally, the project has benefited from numerous interactions with policymakers, researchers, stakeholders, and OECD colleagues (not least from the Mission Action Lab) through various events, interviews, and meetings. The details of the data and information collected during these interactions are available on the online knowledge platform for missions (the OECD MOIP Online Toolkit – https://stip.oecd.org/moip).

Table of contents

Tables

Figures

Boxes

Abbreviations and acronyms

ACCC	Atmosphere and Climate Competence Centre
ARPA-E	Advanced Research Projects Agency-Energy (United States)
AS	Acceleration Strategy (France)
BMK	Federal Ministry for Climate Action, Environment, Energy, Mobility, Innovation and Technology (Austria)
CCSU	Carbon capture, storage or utilisation
CDTI	Centre for the Development of Industrial Technology (Spain) *Centro Para el Desarrollo Tecnológico Industrial*
CO_2	Carbon dioxide
CSIRO	Commonwealth Scientific & Industrial Research Organisation (Australia)
CSTP	Committee for Scientific and Technological Policy
DARPA	Defense Advanced Research Projects Agency (United States)
DG	Directorate-General
EERC	Energy Earthshot Research Centers (United States)
EU	European Union
EUR	Euro
GHG	Greenhouse gas
M&E	Monitoring and evaluation
MMIP	Multiannual mission innovation programme
MOIP	Mission-oriented innovation policy
MPM	Mission portfolio management
NRC	National Research Council (Canada)
OECD	Organisation for Economic Co-operation and Development
PEPR	Priority research programmes and equipment (France) *Programmes et équipements prioritaires de recherche*
R&D	Research and development
RTO	Research and technology organisation
SFI	Science Foundation Ireland
SIA	Strategic Innovation Area (Sweden)
SIP	Strategic innovation programme
STI	Science, technology and innovation
STIO	Science, Technology and Innovation Outlook
TRL	Technology readiness level
UKRI	UK Research and Innovation
USD	United States dollar
VTT	Technical Research Centre of Finland

Executive summary

Conducting thorough analyses of the effectiveness of missions at a critical milestone of this policy approach

Mission-oriented innovation policies (MOIPs) have reached a critical juncture. While still in the early stages of implementation, these policies are already under intense scrutiny to demonstrate their impact and effectiveness. As more countries adopt MOIPs, there remains limited anecdotal evidence on the effectiveness of different designs and practices. Against this backdrop, this report leverages a unique database of 101 "net zero missions" and 17 in-depth case studies to assess the added value of MOIPs in supporting national greenhouse gas emissions reduction commitments, compared to traditional science, technology and innovation (STI) policy approaches.

Setting ambitious goals, but lacking direction

MOIPs encourage the collective development of broad, ambitious goals, engaging a wide array of actors across different sectors. However, despite criticisms of being overly top-down, most missions remain largely bottom-up in practice. Their objectives often lack focus and their target, if any, non-measurable. Their strategic agenda and roadmap are critical in setting negotiated pathways to achieve these objectives but remain indicative and are not systematically used to monitor the progress of their portfolio of activities. To realise their ambitions, **missions need to become more outcome-focused, with clear targets and timelines, including intermediate milestones**.

Engaging actors and committing resources beyond science, technology and innovation

In almost all cases, STI authorities have taken the lead on missions, acting as champions from the outset. They have successfully convened at the "mission table" diverse actors – including policy makers, regulators and stakeholders from sectors like transport and energy – around a common agenda to align their investment and exchange information on progress. Unlike traditional interministerial and cross-sectoral strategies, which often lack actionable mechanisms and dedicated budgets, missions are associated with specific governance structures and tailored interventions designed to achieve their objectives. However, the participation of sectoral policy and regulatory authorities in the mission's governance bodies to set mission agendas and align plans has not yet been confirmed by significant commitments in the form of financial resources or mobilisation of their interventions to support the mission portfolio. To significantly "span the boundaries", **missions should incorporate the necessary policy instruments and incentives to scale-up and deploy the solutions they develop**. As missions progress, securing formal connections to the large-scale national climate funds and sustainability transition resources is critical to complete the "last mile" of the innovation process.

Providing missions with dedicated multiannual funding to expand beyond research and innovation

Missions generally benefit from longer term and more stable funding than traditional STI initiatives, and their budgets can compare with or even exceed those of climate research and development programmes of similar scope. However, these resources are still insufficient to extend beyond research, innovation and demonstration. Additionally, the fragmentation of a mission's budget across diverse funding sources hampers its ability to reap its systemic effects and make it contingent on the goodwill of the mission's partners. **A certain level of central, multiannual funding specifically dedicated to the mission is crucial, notably to incentivise partners to allocate resources to specific mission activities, rally new partners, fill potential portfolio gaps, and enable continuous learning and improvement**.

Furthermore, very few innovative financial models and funding instruments have been used in net zero missions to raise private funding. **There is also a need to design and experiment with new innovative funding mechanisms to increase private engagement in and commitment to the missions**.

Improving mission portfolio management for greater impact

Despite their potential, proactive and flexible portfolio management practices necessary to maximise the systemic benefits of missions remain underdeveloped. Mission managers are only beginning to implement practices that exploit the complementarities and synergies between various activities within a consistent portfolio. Barriers to effective portfolio management include a lack of methodologies and criteria for enhancing synergies, inadequate staffing and skills, fragmented funding, conflicting incentives, and restrictive bureaucratic rules. **Overcoming these challenges requires investment in the development of the needed capabilities, tools and methods for proactive portfolio management.** Acknowledging their specific status, **these initiatives should also be granted enhanced strategic flexibility to operate as required to realise their strategic agenda**. For all these tasks, high-level political backing and strong and well-resourced dedicated teams at both the MOIP initiative and individual mission levels are needed.

Facing the three main challenges of net zero missions, but ready to overcome them

Overall, the analysis reveals that most net zero missions produce many of the effects outlined in their theory of action. In most cases, they represent a marked improvement over traditional STI policy mixes in terms of the ambition, scope and intensity of the collaboration needed to collectively address the complex challenge of climate change. However, these achievements will not be sufficient to scale-up and deploy these innovations on the massive scale needed to fulfil national net zero targets. **Missions need to find their way out of three main challenges – or "traps" – that have emerged at the still early stage of this policy approach**:

- The STI Trap: Net zero missions must extend their focus beyond technological innovation.
- The Orientation Trap: Missions must not only provide targets and strategic agendas but also drive meaningful change in activities and behaviours.
- The Policy Trap: Missions need to leverage resources beyond public budgets through greater engagement with private sector resources and capabilities.

Learning our way towards a third generation of missions

These limitations do not invalidate the MOIP approach but instead highlight the need for more fully developed missions, with different designs and additional resources. The vast majority of missions have been launched recently, with only a few years of implementation behind them. **This report's findings call for a new generation of missions that are genuinely transformative, enlisting public actors and policies beyond the STI realm, effecting changes via joint implementation, and crowding in the missions with resources and capabilities from private actors.**

1 The net zero mission imperative

This chapter shows the urgency of the need for a new policy approach to leverage the potential of research and innovation to tackle climate change in a challenging context. It then sets the study within the context of recent OECD work.

Persisting deviations from scenarios that would keep the world within an acceptable level of global warming combined with greater awareness that traditional policy and governance frameworks are inadequate to close this gap are making it increasingly urgent to find solutions to this global challenge. This study assesses the potential of mission-oriented policies to help countries meet their net zero commitments.

The system transformation imperative

It becomes clearer every day that "change-as-usual" is no longer an option to tackle systemic societal challenges such as climate change. Aside from the slowdown caused by the COVID-19 pandemic and current uncertainties due to geopolitical tensions, clean energy transitions have accelerated in recent years, driven by bold policies (IEA, 2024[1]). An increasing range of country-specific innovation support measures has helped drive the costs of low-carbon technologies down and increase their performances, allowing significant progress in areas such as buildings or transportation (IPCC, 2023[2]). However, in a great majority of countries, meeting 2030 and 2050 greenhouse gas (GHG) emissions reduction targets will require progress that is of a greater order of magnitude and on a much broader sectoral scope than what has been achieved in recent decades. What is at stake to achieve net zero in due time is not accelerating countries' current GHG emissions reduction trajectories but transforming current socio-economic systems. Figure 1.1 shows the logic behind this argument. The remainder of this section will develop this idea.

Figure 1.1. The system transformation imperative

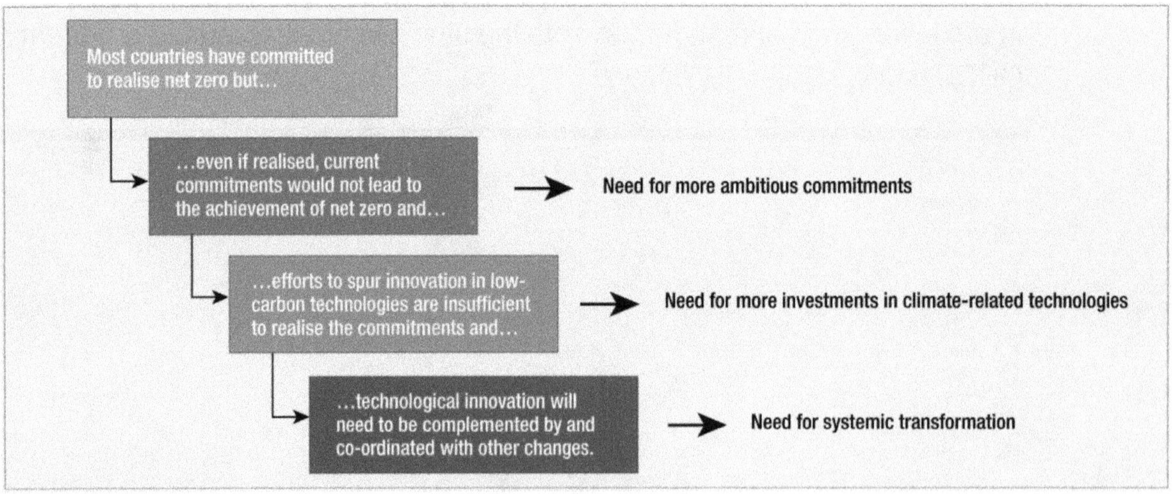

Ambitious but insufficient and ill-defined commitments

Since the Paris Agreement in 2015 and as of March 2024, 110 countries have pledged a net zero target; of these 96 are aiming to reach this target by 2050 or before, accounting for 85% of global carbon emissions (OECD, 2024[3]). However, in most cases, these formal commitments do not meet the minimum level of operational requirements for these strategies to be credible or effective (Net Zero Tracker et al., 2023[4]) and are not binding (OECD, 2023[5]). Most are missing crucial information, not least regarding how these targets are intended to be met and which main pathways and solutions are envisaged (Jeudy-Hugo, Lo Re and Falduto, 2021[6]).[1] Furthermore, even in the unlikely case that all countries implement their pledges and continue at the same pace until 2100, global warming is likely to be around 2.4°C (OECD, 2023[5]).

Climate actions (and results…) are not aligned with commitments

Having set their commitments and targets, most countries are currently turning to the task of translating their net zero commitments into concrete actions that involve immediate decisions. However, current climate actions fall significantly short of what would be needed to achieve these targets (World Resources Institute, 2023[7]). OECD work highlights the decline in the rate of innovations related to emissions reductions since 2012,[2] as measured by patenting trends (Cervantes et al., 2023[8]). This decrease is concomitant with a stagnation of concrete climate policy measures across OECD countries since 2011, following a strong increase from 2000 to 2011, as measured by the OECD Environmental Policy Stringency index (Kruse et al., 2022[9]). While the amount of public investment in research and development (R&D) in low-carbon energy has increased since 2015 and represents the bulk of public spending in energy R&D (IEA, 2022[10]), this spending is still far below that consented by governments after the 1974 and oil shocks (OECD, 2023[11]).

Transition pathways towards net zero require technological and *societal changes*

While currently available technologies can achieve the needed emissions reduction targets of the 2030 commitments (45% reduction from 2010 levels), the net zero objective for 2050 will require significant new advances and a scaling up of technologies that are still in laboratories or at prototype or demonstration stage (IEA, 2021[12]).[3] Research and innovation activities will, therefore, be of paramount importance for all net zero pathways that aim to contain global warming while preserving some level of economic and social progress.

However, the needed changes span far beyond the technological realm and concern user and consumer behaviours (e.g. commuting, eating), manufacturing and maintenance skills, modes of production, infrastructure and equipment, new sourcing of materials, regulatory change, and ways of organising social systems at different levels (buildings, cities, regions, countries). Against this backdrop, rapid progress in the last decade, notably in energy technologies (for instance, in advanced battery technologies – after centuries of rather slow advances punctuated by some rare breakthroughs), can be misleading, as it supports the idea that technical change alone will bring the needed solutions.

Different net zero pathways are still available for a few years, but they will all involve deep national and sectoral system transformations

Changes in a wide range of domains will, therefore, have to co-evolve in a coherent way and toward similar objectives if countries are to transition towards net zero economies. Despite the continuous avalanche of bleak evidences – including regarding the likelihood of crossing climate tipping points even at a lower level of warming (Lenton et al., 2019[13]; OECD, 2022[14]), experts from the Intergovernmental Panel on Climate Change still affirm that different pathways in relation to a 1.5°C global warming scenario are still available.

The window of opportunity to enable climate resilient development is however rapidly narrowing, calling for rapid and deep greenhouse gas emission reductions (IPCC, 2023[2]).The commonality of all pathways and scenarios to transition towards net zero is that they can be realised only at the price of profound transformations of existing systems, be they at the sectoral (IEA, 2021[12]) or national level (The Shift Project, 2022[15]).

New policy approach for addressing complex and ambitious commitments

Established national policy mixes are too fragmented to lead to net zero

Since the 1980s, science, technology and innovation (STI) policies have primarily focused on correcting individual market failures, despite their variations due to national contexts and political configurations. This emphasis on fixing market failures was influenced by New Public Management's impact on political and administrative spheres, which has led to policy devolution and specialisation, resulting in a fragmented policy landscape (Mazzucato, 2016[16]). In several areas, government intervention frameworks consist of multiple policy instruments, each with different objectives, functions, funding sources and executive organisations (ministries, agencies) with specialised professional staff. This approach has resulted in increased efficiency and effectiveness, with gradual improvements of these instruments through evaluation, learning and exchange among policy makers. It has also benefitted from the expertise accumulated by beneficiaries, such as research organisations and firms, on how to best operate and use these instruments (Peters, 2018[17]).

However, policy fragmentation also greatly hinders innovation systems' ability to co-ordinate in a consistent way the multiple changes that are needed to address complex societal challenges such as global warming. It is widely acknowledged that the societal transformation that conditions the achievement of net zero will require a combination of different types of interventions for any given sociotechnical option (D'Arcangelo et al., 2022[18]).

The renewal of proactive innovation and industrial policies: Mission-oriented policies

Awareness of the limitations of prevailing governance and policy frameworks has grown, even among the most traditional policy makers and think tanks. Combined with the urgency to address mounting societal challenges, in the past 10-15 years this has led to a renewed focus on proactive and voluntary innovation policies (Aiginger and Rodrik, 2020[19]).[4] However, this renewal differs from the previous wax and wanes of industrial policy. As the understanding of sustainability crises improved, experts and policy makers increasingly advocated for a new policy approach to address related challenges, which would go beyond a "greening" of traditional industrial policies.

During the first ten years or so, policy experts and practitioners devoted their attention to developing the "terms of reference" of this new policy approach. Among the key genetic traits of the sought-after new policy approach were its purposive and integrated features, in relation to the scale and systemic dimensions of the challenge to be tackled:

- *purposive* to allow gathering willingness, administrative and political power, skills, and financial resources towards some commonly agreed-upon objectives related to a broad challenge
- *integrated* to closely interconnect the different interventions and activities that are needed to address the different complementary facets and components of the challenge.

Pre-empting the traditional critics of top-down policy making stemming from previous experiences such as the US and Japanese pre-competitive consortia or the French "*grand programmes*",[5] additional requirements were that the new policies avoid targeting pre-selected sectors and picking winners and are flexible, agile and clearly linked to potential markets.

Although a few had already identified the shift towards a new "mission-led paradigm" by the end of the 2000s (Gassler, Polt and Rammer, 2008[20]), it was only in the mid-2010s that this quest for a new policy approach crystallised around what became known as mission-oriented innovation policies (MOIPs), named after the popular defence and space missions of the 1960s and 1970s. Relying upon a growing body of literature led by the star economist Mariana Mazzucato, an increasing number of countries have embarked on such an approach under different (often experimental) manners in the last five years. The OECD defines

MOIPs as a co-ordinated package of policy and regulatory measures tailored specifically to mobilise STI to address well-defined objectives related to a societal challenge, within a defined time frame. These measures possibly span different stages of the innovation cycle, from research to demonstration and market deployment; mix supply-push and demand-pull instruments; and cut across various policy fields, sectors and disciplines (Larrue, 2021[21]).

The "missions for net zero" study

Previous OECD work on mission-oriented innovation policies

The OECD started working on MOIPs in 2019 under the aegis of the CSTP. It developed a typology of MOIPs and identified a series of design principles for this policy approach. These analytical inputs were then used to scan the main MOIPs identified at that time (about 40 MOIP initiatives in 2020) in all challenge areas and systematically review and categorise the practices and processes leading the development, co-ordination and implementation of missions. In parallel, more in-depth investigations were performed through "national MOIP studies" in Austria, Japan, Korea and Norway. The results of this work were presented in various reports and an online database structured along the same analytical framework.

Building upon these results, this report focuses on one challenge area to provide a more detailed understanding of the underpinning processes that condition the launch and evolution of these policies and their first results. Box 1.1 presents the rationales for selecting climate change as the focus challenge area.

Box 1.1. Why focus on mission-oriented innovation policies for net zero?

During its first phase (2019-20), the Committee for Scientific and Technological Policy's (CSTP) project on mission-oriented innovation policies (MOIPs) focused on MOIP initiatives irrespective of the challenges they pursued, from reducing cancer fatalities to reducing greenhouse gas (GHG) emissions. Building upon this work, this report focuses on "net zero missions", i.e. missions that aim directly or indirectly to mitigate or adapt to climate change. This approach seeks to refine the understanding of their challenges and opportunities, their practices (related to mission definition, governance and the unfolding of activities) and, as much as possible, their results and the way these are monitored and evaluated.

As the scope of analysis is narrower and consistent, it allows more analytical depth and granularity. In particular, fieldwork and analysis can be conducted at the level of missions, rather than at the upper level of MOIP initiatives (which often include several missions addressing different societal challenges, such as climate change, health, biodiversity, water management, etc.).* This lower level unit of analysis is particularly relevant since MOIPs are expected to create a dedicated (meso-)system of innovation around a specific challenge, with a strategic agenda, a governance structure and a package of interventions that are tailor-made for this challenge.

Furthermore, it enables exploring the influence of a challenge's specific features on the dynamics of the MOIPs to tackle it. These features comprise notably the breadth and intensity of the challenge, its complexity (in relation to its systemic character, whereby potential solutions rely on the interactions between different types of change in various organisations, sectors and disciplines), its contestability (when the problem and/or the solutions at stake are subject to diverging claims, values and framings, conflicts of interest – as defined by Wesseling et al. (2018[22])), and its level uncertainty (when the state of knowledge does not offer clear paths to a solution (Nelson, 2011[23])). This analysis complements previous CSTP work that explored the influence of countries' specific institutional settings (Larrue, 2021[24]; 2021[25]).

Following discussions with the OECD MOIP steering group and in agreement with the CSTP, it was decided to focus on the challenge of global warming. This challenge combines several features that make it a perfect candidate to investigate the added value of the MOIP approach. As argued in the OECD horizontal project "Net Zero+: Climate and Economic Resilience in a Changing World" (OECD, 2023[26]), to fully harness the critical contribution to the net zero challenge, "governments will need to do more than just redirect their science, technology and innovation policies, shifting instead towards a mission-oriented approach to technology development and deployment to ensure that efforts are streamlined across policy areas".

Among the main criteria for choosing the net zero challenge area were notably:

- its level of urgency to find new solutions, as climate change's impacts on people's lives are already significant and rapidly growing
- it is systemic, requiring a combination of several types of changes and innovations
- it lends itself very well to a mission-oriented approach since most countries have adopted clear net zero targets with milestones.

Note: The bulk of the academic work on MOIPs is undertaken at the level of initiatives, not specific missions, which does not allow opening the substantive and political dimensions of these endeavours. The Fraunhofer Institute for Systems and Innovation Research's work on the 12 missions of the German HTS2025 (Roth et al., 2022[27]) is a notable exception.

Objectives of this report

This report aims to assess the added value of an MOIP approach to support countries' efforts to meet their GHG emissions reduction commitments compared to traditional STI policy approaches.

The report lays out conclusions, lessons learnt and recommendations that inform policy makers and their partners about:

- the extent to which and under which conditions MOIPs are better suited than other policy approaches to support countries' efforts towards net zero
- how to design, co-ordinate and implement MOIPs to effectively reduce GHG emissions.

A better understanding of the potential and limitations of this policy approach as well as its enablers and barriers are particularly needed at a time when:

- Countries are actively searching for effective ways to govern and implement their commitments for reducing GHGs as the consequences of climate change become more tangible and devastating every day (extreme climatic events such draughts and floods, deadly heat waves, loss of land space due to rising seas, loss of biodiversity, etc.);
- MOIPs are reaching a pivotal time. While most of these policies are still at an early stage, there is already strong political demand to demonstrate results. These initiatives are often highly visible and have raised high expectations (and sometimes larger budgets), which have attracted public and political attention;
- As MOIPs receive an increasing number of criticisms from both research and innovation actors and some academics, there is now more than ever a need for systematic, robust, non-ideologically biased evidence on missions.

References

Aiginger, K. and D. Rodrik (2020), "Rebirth of industrial policy and an agenda for the twenty-first century", *Journal of Industry, Competition and Trade*, Vol. 20, pp. 189-207, https://doi.org/10.1007/s10842-019-00322-3. [19]

Branstetter, L. and M. Sakakibara (2002), "When do research consortia work well and why? Evidence from Japanese panel data", *The American Economic Review*, Vol. 92/1, pp. 143-159, https://www.jstor.org/stable/3083325. [29]

Cervantes, M. et al. (2023), "Driving low-carbon innovations for climate neutrality", *Science, Technology and Industry Policy Papers*, No. 143, OECD Publishing, Paris, https://doi.org/10.1787/8e6ae16b-en. [8]

D'Arcangelo, F. et al. (2022), "A framework to decarbonise the economy", *OECD Economic Policy Papers*, No. 31, OECD Publishing, Paris, https://doi.org/10.1787/4e4d973d-en. [18]

Gassler, H., W. Polt and C. Rammer (2008), "Priority setting in research and technology policy: Historical developments and recent developments", in Nauwelaers, C. and R. Wintjes (eds.), *Innovation Policy in Europe: Measurement and Strategy*, Edward Edgar. [20]

IEA (2024), *World Energy Outlook 2024*, Licence: CC BY 4.0 (report); CC BY NC SA 4.0 (Annex A), https://www.iea.org/reports/world-energy-outlook-2024. [1]

IEA (2022), "Evolution of public low-carbon energy RD&D budget in IEA member countries, 1974-2021", https://www.iea.org/data-and-statistics/charts/evolution-of-public-low-carbon-energy-rd-and-d-budget-in-iea-member-countries-1974-2021 (accessed on 31 August 2023). [10]

IEA (2021), *Net Zero by 2050: A Roadmap for the Global Energy Sector*, OECD Publishing, Paris, https://doi.org/10.1787/c8328405-en. [12]

Jeudy-Hugo, S., L. Lo Re and C. Falduto (2021), "Understanding countries' net-zero emissions targets", *OECD/IEA Climate Change Expert Group Papers*, No. 2021/03, OECD Publishing, Paris, https://doi.org/10.1787/8d25a20c-en. [6]

Kruse, T. et al. (2022), "Measuring environmental policy stringency in OECD countries: An update of the OECD composite EPS indicator", *OECD Economics Department Working Papers*, No. 1703, OECD Publishing, Paris, https://doi.org/10.1787/90ab82e8-en. [9]

Larrue, P. (2021), "Mission-oriented innovation policy in Japan: Challenges, opportunities and future options", *OECD Science, Technology and Industry Policy Papers*, No. 106, OECD Publishing, Paris, https://doi.org/10.1787/a93ac4d4-en. [25]

Larrue, P. (2021), "Mission-oriented innovation policy in Norway: Challenges, opportunities and future options", *OECD Science, Technology and Industry Policy Papers*, No. 104, OECD Publishing, Paris, https://doi.org/10.1787/2e7c30ff-en. [24]

Larrue, P. (2021), "The design and implementation of mission-oriented innovation policies: A new systemic policy approach to address societal challenges", *OECD Science, Technology and Industry Policy Papers*, No. 100, OECD Publishing, Paris, https://doi.org/10.1787/3f6c76a4-en. [21]

Larrue, P. and M. Rebuffet (2008), "Des grands programmes technologiques aux grands projets d'innovation: Les transformations d'un outil de politique technologique", in Lesourne, J. and D. Randet (eds.), *La Recherche et l'Innovation en France*, Odile Jacob. [30]

Lee H., A. (ed.) (2023), *Summary for policy makers*, Intergovernmental Panel on Climate Change, http://www.ipcc.ch/report/ar6/syr/downloads/report/IPCC_AR6_SYR_SPM.pdf. [2]

Lenton, T. et al. (2019), "Climate tipping points – too risky to bet against", *Nature*, https://doi.org/10.1038/d41586-019-03595-0. [13]

Mazzucato, M. (2016), "From market fixing to market-creating: A new framework for innovation policy", *Industry and Innovation*, Vol. 23/2, pp. 140-156, https://doi.org/10.1080/13662716.2016.1146124. [16]

Nelson, R. (2011), "The moon and the ghetto revisited", *Science and Public Policy*, Vol. 38/9, pp. 681-690, https://doi.org/10.1093/scipol/38.9.681. [23]

Net Zero Tracker et al. (2023), *Net Zero Stocktake 2023: Assessing the Status and Trends of Net Zero Target Setting Across Countries; Sub-national Governments and Companies*, Net Zero Tracker et al., https://zerotracker.net/analysis/net-zero-stocktake-2023. [4]

OECD (2024), *International Programme for Action on Climate Dashboard*, web page. [3]

OECD (2023), *Net Zero+: Climate and Economic Resilience in a Changing World*, OECD Publishing, Paris, https://doi.org/10.1787/da477dda-en. [26]

OECD (2023), *OECD Science, Technology and Innovation Outlook 2023: Enabling Transitions in Times of Disruption*, OECD Publishing, Paris, https://doi.org/10.1787/0b55736e-en. [11]

OECD (2023), *The Climate Action Monitor 2022: Helping Countries Advance Towards Net Zero*, OECD Publishing, Paris, https://doi.org/10.1787/43730392-en. [5]

OECD (2022), *Climate Tipping Points: Insights for Effective Policy Action*, OECD Publishing, Paris, https://doi.org/10.1787/abc5a69e-en. [14]

Peters, B. (2018), "The challenge of policy coordination", *Policy Design and Practice*, Vol. 1/1, pp. 1-11, https://doi.org/10.1080/25741292.2018.1437946. [17]

Roth, F. et al. (2022), "Putting mission-oriented innovation policies to work: A case study of the German High-Tech Strategy 2025", *Fraunhofer ISI Discussion Papers Innovation Systems and Policy Analysis*, No. 75, https://www.isi.fraunhofer.de/content/dam/isi/dokumente/cci/innovation-systems-policy-analysis/2022/discussionpaper_75_2022.pdf. [27]

Sakakibara, M. (1997), "Evaluating government-sponsored R&D consortia in Japan: Who benefits and how?", *ELSEVIER Research Policy*, Vol. 26, pp. 447-473, https://doi.org/10.1016/S0048-7333(97)00018-8. [31]

The Economist (2022), "Many countries are seeing a revival of industrial policy", *The Economist*, https://www.economist.com/special-report/2022/01/10/many-countries-are-seeing-a-revival-of-industrial-policy (accessed on 28 July 2022). [28]

The Shift Project (2022), *Plan de transformation de l'économie française*, Odile Jacob, https://ilnousfautunplan.fr/le-plan. [15]

Wesseling, J. et al. (2018), “A framework for mission-oriented innovation policy: Alternative pathways through the problem-solution space”, *Technological Forecasting and Social Change*, Vol. 110, pp. 117-125, https://doi.org/10.31235/osf.io/njahp. [22]

World Resources Institute (2023), *State of Climate Action 2023: Assessing Progress Toward 2030 and 2050*, World Resources Institute, Washington, DC, https://www.wri.org/research/state-climate-action-2023. [7]

Endnotes

[1] For instance, only 60% of commitments include interim targets and 62% are associated with a reporting mechanism.

[2] For all climate-related technologies (but batteries) and almost all major innovating countries.

[3] The International Energy Agency estimates that 50% of the emissions reductions in 2050 would need to come from technologies that are still currently under development, in particular solid-state batteries, hydrogen electrolysers and direct air capture technologies. This ratio is even higher in heavy industry and long-distance transport applications (IEA, 2021[12]).

[4] See also The Economist (2022[28]).

[5] See notably Branstetter and Sakakibara (2002[29]) and Sakakibara (1997[31]) on research consortia and Larrue, P. and M. Rebuffet (2008[30]) on the French *grands programmes*.

2 The underpinning mission-oriented innovation policy analytical framework

This chapter synthetises the analytical framework upon which the new developments presented in the remainder of the report rely. It emphasises the specific characteristics of missions that differentiate them from traditional policy frameworks, notably their integrated nature, from objectives to implementation, as well as their multidimensional and multilevel features. It also presents the different types of missions revolving around these common features.

Since the OECD started working on mission-oriented innovation policies (MOIPs) in 2019, it has followed and deepened the same analytical framework based on the MOIP "design principles" and a typology, which have been further refined in recent years to develop mission implementation support tools, notably a "mission theory of action" and a "mission monitoring tool".

Mission-oriented innovation policies integrate strategy, co-ordination and action to tackle complex societal challenges

The three integrated building blocks of mission-oriented innovation policies

Although they can differ significantly in their design and type of objectives, MOIPs revolve around three building blocks (Figure 2.1.):

1. Strategic orientation: They are oriented toward the achievement of clear objectives, formalised in terms of expected results (not inputs invested or actions to be implemented) and developed collectively.
2. Policy co-ordination: They align the plans of various government actors in charge of different components (e.g., knowledge, technologies, funding, instruments pertaining to different policy fields, regulations) that are essential for achieving the collectively agreed-upon objectives.
3. Policy implementation: They are implemented via a comprehensive mix of policy interventions and various initiatives to support a range of activities, from research to market launch and the formation of the required skills. These packages of interventions are deliberately designed to achieve the policy's objectives. They can include joint implementation initiatives (from joint calls for proposal to co-operative, co-funded schemes and programmes) that bring together multiple partners across policy fields and sectors.

Collective action lies at the core of each of these building blocks: an MOIP involves a collectively developed agenda; a dedicated structure of governance to take and monitor the effects of common or mutually consistent decisions; and, finally, a deliberately designed "joined-up" policy mix. What is unique about MOIPs is not the presence of any of these building blocks taken in isolation (which are found in all STI systems) but rather their integration into a common organisational and institutional framework. Neither a whole-of-government national strategy for green hydrogen nor a high-level cross-ministerial council for industry decarbonisation or a large-scale co-operative programme for a circular economy are sufficient to form an MOIP. For any given challenge, an MOIP, by definition, combines and maintains close bi-directional flows of decisions and information between the three building blocks.

Figure 2.1. The three integrated building blocks of mission-oriented innovation policies

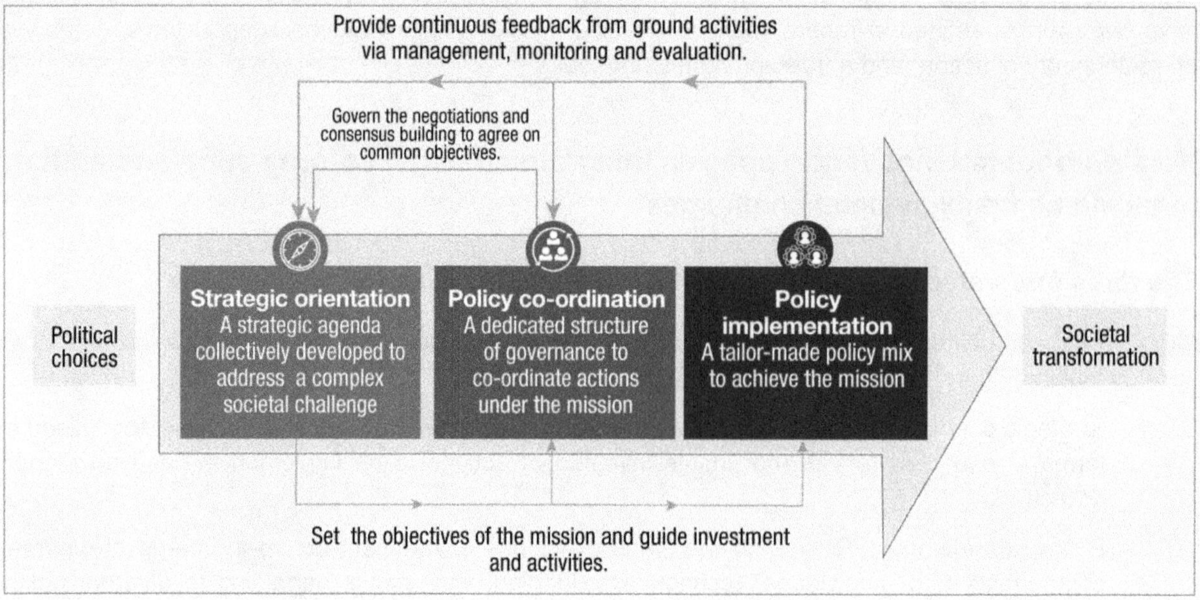

Strategic orientation

The substantive and political issue of the directions of change has been largely absent from STI policy for decades, resulting in broad functional strategic frameworks and neutral and indirect policy measures. The focus on complex and systemic societal challenges and the transformations they require has revealed the "directionality failures" of existing STI systems inherited during this period. As argued by Weber and Rohracher (2012[1]), "transformative change, on the contrary, is intimately linked to the question of direction and requires the setting of collective priorities". The first function of MOIPs is to provide an institutional space in which public and private actors of a challenge community can become aware of their complementarities and interdependencies and set a process for collectively developing objectives and a strategic agenda to solve these challenges.

All missions, therefore, produce sets of well-accepted objectives related to the realisation of the complex challenge they tackle. These "directions for change" are the cornerstone of any mission that set the ground for subsequent collective action. They are developed in very different ways and take various forms. They can be packaged in a catchy and inspiring mission statement (e.g., "reduce emissions from road transport by 50% by 2030") but most often start with very broadly defined challenge areas and are further specified into co-developed strategic agendas as the mission unfolds.

This is certainly where the main misunderstanding regarding MOIPs resides: they are still often characterised as (and criticised for) being top-down, while the definition of their objectives is often mostly bottom-up, involving a wide array of public and private stakeholders. Previous OECD work on MOIPs has revealed that the process of developing mission orientations is gradual and involves progressively refining the objectives. Missions often begin from broad challenges and the bulk of the mission work is, based on these, to collectively develop a strategic agenda that is both consensual and precise enough to guide collective action. Important implications of this observation are that:

- The objectives of the mission are often the result of the mission process itself rather than its starting point.
- The distinction between "top-down" and "bottom-up" missions is blurred; most missions proceed through successive top-down and bottom-up stages.

- Public authorities find a new role in several MOIPs as "moderators". The state often orchestrates the process of co-creating the strategic agenda with little intervention in the actual directional decisions.

The active involvement of mission stakeholders in the definition of the strategic agenda is particularly crucial to ensuring their subsequent engagement in the implementation of the mission. It is also, along with high-level political and administrative back-up, a condition of their legitimacy, which, in turn, can help justify large budget requests and some possible derogations to "policy-as-usual" practices (i.e. multiannual funding, more hands-on project management). It is also instrumental to prepare the acceptance of societal transformation whose potential social impacts may be significant.

MOIPs rely on multiple but rather traditional ways of engaging stakeholders (online consultations, consultation events, etc.). One difference is that they tend to be more systematic and better resourced as they are considered to be a key component of the MOIP approach. More recently, new participatory practices seem to diffuse among missions, notably the common definition of road maps, theory of change and pathways.

> *The main "how-to" conundrums of strategic orientation in missions*
>
> *How to set the adequate level and scope of mission objectives that are both ambitious and realistic?*
>
> *How to combine the solution neutrality of objectives while providing clear directionality to focus collective efforts?*
>
> *How to set firm and credible common objectives while leaving enough flexibility to make them evolve as new information and knowledge are accumulated?*
>
> *How to ensure the high-level political legitimacy of missions while avoiding*
>
> *short-term political interferences and ensuring longevity beyond electoral cycles?*
>
> *How to ensure strong stakeholder involvement in the collective development of the strategic agenda while avoiding mission capture by powerful incumbents?*
>
> *How to engage a wide array of partners while maintaining clear direction and consistency in the objectives and avoiding "mission dilution"?*

Policy co-ordination

As stated by Peters (2018[2]), "attempting to deal with a problem such as climate change or sustainable development requires the involvement of much of government, and hence co-ordination". To tackle such complex and systemic challenges, whether climate change, the reduction of biodiversity or cancer, MOIPs bring together different policy bodies responsible for various stages of the innovation chain (from research to deployment) and different components of innovation systems (such as skills, infrastructure, research and development [R&D], regulations), possibly at different levels of governance (supranational, national, regional, local). This wide set of mission partners uses different types of committees to agree on common objectives, monitor and refine them, align their plans towards these goals, and decide upon needed investments and actions. They vary greatly according to their composition, their mandate (e.g. decision making, monitoring and evaluation, consultation), their level (strategic, operational), and the status of the decisions they take (more or less binding).

Governance bodies (e.g. steering committees, orientation committees, governing boards) and other formal co-ordination mechanisms (such as roundtables) are found at the levels of an MOIP initiative and of each of its missions. At the level of missions, a key complement to these bodies is often a unique mission co-ordinator with strong prerogatives.

Previous analysis based on numerous interviews and workshops with mission leaders has shown that cross-governmental co-ordination is one of the main practical challenges. This is confirmed by a recent survey of mission practitioners and stakeholders, who rank "silo effects" as the highest barrier to a mission's success (OECD and DDC, 2022[3]). MOIP partners strive to work horizontally across administrative silos while navigating vertical funding streams, reporting lines, incentives and mindsets.

To be able to co-ordinate actions, these bodies have set formal or informal rules, defined specific roles for each member, and some have signed formal co-operation and commitment agreements. They are also governed by more "underground" aspects inherent in all collective action, namely power relationships, and competitive games between partners (particularly in terms of the scope of intervention and budget (OECD, 2024[4]).

> ▸ *The main "how-to" conundrums of policy co-ordination in missions*
>
> *How to ensure the consistency of different policy makers' plans across policy sectors and levels of governance in a context characterised by fragmentation, political and administrative turf, conflicting objectives, and compartmentalised funding?*
>
> *How to ensure broad holistic co-ordination across all silos while ensuring sufficient leadership to allow swift and agile decision making within the mission?*
>
> *How to match the scope of the missions that aim to support sustainability transitions and the level of authority of the mission in the government structure (agency, ministry, centre of government)?*

Policy implementation

Once the policy makers and stakeholders in a given challenge area have defined a shared strategic agenda and set governance arrangements to co-ordinate their plans and investments, a mission requires policy integration, i.e. the operational articulation of a consistent and tailor-made package of policy interventions and activities to realise the mission objectives.[1] The degree of integration varies between missions. Some missions function as "one initiative" integrating the different interventions, or at least appear as such to beneficiaries ("one-stop shop missions"), while others only ensure regular operational co-ordination and information exchange meetings between the different responsible policy bodies.

Novel portfolio management practices are essential to successfully integrate the policy interventions and activities. However, these practices require specific skills, mindsets, and human and financial resources to provide hands-on support that significantly differs from traditional arm's-length and formal management. The portfolio manager (most often the mission co-ordinator or leader) must build the portfolio backward from the objectives and make it evolve as new information is unveiled and progress is made. This also requires new management tools and techniques, such as visualisation tools to dynamically map the portfolio. Portfolio management also involves promoting interactions between the different complementary activities of the mission (OECD, 2024[5]).

Despite progress in the evaluation of systemic and complex programmes and policies (or portfolios thereof), current methodologies and frameworks still fall short of providing the resources needed for mission evaluations. Missions require different evaluation perspectives, frameworks, methods, criteria and practices, including the very questions to be asked, the data to be collected and other markers of change. The literature on missions and other types of transition or transformative policies widely acknowledges this need for some renewal in evaluation (Haddad et al., Molas-Gallart et al., 2021). Recent OECD work recommends that mission monitoring and evaluation focus on tracking processes with specific tools to capture the specific additional effects of missions, in addition to the various policy instruments they mobilise. A range of academic and practical works are underway to develop and test these tools and methods (Larrue, Tõnurist and Jonason, 2024[6]).

> *The main "how-to conundrums" of policy implementation in missions*
>
> *How to practically combine different instruments with different funding sources, selection criteria, operating procedures, reporting systems, information systems?*
>
> *How to promote information and knowledge exchange between different instruments and activities to ensure synergies while taking into account confidentiality and competitive relations between some of the actors?*
>
> *How to perform hands-on mission portfolio management in administrations suffering from staff shortages, limited budgets and inadequate skills forged in previous practices?*
>
> *How to ensure the cohesion of the horizontal (cross-departmental) mission teams when all reporting lines and funding streams are vertical (departmental)?*
>
> *How to design monitoring and evaluation processes that ensure mission accountability while recognising their long-term and exploratory nature?*
>
> *How to attribute mission effects and failures to ensure a sense of responsibility and engagement in multi-partner, co-funded, collective missions?*

Mission-oriented innovation policies articulate different levels of interventions to tackle complex systems

MOIPs are multi-level systems, which include an overarching policy framework "hosting" several missions that steer, co-ordinate and integrate existing policy interventions and activities (Figure 2.2):

- Most missions are grouped in a common policy framework: the MOIP initiative. At this level, the directions remain general (e.g., solving the most pressing societal challenges while improving national competitiveness) and functional (i.e. using a mission and transformative approach to solve these challenges). The role of the governance bodies is to select the challenge areas and missions, provide overarching advice, ensure linkages to the political sphere and high-level co-ordination across policy fields, and monitor and evaluate the implementation of the missions. [25] Some support services can also be found at this level to manage budgets, improve and harmonise practices (including by promoting interaction between missions), and set the appropriate framework conditions for their successful realisation.
- Missions are the collective action vehicles focused on a specific challenge, with a corresponding strategic agenda, governance structure and policy mix. It is at this level that actors become aware of their common fate and opportunities for collective action and, consequently, where most systemic effects are produced.
- Policy interventions and activities are the concrete actions undertaken to realise the mission objectives. They pertain to different stages of the innovation chain (from research to scale-up and deployment), components of the underpinning innovation system (from R&D to skills and regulations), and generations of innovative solutions (from the least to the most mature) of various types (technological, organisational, behavioural, social and all possible combinations of these).

Figure 2.2. Mission-oriented innovation policies as multi-level systems: An example of a "mission-oriented innovation policy initiative with three missions"

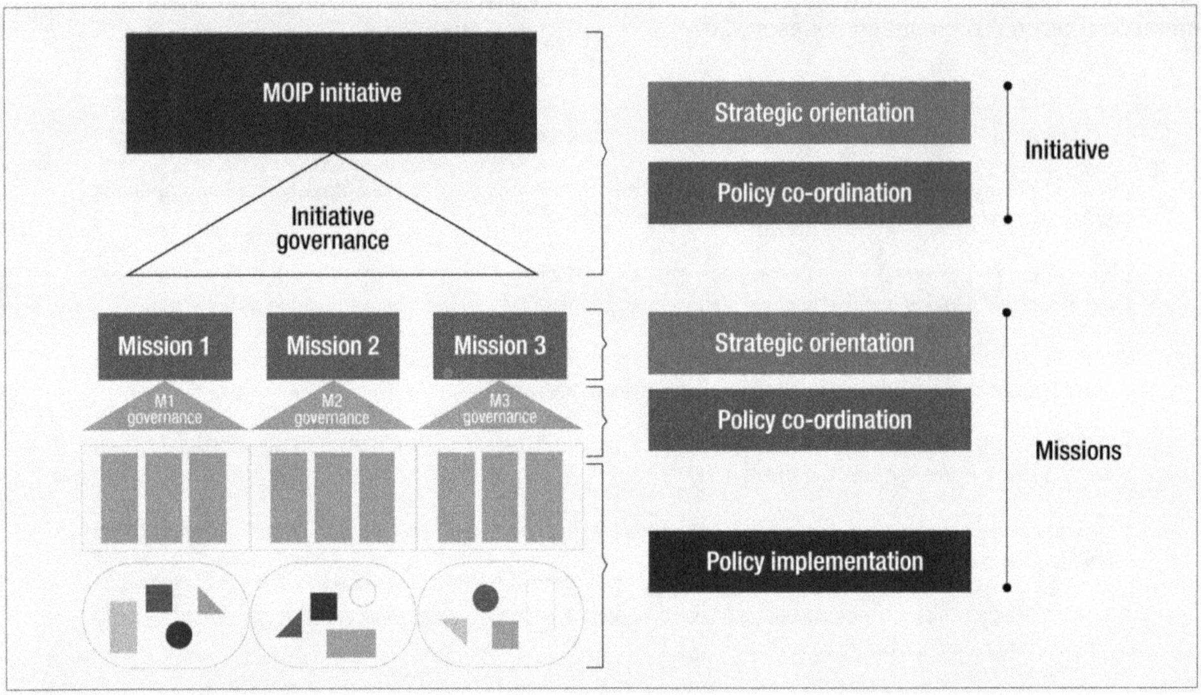

Note: MOIP: mission-oriented innovation policy.

Mission-oriented innovation policies take different forms revolving around common design principles

While MOIP initiatives and missions can have very diverse designs, scales and scopes, they still share fundamental common features.

The mission-oriented innovation policy design principles

The three building blocks can be further broken down into "design principles". They define the features that are anticipated in MOIP initiatives that match the OECD definition. They apply to an MOIP ideal type, as very few initiatives – if any – will meet every criterion. In reality, these principles are often mixed and adapted according to the vast differences in MOIP designs, influenced by country-specific factors, thematic nuances and other variables. While these design principles provide a normative framework to guide policy direction, they remain versatile, accommodating various types of initiatives tailored to different mission and governance contexts.

The design principles pertaining to the three building blocks are:

1. strategic orientation: directionality and intentionality, legitimacy, flexibility
2. policy co-ordination: horizontality and verticality, novelty, demand articulation
3. policy implementation: policy-mix consistency, fundability, evaluability and reflexivity.

Figure 2.3 presents a succinct definition of each design principle.

Figure 2.3. Mission-oriented innovation policy design principles

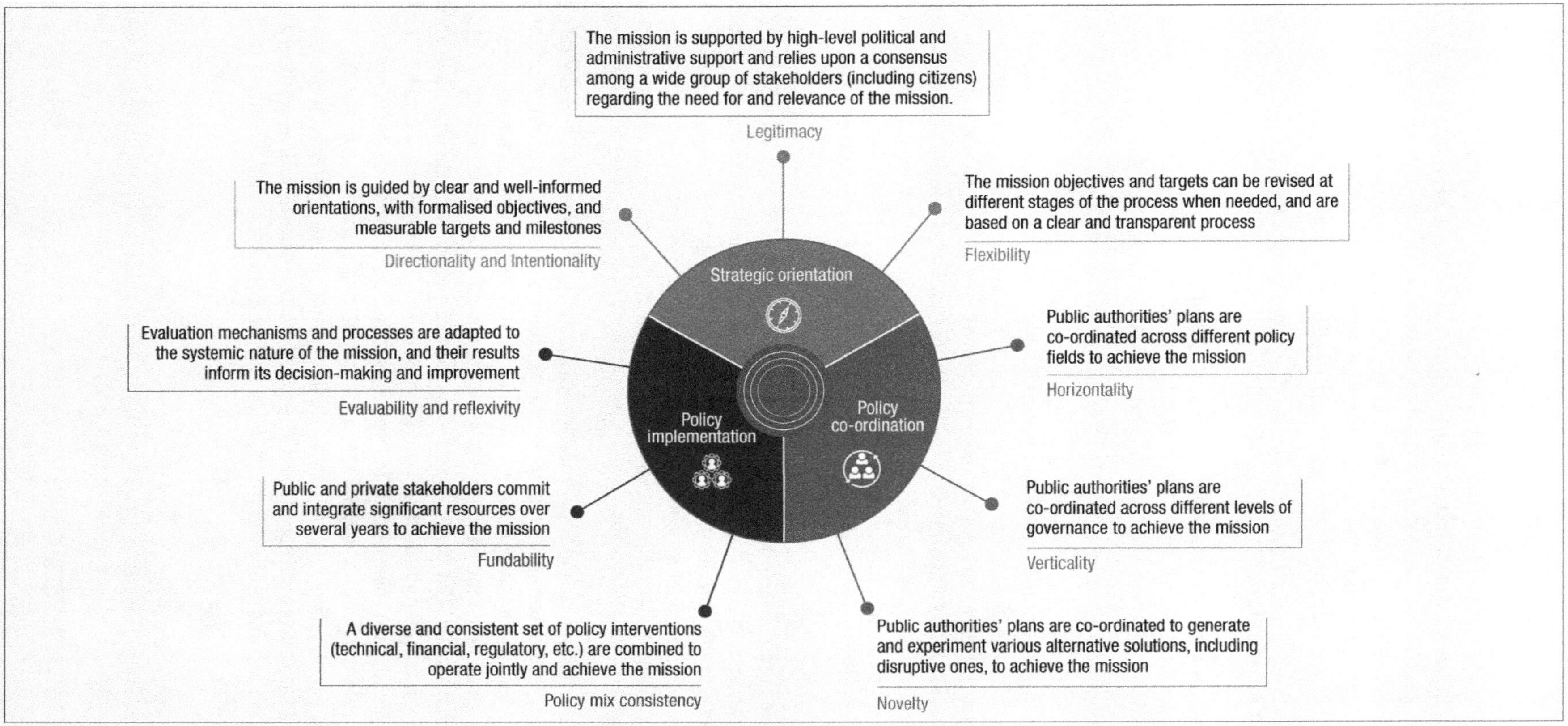

Annex A provides definitions of the design principles and corresponding questions to assess their degree of realisation. Each of these design principles represents a potential line of improvement, as needed in each specific mission case. The general and gradual improvement of a mission across these design principles increases the degree of "mission orientation" or, more colloquially, "degree of missionness". Building on this analytical framework, the OECD Mission Action Lab developed a monitoring tool which was tested in real conditions in the context of the "Austrian EU missions" (see Box 4.2).

The different types of missions

The different types of missions vary notably in their scope and the extent to which they embrace the mission-oriented policy approach, i.e., how far they go in steering, co-ordinating and integrating activities to address a specific challenge (hereafter, the degree of maturity) (Figure 2.4).

Missions distinguish themselves from the most traditional STI policy frameworks (1) composed of individual instruments with single goals (e.g. increasing R&D investment) to alleviate specific market failures (e.g. underinvestment in R&D due to the low appropriability and high uncertainty of research results). These policies, inherited from decades of influence of the New Public Management doctrine, are characterised by a narrow scope and a low level of integration of the instrument portfolio. Large "umbrella missions" (2) gather in a single institutional vehicle (whether officially termed as a "mission" or not), multiple public interventions addressing various needs to tackle a common goal. However, these interventions are loosely integrated, only involving, for the most part, an exchange of information between the various responsible authorities and common ex post monitoring rather than ex ante collective decision making and real joint action.

The two remaining missions correspond to the two most traditional types of missions depicted in the literature: the acceleration and transformative missions. Acceleration missions (3) closely integrate a portfolio of instruments to pursue focused and well-delineated goals, in most cases related to the development of green technological innovations. Transformative missions (4) combine a wide systemic scope and a significant level of integration to commonly steer activities along a collectively defined pathway to address a challenge.

Yet, as the difficulty of designing and implementing missions increases with the scope, only very few mission initiatives (if any) have managed to achieve a high degree of "mission orientation" on a wide scope. However, missions evolve as organisations involved in MOIPs learn and gradually improve how to do missions and MOIPs gain legitimacy and enlist new partners. Two main evolution pathways toward transformative missions can be identified: 1) the evolution of large umbrella missions to become more integrated (for instance in Germany from the High-Tech Strategy 2025 missions and its 12 missions to the new "Future Strategy" and its 6 missions). This requires time, as it involves building trust between the involved parties and reforming many incentives and formal and informal processes; and 2) efforts to broaden the scope of acceleration missions to establish larger, more systemic national missions while maintaining their close co-ordination (for instance in Norway from the Pilot-E scheme to the two recent national missions embedded in the Long-term Plan for Higher Education and Research 2023-2032).

Figure 2.4. Typology of missions according to their scope and degree of "mission orientation"

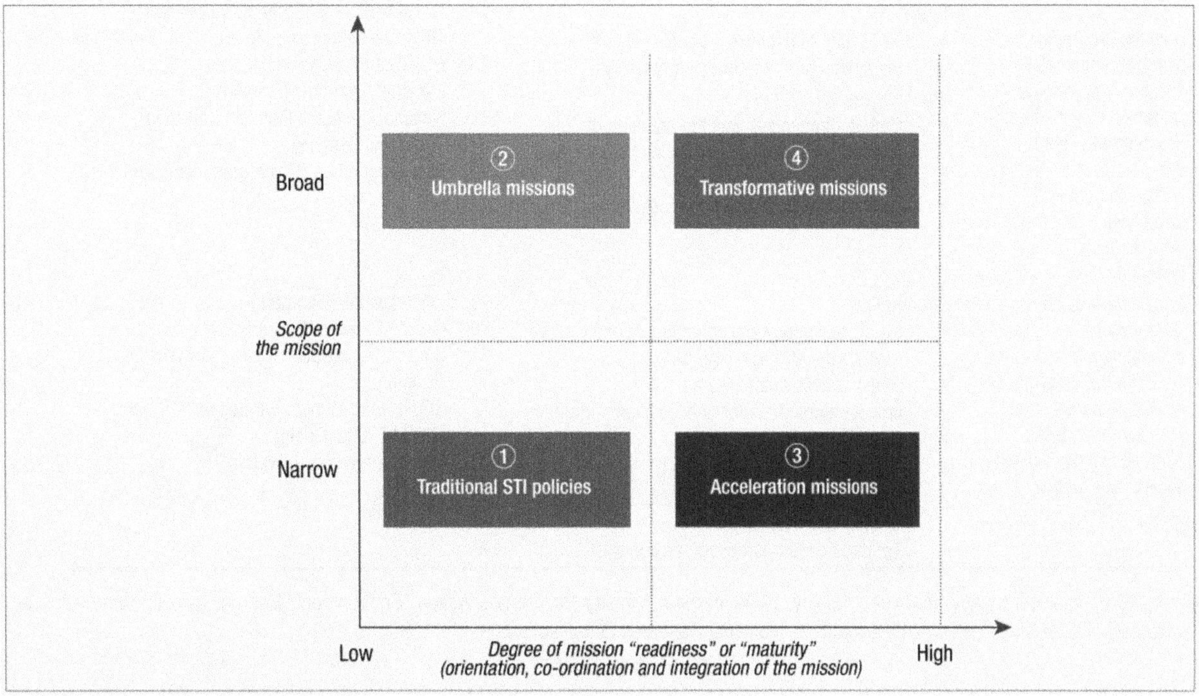

Note: STI: science, technology and innovation.

A typology developed in previous OECD work identified four main MOIP types (Larrue, 2021[7]). Table 2.1 presents each type, a selection of corresponding examples of MOIPs, and their distinctive strengths and weaknesses.

Table 2.1. Basic characteristics of the four main types of mission-oriented innovation policies

Types of MOIP initiatives	Strengths and weaknesses	Example of MOIP initiatives (country)
Overarching mission-oriented strategic framework:Large policy framework aiming to achieve ambitious, high level, national or transnational missions to address systemic challenges	Strengths: • High visibility and (societal and political) legitimacy • Broad scope covering a wide range of potential solutions • Systemic intervention, "all-hands on-board" approach, nationwide effort Weaknesses: • Loose co-ordination, can take the form of broad umbrella programmes • Higher transaction costs	1. Austrian Transition Missions (Austria) 2. Horizon Europe's missions (European Union) 3. Mission-driven Top Sectors and Innovation Policy (Netherlands) 4. Future Strategy (Germany) 5. France 2030 Acceleration Strategies (France) 6. Energy Earthshots™ (United States) 7. Moonshot R&D Program (Japan)
Challenge-based programmes and schemes: Targeted agency schemes, using competitive mechanisms to accelerate the development of concrete solutions to a specific challenge	Strengths: • Co-ordination of public support along the innovation chain • Hands-on management of projects/project portfolios • Articulation of supply and demand for knowledge Weaknesses: • Niche solutions, need additional scale-up interventions often outside the scope of the mission	8. UKRI Industrial Strategy Challenge Fund (United Kingdom) 9. Pilot-E and Pilot-T (Norway) 10. National Challenge Fund (Ireland) 11. The Alchemist (Korea) 12. Energy Storage Grand Challenge (United States) 13. Challenge-Driven Innovation Initiative (Sweden)

	• Narrow scope, focused on technological/engineering options	
Thematic mission-oriented programmes: Traditional thematic research programme reformed to make them progressively more directional, co-ordinated across sectors and disciplines, and broader in their means of intervention	Strengths: • Continuity with former thematic research and innovation programmes, progressivity Weaknesses: • Path dependencies limit the adoption of mission-oriented policy practices (result-driven, cross-sectoral co-ordination) • Tend to remain focused on research	14. Cross-ministerial Strategic Innovation Promotion Program (Japan) 15. CSIRO's missions (Australia) 16. Flagship Programs (Finland) 17. National Research Council Challenge Program (Canada) 18. Mission-oriented STI programmes (Lithuania)
*Ecosystem-based mission programmes:*Mechanisms delegating to ecosystems of actors the development and implementation of strategic agendas to address broadly defined societal challenges	Strengths: • Strong legitimacy and commitment of all actors towards the strategic agenda • Role of public authorities as orchestrators/facilitator of ecosystem formation Weaknesses: • Less challenge/mission-based • Risk of capture of missions by and in favour of leading/historical players • Tend to be less disruptive/transformative	19. Innomissions (Denmark) 20. Growth Engines (Finland) 21. Smart Specialisation Strategy of Wallonia (Belgium) 22. Smart Specialisation Strategy of Catalonia – RISCAT2030 (Spain) 23. Impact Innovation (Sweden)

Note: MOIP: mission-oriented innovation policy; BMK: Federal Ministry for Climate Action, Environment, Energy, Mobility, Innovation and Technology: CSIRO: Commonwealth Scientific & Industrial Research Organisation.

References

Larrue, P. (2021), "The design and implementation of mission-oriented innovation policies: A new systemic policy approach to address societal challenges", *OECD Science, Technology and Industry Policy Papers*, No. 100, OECD Publishing, Paris, https://doi.org/10.1787/3f6c76a4-en. [7]

Larrue, P., P. Tõnurist and D. Jonason (2024), "Monitoring and evaluation of mission-oriented innovation policies: From theory to practice", *OECD Science, Technology and Industry Working Papers*, No. 2024/09, OECD Publishing, Paris, https://doi.org/10.1787/5e4c3204-en. [6]

OECD (2024), "Governing missions: Securing effective governance to enable mission success", *OECD Science, Technology and Industry Policy Papers*, OECD Publishing, Paris, forthcoming. [4]

OECD (2024), "Mission portfolio management: Towards a dynamic practice", *OECD Science, Technology and Industry Policy Papers*, OECD Publishing, Paris. [5]

OECD and DDC (2022), *Mission-oriented Innovation Needs Assessment Survey*, OECD and Danish Design Center, https://ddc.dk/wp-content/uploads/2021/10/REPORT-mission-needs-assessment-survey-110222-.pdf. [3]

Peters, B. (2018), "The challenge of policy coordination", *Policy Design and Practice*, Vol. 1/1, pp. 1-11, https://doi.org/10.1080/25741292.2018.1437946. [2]

Tosun, J. and A. Lang (2017), "Policy integration: Mapping the different concepts", *Policy Studies, Taylor & Francis Journals*, Vol. 38/6, pp. 553-570, https://doi.org/10.1080/01442872.2017.1339239. [8]

Trein, P., M. Iris and M. Martino (2019), "The integration and coordination of public policies: A systematic comparative review", *Journal of Comparative Policy Analysis: Research and Practice*, Vol. 21/4, pp. 332-349, https://doi.org/10.1080/13876988.2018.1496667. [9]

Weber, K. and H. Rohracher (2012), "Legitimizing research, technology and innovation policies for transformative change: Combining insights from innovation systems and multi-level perspective in a comprehensive "failures" framework", *Research Policy*, Vol. 41/6, pp. 1037-1047, https://doi.org/10.1016/j.respol.2011.10.015. [1]

Endnotes

[1] A voluminous amount of research exists on the concept of policy integration since the 1990s and since the beginning the OECD has been one of the most active organisations to operationalise this concept. There are different views on and definitions of policy integration and how it is a form of or differs from policy co-ordination (see, for instance, Trein, Iris and Martino (2019[9])). In the MOIP analytical report, policy integration is distinct from policy co-ordination and refers exclusively to the consistent and cross-sectoral implementation of policy instruments, including its most practical implications. Following the distinction made by Tosun and Lang (2017[8]), policy integration is realised by means of policy instruments and is of *procedural* nature. Co-ordination, which refers to plans' alignment with shared goals, is of a *substantive* nature.

3 Methodology and evidence base to assess the added value of net zero missions

This chapter presents the methodology and evidence base specifically developed to assess the added value of mission-oriented innovation policies. In particular, a mission theory of action is used to systemically track the process on which the expected mission "systemic effects" rely.

There exist very few fully fledged evaluations of mission-oriented innovation policies (MOIPs) that could provide evidence of whether they meet their ambitious objectives and, given their long-term and impact-based objectives, it is likely that there is still a long way to go before enough evaluations are available to draw robust conclusions on their ability to deliver on their many promises. However, as previously mentioned, many missions were launched three to five years ago and are facing increasing political and administrative pressures to justify their co-ordination efforts and budgets.

In response to this emerging demand for accountability, a complementary approach is proposed: while direct evidence of MOIPs' contributions to objectives such as greenhouse gas (GHG) emissions reductions or job creation might be elusive at this stage, it is possible to track the key processes that lie at the heart of the MOIP approach and which should lead to such impacts and assess whether they unfold as expected and produce their "systemic effects". Rather than a substantive evaluation (is the mission being realised and the selected challenge solved?), this chapter focuses on a process-tracking evaluation in the early years of this policy approach (is the MOIP approach relevant to tackle the selected challenge?).

For that purpose, it is necessary to develop a theory of action, a tool that is increasingly used in evaluation of complex interventions, along theories of change (Box 3.1). In the case of MOIPs, the theory of action should surface the expected causal relationships between the problems MOIPs tackle and their desired goals, inputs, outputs, outcomes and impacts. This theory of action is presented in this chapter and used in subsequent chapters to analyse the database of 101 net zero missions and 17 in-depth case studies. It is also used to present the results of this work, distinguishing between the outputs and outcomes of net zero missions and structures this report, providing insights on the contribution of net zero missions to three expected outputs, followed by three expected outcomes.

Box 3.1. What are theories of change and theories of action and how are they used in public policy evaluations?

In its most general understanding, a theory of change is a set of beliefs about how change happens (Church and Rogers, 2006[1]). More precisely, in the context of a policy intervention or programme, it is the logical model that explains how the objective of the intervention is achieved, including the underlying assumptions and beliefs on causal relationships. It follows step-by-step the result chains that link the interventions' inputs and activities to the attainment of its stated objectives (usually working backwards from the objectives). It was first proposed as a tool for evaluating complex programmes, whose basic assumptions about the relations between inputs, outcomes and impacts were most often poorly articulated (Weiss, 1995[2]).

A theory of change is usually presented in a visual diagram that provides at a glance the main expected impact linkages. It does not provide a specific implementation plan but is a tool to collectively make explicit and discuss the hypotheses that guided the design of the intervention in the first place and create a consensus on these hypotheses in the likely advent of diverging views. Once agreed upon, these hypotheses are represented as causal relationships in the diagram. The tool's main benefits are, therefore, as much in the process as in the final results (i.e. the diagram obtained at the end).

Alongside these theories of change, 'theories of action' (ToAs) are proposed as a tool to track the specific mission processes and the systemic effects they are expected to generate to tackle a specific challenge. In a nutshell, a theory of action is inward-looking and process-oriented. It is "the delivery model for a Theory of Change" (Georges, 2024[3]). It describes how the mission is designed and set up to realise the mission. It maps the chains of causality that connect the way missions are designed and governed to the impact they are expected to produce. Rather than only focusing on the substantive dimension of missions (is the mission being realised and the selected challenge solved?), mission theories of action track the key processes that lie at the heart of the MOIP approach and allow assessing whether they unfold as expected and produce their 'systemic effects' (i.e., is the adopted approach effective to tackle the selected challenge?)

Theories of change and theories of action are therefore the two faces of the same coin, providing complementary views on the expected process of change that should lead to the realisation of the mission. It is argued that mission theories of action can prove particularly instrumental to both mission managers and evaluators in a developmental approach. In the case of MOIPs, ToC should surface the expected causal relationships between the problems these policies tackle and their desired goals, inputs, outputs, outcomes, and impacts (Janssen et al., 2021[4]; Hekkert et al., 2020[5]). These maps of mission 'contribution claims' can prove particularly instrumental to guide and monitor their portfolio of diverse activities, in order to check that they are consistent among themselves and aim in the right direction.

When used for evaluating a given programme, the theory of change can be mobilised to systematically examine the causal relationships at each step. Depending on the type of policy or programme, indicators or markers can be associated with the different connections.

Sources: Church and Rogers (2006[1]); Weiss (1995[2]); (Janssen et al., 2021[4]; Hekkert et al., 2020[5]).

The double additionality of missions

As previously mentioned, MOIPs are an additional institutional layer to direct, co-ordinate and integrate new – and most often already existent – interventions. To validate this policy approach, it is necessary to substantiate that they produce additional benefits relative to traditional STI policy frameworks, and that these benefits outweigh the additional transaction costs. The validation of this policy approach thus depends on them successfully passing a stringent double test: not only must they accomplish their missions, but they should do so more effectively and more efficiently than would have been the case with traditional approaches, or they should fulfil objectives that are beyond the reach of these traditional approaches (Larrue, Tõnurist and Jonason, 2024[6]).

Using the evaluation terminology, MOIPs must prove two types of additionality (Figure 3.1):

1. The "first-order" additionality relates to the additional net effects of any given intervention relative to what would have been the case in the absence of public intervention.
2. The "second-order" additionality is specific to MOIPs. It captures the additional effects relative to a counterfactual scenario that is not a "no intervention" scenario but a "traditional STI policy" scenario.

Figure 3.1. The double additionality of missions

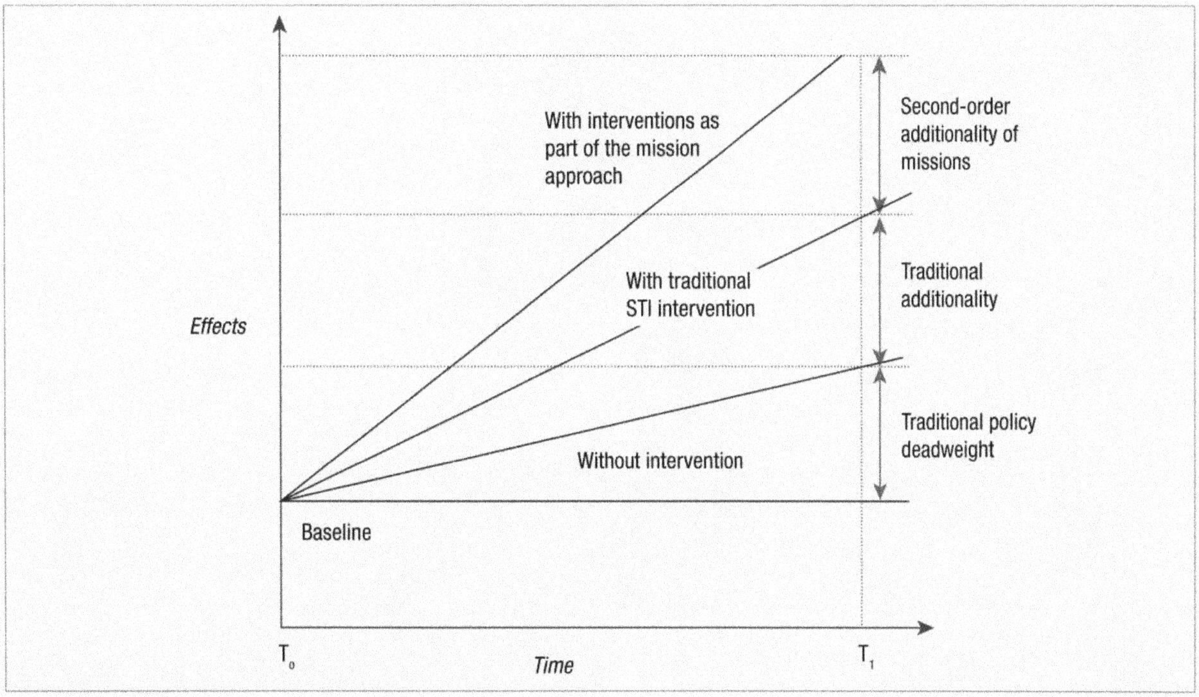

Note: STI: science, technology and innovation.

Quantitative assessments of "first-order" additionality have often proven difficult due to the difficulty to run counterfactual scenarios through pairing techniques used in random control trials, for instance in clinical, development aid or education programme evaluations. In the STI domain, the beneficiaries of an innovation scheme are most often of a different nature than those who did not apply to the scheme or were not selected. The resulting selection bias makes any comparison between beneficiaries and non-beneficiaries (constituting the counterfactual sample) hardly meaningful.

Assessing the "second-order" additionality is even less suited to quasi-experimental evaluation methods since the MOIP intervention scenario is not a substitute for but an addition to the "baseline" scenario. It is, therefore, necessary to recourse to mainly qualitative evidence drawn from desk review and interviews with mission leaders and partners.

Against this backdrop, the MOIP theory of action seeks to lay the expected additional effects on top of those produced by existing policy instruments to guide field work. It is used as a map upon which the net zero mission instruction templates and interview guidelines were directly based.

The theory of action of net zero missions

Building upon the analytical framework presented above, the net zero theory of action describes how MOIPs are expected to produce their impacts, in direct relation to their specific features. More precisely, it presents the set of expected causal relationships between the design principles of this policy approach and its intended outputs, outcomes and impacts (Figure 3.2). Along the lines of the aforementioned typology of missions (Kuittinen, Polt and Weber, 2018[7]), two types of impacts are distinguished: 1) change acceleration; and 2) system transformation. The various causal relationships are based on the results of previous OECD work on MOIPs, a review of the literature on missions and multiple interactions with scholars during the project.[1]

Figure 3.2. The net zero mission theory of action

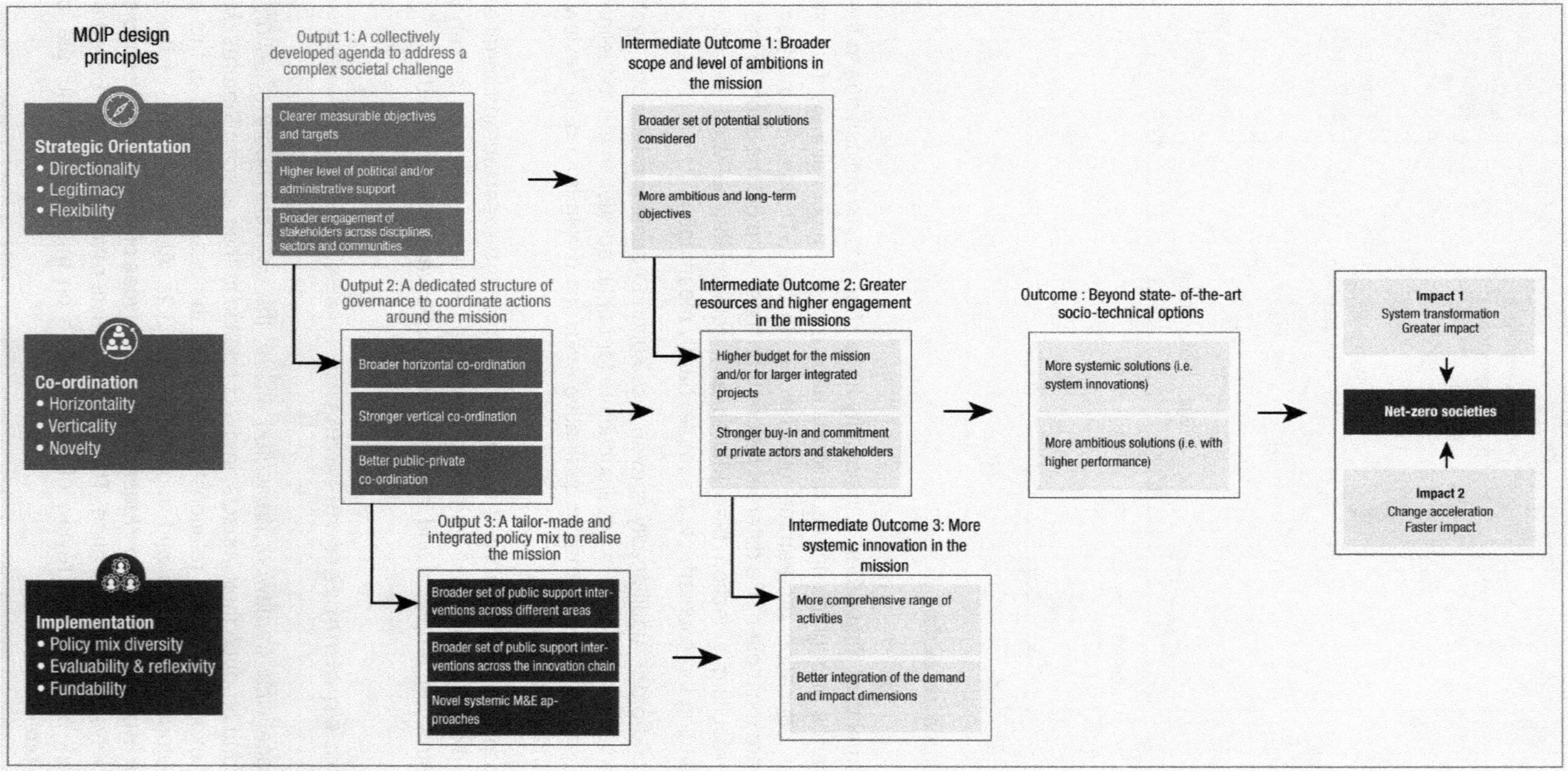

Note: MOIP: mission-oriented innovation policy.

The MOIP design principles are the starting point of the theory of action. Together they constitute the "genetic traits" of a given mission. For instance, in the strategic orientation building block, the direct expected outputs of the directionality and intentionality, legitimacy and flexibility design principles are notably clearer and flexible objectives and directions to realise the missions, a broader and higher degree of consensus among stakeholders and possibly citizens on the necessity to realise these objectives, and stronger backing of high-level political and policy officials.

The second stage of the theory of action includes the intermediate outcomes of the MOIPs. For instance, the clear and legitimate shared agenda is expected to include a broader set of potential options directed towards more ambitious and long-term objectives. In combination with elements of the policy co-ordination building-block, this shared agenda should also result in a higher budget for the mission, as well as stronger buy-in and commitment from private actors and stakeholders involved in the realisation of the mission, and the support to a more comprehensive range of activities being supported (i.e. not only technological aspects but also elements related to the needed skills, infrastructure, regulatory framework, user awareness, etc.). Finally, a wide range of actors across all silos, strongly committed to achieving the mission through the exploration of a broader set of potential options and a wider range of supported activities, benefitting from greater resources, could obtain solutions with higher performance, which can be articulated in a more systemic way. Down the causal thread, as previously mentioned, this should result in either change acceleration or system transformation.

Methodology

The study proceeded through two parallel strands of field work: 1) extensive fieldwork based on the analysis of a database of over 100 net zero missions; and 2) intensive fieldwork by undertaking case studies of 17 net zero missions.

The Net Zero Mission Database

The OECD has identified 148 net zero missions pertaining to 43 MOIP initiatives in 23 countries based on previous work done on MOIPs and other projects under the Committee for Scientific and Technological Policy (Figure 3.3). These missions directly or indirectly aim to address climate change through mitigation or adaptation.[1] The database[2] provides information on each mission's objectives, targets, funding, technological areas and application sectors, as well as more exploratory features like mission rationales.

While the *Net Zero Mission Database* is not exhaustive, it includes the main missions that match the OECD definition. It is, however, worthwhile keeping in mind a few caveats, as presented in Box 3.1.

Box 3.2. The caveats of the *Net Zero Mission Database*

Although the *Net Zero Mission Database* is meant to be as exhaustive as possible, some relevant initiatives are not included for different reasons. First, the mission-oriented innovation policy (MOIP) definition leaves some room for interpretation as to which initiatives are mission-oriented or not. Although it obeys clear design principles, this policy approach is not totally new and distinct *vis-à-vis* the existing policy landscapes. The difference is at times more a matter of degree than of nature and the question of where to draw the line between what is and what is not mission-oriented relies on the analysts' appreciations. Furthermore, some proto-missions, still at the stage of thematic calls for proposals, evolve and become gradually closer to MOIPs. The abusive use of the term "mission-oriented", which has now become a buzzword in some domains ("mission washing"), sometimes makes the distinction even more complicated. A key element that makes this appreciation more robust is the comparison between different initiatives to obtain a rather consistent group of policies in terms of how far they go on the different dimensions of mission orientation. Moreover, besides a few borderline cases, most identified initiatives are clearly mission-oriented, recognised as such by policy makers and analysts.

Other reasons for not including some missions are related to the nature of these initiatives or the scope of this study:

- Some MOIP initiatives are too novel to be included. New initiatives arise every year, including at regional levels, and several countries and regions are currently considering the adoption of an MOIP approach or the creation of new initiatives.
- Very few missions have yet been identified outside advanced economies. This does not mean that other, emerging, economies do not apply any of the MOIP design principles such as stakeholder engagement or cross-sectoral co-ordination. However, it is less likely to find initiatives that combine these principles in a consistent way due to problems of policy and governance capacity in emerging countries. As part of the Mission Action Lab, the OECD is working on the potential of the MOIP approach to support sustainable development in developing countries (Kumpf, Mucarsel and Zavarella, 23 June 2023[8]).
- The database focuses on missions led by national public authorities. Only one regional mission (in Wallonia) is included, although several local initiatives come close to the design and "spirit" of ecosystem-based MOIP initiatives, in particular in the context of the new generation of Smart Specialisation Strategies that drive the allocation of European Union Structural Funds dedicated to research and innovation during the programming period 2021-27.[1] Many cities also use a mission approach to drive their efforts towards carbon-neutrality, not least in Europe in the context of the EU 'Climate-Neutral and Smart Cities' mission. These missions at city level are not included in the database. Only the national frameworks to support these cities are included.
- All missions included in the database aim to act primarily upon research and innovation to tackle climate change, as per the OECD MOIP definition. Other policies adopting an MOIP approach exist in other policy areas, involve little or no STI development.[2] However, to date, these missions seem rare.
- Finally, this database focuses on mission-oriented policies, not mission-oriented organisations. It, therefore, does not include the specialised mission-oriented and high-risk high-reward agencies such as the Defense Advanced Research Projects Agency (DARPA) and Advanced Research Projects Agency-Energy (ARPA-E) in the United States, and the Advanced Research and Invention Agency in the United Kingdom. These agencies operate activities that match several of the MOIP design principles, which make them close to "acceleration missions" as previously defined but remain, however, mostly confined to calls for proposals to address scientific and technological obstacles.

Notes: 1. For instance, the Research and Innovation Strategy for the Smart Specialisation of Catalonia (RISCAT3), which promotes the development of territorial shared research and innovation agendas. These shared agendas "articulate, through a participatory model of governance, the collective action of various actors aimed at addressing a common challenge (usually related to the SDGs) in the territory and the problems that this challenge may generate" (Fernández and Romagosa, 2020[9]). 2. For instance, the Delta Programme in the Netherlands was included in the mission-oriented policy observatory commissioned by the European Commission (European Commission, 2018[10]). This mission aims to protect the country from flooding, mitigate the impact of extreme weather events and secure supplies of freshwater. <!!Best practice on boxes: see page 20 of the OECD Style Guide.

As shown in Figure 3.3, most of the identified net zero missions are implemented in European countries (around 80% of missions), with a strong concentration in northern Europe. Nordic countries alone represent 33% of the net zero missions in this study (31% of MOIP initiatives). Their missions are not only more numerous, but also have a higher degree of "mission orientation" as previously defined, while missions such as the Spanish "*CDTI misiones*" are "borderline cases". Outside the European Union, represented countries include Australia, Brazil, Canada, Chile, Colombia, Japan, Korea, the United Kingdom and the United States.

Figure 3.3. Map of mission-oriented innovation policy initiatives and number of net zero missions

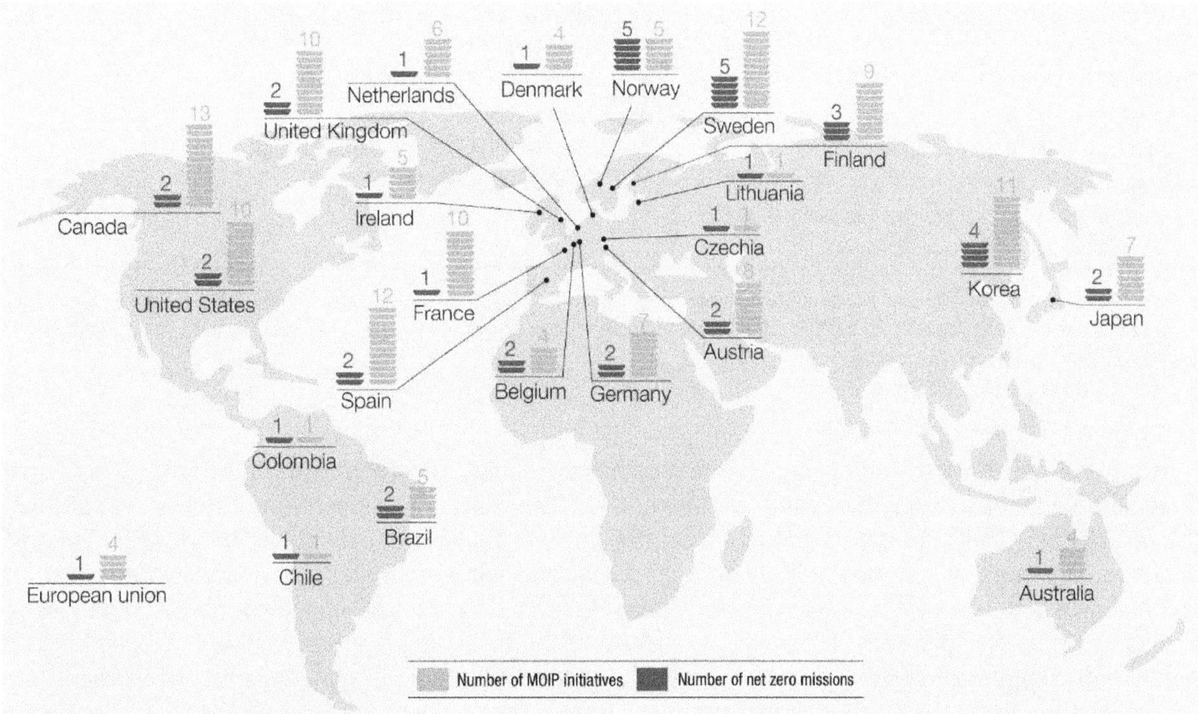

Note 1: MOIP: mission-oriented innovation policy. Note 2: This map includes all net zero missions identified as of October 2024. Note 3: The list of net zero missions is available in Annex B.
Source: OECD Net Zero Mission Database.

Among the net zero missions identified as of October 2024, 101 related to 30 MOIP initiatives in 20 countries have been included in the analyses of this report (Table 3.1). The Table 3.1 includes the subset of these net zero missions that are included in this report's analysis.

Table 3.1. Mission-oriented innovation policy initiatives and number of net zero missions included in the study per country

Australia	4	**Korea**	3
CSIRO's missions	4	Korean Advanced Research Programme Accelerator (KARPA)	1
Austria	8	The Alchemist	2
Austrian Transition Missions	4	**Lithuania**	1
Belgium	3	Mission-oriented science and innovation programmes	1
Smart Specialisation Strategy of Wallonia	3	**Netherlands**	6
Canada	3	Mission-driven Innovation and Top-Sector Policy	6
NRC Challenge programme	1	**Norway**	5

Colombia	1	CLIMIT	1
Bioeconomy mission	1	Green Platform Initiative	1
Denmark	4	Norwegian national missions	1
Green missions/Inno missions	4	Pilot E	1
European Union	4	**Spain**	10
Horizon Europe's missions	4	Science and innovation missions	10
Finland	7	**Sweden**	9
Flagship programmes	2	Challenge-driven Innovation Initiative	3
Growth engines	5	Innovation partnership programmes	2
France	7	Strategic innovation programmes	1
National acceleration strategies	7	Vinnova's pilot missions	3
Germany	4	**United Kingdom**	9
Hightech Strategy 2025	4	Industrial Strategy Challenge Fund	9
Ireland	5	**United States**	9
Research Ireland Challenge programmes	4	Department of Energy's Grand Challenge	2
Japan	3	Energy Earthshots™	7
Cross-ministerial Strategic Innovation Promotion Program	1		
Moonshot Research and Development Program	2		

Note 1: CSIRO: Commonwealth Scientific & Industrial Research Organisation; NRC: National Research Council. Note 2: Detailed information on most of these MOIPs is available on the OECD online MOIP Toolkit: https://stip.oecd.org/moip. Note 3: This table only include the 101 missions included in this report's analysis.
Source: OECD Net Zero Mission Database.

A majority of net zero missions pertain to the most widely known "stereotypes" of MOIPs, i.e., challenge-based programmes and schemes (44 missions) and the overarching mission-oriented strategic framework (32 missions). Challenge-based programmes draw on a significant extent on the "DARPA model" characterised notably by clearly defined objectives and targets related to a challenge (often of technological nature); continuity of support across the innovation stages, including market deployment, thanks to strong linkages with potential users/buyers of the technology; and proactive management and hands-on management of the portfolio of activities by a powerful "programme director" (Bonvillian, Van Atta and Windham, 2019[11]). Overarching strategic frameworks correspond more closely – at least in the initial intentions – to the model of MOIPs presented by Mazzucato, in which a wide range of public and private actors jointly develop broad systemic missions associated with targets and milestones and pool together their resources and modes of intervention to realise them through collective action (Mazzucato, 2018[12]). Building upon the OECD typology, Uyarra (2023[13]) added a fifth type, namely the place-based micro missions that encapsulate the many local and city missions, such as Greater Manchester's net zero mission. These missions are numerous and extend beyond the 100 cities of the EU "Climate-neutral and smart cities"' mission. As explained in Box 3.2, the OECD database only includes the national frameworks to support these cities, e.g. the Austrian Climate-neutral City mission, the Swedish Viable Cities mission and the EU mission itself.[3]

Table 3.2. Breakdown of mission-oriented innovation policy initiatives and net zero missions by type of mission

	Number of missions	Number of MOIP initiatives
Ecosystem-based mission programmes	15	5
Thematic mission-oriented programmes	10	6
Overarching mission-oriented strategic frameworks	32	9
Challenge-based programmes and schemes	44	10

Notes: MOIP: mission-oriented innovation policy. See Chapter 2 for the definitions of the MOIP types.

While the reference to mission orientation in the STI policy area dates back several decades, the earliest "modern" mission-oriented policies, i.e., those aiming primarily to address societal challenges through a targeted and co-ordinated approach, were launched in the 2010s. Most net zero missions were launched between 2018 and 2021 (81%) (Figure 3.4). This coincides with the growing communication around this new policy approach in relation to the launch of the EU missions as part of Horizon Europe. This sudden surge of MOIPs is also related to the general increase of funding for research and innovation activities aimed at mitigating GHG emissions. However, a similar trend for missions in health and other areas can be observed, which indicates that it is more related to a policy rather thematic dynamic. Only a limited number of missions were launched before 2017 (2% of net zero missions). These "early" MOIPs, which were developed even before the policy approach itself gained salience, are not only less numerous, but also more remote from the specific, target or metrics-driven mission, along with strong governance structure and measurable progress.

There has been a significant slowdown in new missions since 2022 as countries strive to implement existing missions, incrementally increase their "degree of mission orientation", and wait for the results of assessments and evaluation before launching new ones. However, some missions have been launched more recently (for instance two MOIP initiatives have been launched in Brazil)[4] or are being developed (such as in the United Kingdom, where the new government elected in 2024 intends to use a 'mission-driven government' approach).

Figure 3.4. Breakdown of net zero mission-oriented innovation policy initiatives and missions analysed in this study by starting date

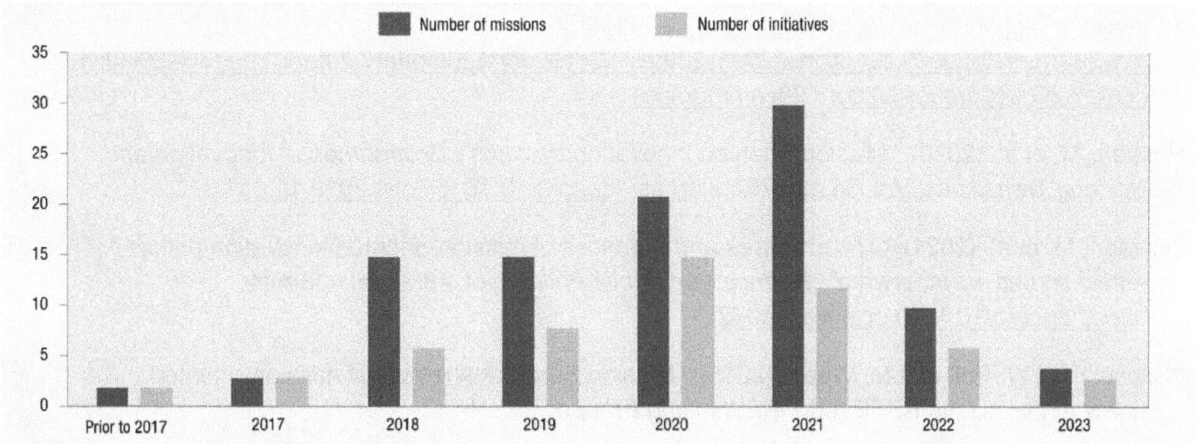

Source: OECD Net Zero Mission Database.

In-depth case studies of net zero missions

Seventeen net zero missions have been selected to form a sample that reflects the diversity of MOIP types and thematic areas. The case studies included two main steps. First, the OECD pre-filled a dedicated template for individual cases based on available desk research and materials.[5] This template was used as the main background document to support interviews with one or several persons directly involved in the mission, including the identified "mission leader" then relevant partners to fact-check and complement the template. About 40 interviews had been performed in the context of this study, representing 63 interviewees. The interview guidelines were structured along the net zero mission theory of action.

A series of dedicated sessions within the Committee for Scientific and Technological Policy meetings enabled a comparison of some net zero missions and provided a platform for discussion among policy makers and the relevant stakeholders.[6]

References

Bonvillian, W., R. Van Atta and P. Windham (2019), *The DARPA Model for Transformative Technologies: Perspectives on the US Defense Advanced Research Projects Agency*, Open Book Publishers, Cambridge, United Kingdom, https://doi.org/10.11647/OBP.0184. [11]

Church, C. and M. Rogers (2006), *Designing for Results: Integrating Monitoring and Evaluation in Conflict Transformation Programs, Search for Common Ground*, Search for Common Ground, Washington, DC, https://documents.sfcg.org/Documents/manualpart1.pdf. [1]

European Commission (2018), *Mission-oriented Research and Innovation Inventory and Characterisation of Initiatives: Final Report*, Publications Office of the European Union, https://doi.org/10.2777/697082. [10]

Fernández, T. and M. Romagosa (2020), *Articulating Shared Agendas for Sustainability and Social Change: A Contribution from the Territory to the EU Debate on Transitions to Sustainability*, http://catalunya2020.gencat.cat/web/.content/00_catalunya2020/Documents/angles/fitxers/shared-agendas.pdf. [9]

Georges, R. (2024), *What is a theory of action*, https://intdev.tetratechasiapacific.com/what-is-a-theory-of-action/#:~:text=the%20program%20theory.-,A%20Theory%20of%20Action%20is%20the%20delivery%20model%20for%20a,for%20individuals%2C%20groups%20or%20communities. [3]

Hekkert, M. et al. (2020), "Mission-oriented innovation systems", *Environmental Innovation and Societal Transitions*, Vol. 34, pp. 76-79, https://doi.org/10.1016/j.eist.2019.11.011. [5]

Janssen, M. et al. (2021), "The promises and premises of mission-oriented innovation policy: A reflection and ways forward", *Science and Public Policy*, Vol. 48/3, pp. 438-444, https://doi.org/10.1093/scipol/scaa072. [4]

Kuittinen, H., W. Polt and M. Weber (2018), "Mission Europe? A revival of mission-oriented policy in the EU", in RFTE (ed.), *RE:thinking Europe*. [7]

Kumpf, B., L. Mucarsel and A. Zavarella (23 June 2023), "Mission-oriented innovation: A suitable approach for just net zero transitions in the Global South?", *OECD Development Matters Blog*, https://oecd-development-matters.org/2023/06/23/mission-oriented-innovation-a-suitable-approach-for-just-net-zero-transitions-in-the-global-south (accessed on 23 June 2023). [8]

Larrue, P., P. Tõnurist and D. Jonason (2024), "Monitoring and evaluation of mission-oriented innovation policies: From theory to practice", *OECD Science, Technology and Industry Working Papers*, Vol. No. 2024/09, https://doi.org/10.1787/5e4c3204-en. [6]

Mazzucato, M. (2018), "Mission-oriented innovation policies: Challenges and opportunities", *Industrial and Corporate Change*, Vol. 27/5, pp. 803-815, https://doi.org/10.1093/icc/dty034. [12]

Uyarra, E. (2023), *Creating National Governance Structures for the Implementation of EU Missions*, Discussion Paper for the Mutual Learning Exercise on EU Missions Governance, PSF Challenge – Horizon Europe Policy Support Facility, Directorate-General for Research and Innovation. [13]

Weiss, C. (1995), "Nothing as practical as good theory: Exploring theory-based evaluation for comprehensive community initiatives for children and families", in Connell, J. (ed.), *New Approaches to Evaluating Community Initiatives: Concepts, Methods, and Contexts*, pp. 65-92, Aspen Institute, https://canvas.harvard.edu/files/1453087/download?download_frd=1&verifier=lVZpf0ynt3iriSXpb8lE7WirRBXUHfbceDQUHleG. [2]

Endnotes

[1] As a theory of action is a living tool that can evolve though interactions and reality checks, the present version should be considered as a milestone, not a final product.

[1] Detailed information on most of these MOIP initiatives and their missions is available on the OECD MOIP Online Toolkit. This platform went through a major update in October 2024 and is updated regularly. See https://stip.oecd.org/moip/.

[2] As of 30 October 2024. See annex B.

[3] These missions are, therefore, included in the database as "overarching mission-oriented strategic frameworks". However, each city involved in these frameworks should, in principle, be considered as a mission in itself since they all have their own objectives, cross-departmental governance structure and portfolio of interventions.

[4] The ten structuring and mobilizing programmes are a new approach to focus the investments that the National Fund for Scientific and Technological Development (FNDCT) funds on national sustainable development priorities. In addition to the FNDCT's mission-oriented approach, Brazil has another set of six missions that have been guiding its new industrial policy – Nova Indústria Brazil – since January 2024.

[5] Completed templates are about 20-25 pages long. They are structured around four sections: 1) the mission-oriented policy initiatives section provides synthetic information on the policy initiative that "hosts" the net zero mission, including the overall context, how and why it was launched, how it is governed, funded, implemented and evaluated; 2) the net zero mission basic characteristics section contains information on the main features of the net zero mission, including its objectives, timeline, scale and scope, and its evolution; 3) the net zero mission process section provides detailed information on the main processes and mechanisms to design/select the mission, govern and implement it, manage its portfolio, and evaluate it; and 4) the net zero mission strengths and weaknesses section.

[6] A first "net zero mission seminar" was organised as part of the 119th meeting of the CSTP on 20-22 October 2021. The mission leaders of three missions were invited to present and discuss the strengths and weaknesses of their mission to tackle the climate neutrality challenge: V. Bryony Livesey, Director at the Industrial Strategy Challenge Fund (Industrial Decarbonisation Challenge); Stine

Jørgensen, Deputy Director at the Danish Agency for Education and Research (Green Missions); and Lisa Higgins, Director at Research Ireland (Net Zero Research Challenge). A second "net zero mission seminar" was organised at the 121st meeting of the CSTP. It convened Joanna Franzén, Strategic Area Lead Sustainable Food Systems, Innovation Management, Vinnova (Healthy Sustainable Food, Vinnova's pilot missions); Guus Mulder, Program Manager, Top Consortium for Knowledge and Innovation Urban Energy (A Carbon-free Built Environment by 2050, Mission-driven Top Sectors and Innovation Policy); and Hans-Günther Schwarz, Federal Ministry for Climate Action, Environment, Energy, Mobility, Innovation and Technology, DG Innovation (Climate-neutral Cities, Austrian Transition Missions).

A panel on mission-oriented policy for net zero was also organised on 25 October 2022 as part of the *Science, Technology and Innovation Outlook* 2023 High-level Debate, using the synthesis of the net zero mission study published in the *Science, Technology and Innovation Outlook* (OECD, 2023) to feed discussions on the added value of the mission approach to reduce greenhouse gas emissions. The panel was composed of Christina Abildgaard, Executive Director, Research Council of Norway; Julien Guerrier, former Director for Research and Innovation, European Commission; and Jeroen Heijs, Director for Innovation and Knowledge, Ministry of Economic Affairs and Climate, Netherlands. The panel was moderated by Christian Naczinsky, Head of EU and OECD Research Policy Department, Austrian Ministry of Education, Science and Research.

4 What are the outputs of net zero missions?

This chapter presents the results of the assessment of net zero missions' outputs, which is the first layer of systemic effects. Net zero mission outputs are produced through three main processes: the collective development of a strategic agenda to address a complex societal challenge, the alignment and holistic monitoring of various actors' plans, and the articulation and management of a portfolio of activities.

In direct relation to their design principles, mission-oriented innovation policies (MOIPs) are expected to deliver three policy outputs (see: Figure 3.2) a collectively developed strategic agenda; 2) a dedicated governance structure to co-ordinate actions towards this agenda; and 3) a consistent package of policy and regulatory interventions to implement the mission. This section questions each of these outputs successively. Table 4.1 summarises the results of this analysis.

Table 4.1. Synthesis of the main outputs of net zero missions

Expected effects	Main outputs
A) Collective development of a strategic agenda to address a complex societal challenge	
Clearer measurable objectives and targets	Missions have enabled setting clearer goals than in traditional programmes, although few correspond to the expected "SMART" goals. Only half of these goals have clear targets. Strategic agendas allow "continuous directionality" and complement mission objectives in a context of high uncertainty and contestation. In stark contrast with traditional strategies and road maps, strategic agendas are directly associated with mission budgets, co-ordination structures and modes of implementation, increasing their influence on interventions.
Higher level of political/ administrative support	Missions are political by nature, owing to normative goals related to societal impacts. Broad national missions attract more attention from politicians and high-level administrative levels, which strengthens their legitimacy but can add pressure to obtain early results.
Broader stakeholder engagement	Strategic agendas are developed by a wide range of actors from different communities, increasing their ownership of the mission and subsequent engagement.
B) Alignment and holistic monitoring of various actors' plans	
Broader horizontal co-ordination	Almost all net zero missions subject to a case study have significantly expanded the scope of co-ordination between different actors across the government structure. Leadership is assumed by the science, technology and innovation authorities that have launched the mission. Cross-sectoral co-ordination is the main challenge of net zero missions, generating significant transaction costs in the largest and most integrated missions.
Stronger vertical co-ordination	Most net zero missions are led by national (or European Union) authorities; some include local authorities in their governance. Local authorities are involved in many mission activities to enable demonstrating solutions and their early transition to market. A few net zero missions are implemented at the regional level, particularly in the context of the new generation of EU Smart Specialisation strategies.
Better public-private co-ordination	Missions complement (and often benefit from) the existing public-private science, technology and innovation (STI) concertation platforms. They add a well-targeted purposive framework and ensure a more direct link to policy interventions.
C) Articulation and management of a portfolio of activities	
Broader set of public support interventions across different areas	All net zero missions are bundled under a common strategic and governance framework featuring different types of interventions, from research and development grants to skill formation or advocacy. Only a few missions include policy instruments that support the market deployment of current or new solutions. Net zero missions allow co-ordinating public support for different aspects of systemic solutions.
Broader set of public support interventions across the innovation chain	Several net zero missions map and connect the various support instruments across the different technology readiness levels, with a view to providing more continuous support to different stages of the innovation chain.
Novel systemic monitoring and evaluation approaches	There is a pervasive perception among mission partners that new evaluation methodologies and processes are needed to evaluate this approach, but very few mission-oriented innovation policy evaluations have been undertaken to date, and they do not significantly depart from traditional STI policy evaluations.

Note: SMART: specific, measurable, achievable, relevant and time-bound.

The collective development of strategic agendas to address societal challenges

One of the key specificities of MOIPs relative to most traditional policies is their strong directionality: the mission is specifically designed to achieve specific objectives. In principle, all decisions regarding what investments and actions are taken thinking backward from the final objectives to be realised. The injunction for science, technology and innovation (STI) policies to be impact-driven is, of course, not new, but it has been unevenly implemented. Furthermore, the expected impacts have remained vague and often closer to outputs (e.g. publications, patents, excellence) and outcomes (e.g. excellence, innovation) than impacts outside the STI domain (e.g. reduction of emissions, job creation).

A diversity of mission objectives

Even before the formulation of mission objectives, the first stage of mission orientation takes place at the MOIP initiative level and consists in choosing the missions themselves, most often in the form of mission or challenge areas. Countries have used different staged combinations of top-down and bottom-up processes, most often involving a mix of political influence; stakeholder consultation, including citizen for the broadest societal missions; and evidence-based studies.

> *Net zero mission cases*
>
> *Moonshot Research and Development Programme, Japan. A Visionary Council was set up in 2019 composed of seven members, industry leaders, renowned academics but also media artists and a writer of science-fiction novels. It was tasked between March and July 2019 with proposing Moonshot areas and potential goals. With support from the Cabinet Office secretariat, the Visionary Council adopted a progressive approach starting from broad societal challenges, opening up to numerous Visions and Goals and finally narrowing-down the number of potential options. It went from 3 'Target Areas', to 13 'Visions' to 25 examples of potential goals. 6 Moonshot goal candidates were finally drafted based on the Council's proposal and the discussion at the December 2019 international symposium where 6 working groups discussed subsets of goal candidates and scenarios for achieving them. One additional working group addressed cross-sectional issues. These goals were then discussed and validated by the Council for Science, Technology, and Innovation in January 2020. An additional goal in the healthcare area was discussed and validated in July 2020. Extensive consultations with various ministries and agencies took place during the process. The Visionary Council also received about 1 800 comments to online open call for inputs from the general public (Larrue, 2021[1]).*
>
> *The UK Research and Innovation (UKRI) Challenge Fund, United Kingdom. The MOIP includes 23 'Challenges' in four large challenge areas. The challenges were selected through a multistage selection process. 1) A call for expressions of interest was first issued to identify issues linked to the grand challenges that 'the bidders wished to address but which, in the absence of public money, might not otherwise receive investment'. 2) UKRI selected, against criteria linked to the grand challenge, a shortlist of potential challenges for support. 3) UKRI discussed the shortlisted challenges with officials from the Department and ministers, and the Secretary of State decided on which challenges to approve based on UKRI recommendations. 4) Once the Challenges were approved (in three different waves) the work started in each of them to determine the objectives. For each of Challenge, UKRI was mandated to develop a 'business case' included details of the Challenge objectives, the rationale for funding, information on the shortlisted challenges, a target for co-investment and a plan for management, monitoring and evaluation (National Audit Office, United Kingdom, 2021[2]).*

Mission objectives vary greatly in their scope, focus and formulation of the expected impact (Table 4.2). Other important variables that differentiate mission objectives are their level of ambition (relative to the state-of-the-art) and clarity.

Table 4.2. Selected mission objectives by scope, impact and focus

Scope	*Broad:* Build Australia's national capability to support the transition to net zero emissions by enabling Australia to prosper and grow in a global low emissions world through new economic, societal and environmental value (Towards Net Zero, CSIRO missions, Australia) *Narrow:* All feed for farmed fish and livestock shall come from sustainable boilers and contribute to reducing greenhouse gas emissions in the food system (Sustainable feed, Norwegian national missions, Norway)
Expected impact	*Technological impact*: Support research and innovation projects and facilities to develop advanced battery technologies that can drive the growth of a strong battery business in the United Kingdom (Faraday battery challenge, Industrial Strategy Challenge Fund, United Kingdom) *Societal impact*: To boost adaptation and resilience to climate change (adaptation to climate change including societal transformation, Horizon Europe missions) *Ecosystem impact*: Establish an ecosystem that makes the compensation of carbon dioxide emissions easier at the international scale while creating business opportunities for Finnish companies (Compensate Growth Engine) *Economic impact*: Make Germany the leading supplier and market for electromobility (safe, networked and clean mobility; High Tech 2025 missions, Germany)
Focus	*Research*: To support interdisciplinary teams to develop disruptive solutions that accelerate progress towards net zero greenhouse gas emissions in Ireland by 2050 (Zero Emissions Challenge, Research Ireland Challenge Programme, Ireland) *Innovation and demonstration*: To develop and scale usage of near-infrared red technology to sort textiles to promote high-quality recycled products suitable for fiber-to-fiber recycling (Challenge Driven Innovation Initiative, The Swedish Innovation Platform for Textile Sorting)

Note: CSIRO: Commonwealth Scientific & Industrial Research Organisation.
Source: OECD *Net Zero Mission Database*.

Regardless of the form these objectives take, programme managers claim that the mission approach has allowed them to set clearer and more inclusively developed goals than the usual programmes and schemes developed by their organisations. In other words, the goals are formulated to be more impactful, rather than simply focusing on inputs or immediate outputs. Against this backdrop, all activities are geared towards the desired outcomes. Even in the most research-intensive mission, the intended results are at the heart of the projects and a cornerstone of research activities. Although many of these objectives are not "inspirational" to the general product as it is expected (Mazzucato, 2018[3]), these clearly enunciated objectives act as a "focusing device" and a reference point for interactions between the different actors all along the innovation chain, and across the various involved communities.

A majority of net zero missions have no clear targets at the outset

The objectives of MOIPs can be diverse. Ideally, a mission's objectives should be translated into concrete and measurable targets (Mazzucato, 2016[4]). However, only approximately 38% of the identified net zero missions (28 missions in 16 initiatives) have established such targets (and 55% of these missions, or 21, have specified greenhouse gas [GHG] emissions reduction targets). In clear contrast with the "mission theory", many missions are characterised by traditional – sometimes lengthy – descriptions of the objectives, blended in elements of context.[1]

Three main reasons explain this derogation to one of the main expected features of MOIPs:

- As previously mentioned, many missions start with a broad challenge and set a specific process for developing goals and targets from the bottom up, i.e. by the stakeholders themselves as part of their proposals to tackle the selected challenge. It is often a requirement in project or strategic agenda calls for proposal to specify clear targets with milestones. While this may lead to stronger buy-in from project partners or ecosystem stakeholders to the goals they have set themselves, it falls short of providing a common focal point, which in turn allows scale and synergetic effects between consistent or competing activities. Another key limitation is that the goals set in these initiatives might be less ambitious and transformative, as revealed by an evaluation of the Swedish strategic innovation programmes (Technopolis, 2022[46]).

- Setting clear targets agreed upon by a multiplicity of actors from different policy domains and industry sectors is a daunting task, especially at the start of the mission, when trust has yet to be built between the new partners. The broad challenge area and mission objective is the "best consensus" reached at the launch of the mission.
- While not specifying mission targets, often missions' objectives refer to their contribution to the 2030 and 2050 national agendas' targets. However, as they do not translate these net zero targets in their specific technological, thematic or industry areas, their directionality remains limited.

The decision of not setting clear targets is, in some cases, part of the MOIP process, notably in ecosystem-based MOIPs, which aim to empower new ecosystems and incrementally lead them to develop their own transition agenda. However, in several other cases, target setting depends on mission-specific factors, which can raise different technical and political debates. This is evidenced by the fact that in the same MOIPs, some missions have targets while others do not. For instance, among the France 2030 acceleration strategies (AS), the Clean Hydrogen AS has precise targets while the two acceleration strategies in the agriculture and agro-food areas do not, revealing the difficulties in achieving consensus on the best pathways to reduce emissions in these areas between the authorities in charge of industry, environment and agriculture.

As the selected cases show (Table 4.3), there are different ways to specify the mission targets in terms of reducing GHG emissions. They vary notably with the scope of the mission, which can be focused on one or several industries (e.g., "hard-to-abate sectors", construction) or technology (e.g. carbon capture, storage and utilisation [CCSU], carbon-removal technologies).[2]

Table 4.3. Selected examples of net zero mission targets

Missions and mission-oriented innovation policies	Targets
Towards Net Zero mission, CSIRO missions, Australia	Help Australia's hardest to abate sectors – including steel, sustainable aviation fuel and agriculture – halve their emissions by 2035
A carbon-free built environment by 2050 mission, Mission-Driven Top-Sector Policy, Netherlands	To achieve a CO_2-free built environment in 2050, requiring a reduction of 3.4 Mt CO_2 in 2030
Industrial Heat Shot mission, Energy Earthshots™, United States	Develop cost-competitive industrial heat decarbonisation technologies with at least 85% lower greenhouse gas emissions by 2035
Carbon-neutral hydrogen mission, France 2030 Acceleration Strategies, France	Develop clean mobility solutions, particularly for heavy vehicles, which will enable savings of more than 6 Mt CO_2 by 2030 (equivalent of the annual CO_2 emissions of the city of Paris).

Note: CSIRO: Commonwealth Scientific & Industrial Research Organisation.
Source: OECD *Net Zero Mission Database*.

Occasionally, objectives and targets may be merged into a concise mission statement, which, if well crafted, can be both inspirational and clear, detailing an ambitious goal within a specific time frame. Such statements act as recognisable "entry points" for the mission.

> *Net zero mission cases*
>
> *▸ Moonshot Goal 5, Moonshot R&D Programme, Japan. The mission aims for the "creation of industry that enables sustainable global food supply by exploiting unused biological resources by 2050.".*
>
> *▸ Hydrogen Earthshot™, Energy Earthshots™, United States. The mission has formalised its main objective as the "1 1 1" goal, i.e. the objective of "reducing the cost of clean hydrogen by 80% to USD 1 per 1 kilogram in one decade".*
>
> *▸ Soil Mission, Horizon Europe Missions, European Union. The mission's objective at its inception was to ensure that "75% of soils are healthy by 2030 for healthy food, people, nature and climate". It has changed to become '100 living labs and lighthouses to lead the transition towards healthy soils by 2030'.*

Missions set common objectives in uncertain and contested environments

As noted, engaging a diverse array of public and private stakeholders in defining mission objectives is fundamental to Mission-Oriented Innovation Policies (MOIPs). However, this process is not always straightforward and can be marked by contestation, conflicts, and power games. Setting clear objectives and targets requires that the mission partners have come to an agreement not only on what must be achieved but also to a certain extent on a subset of pathways to realise these targets, hence excluding others. This is particularly difficult when dealing with the transition to net zero, since it involves delicate trade-offs and balances between different categories of actors and sectors and possible "phasing out" compensation measures for all those who might be negatively affected by the coming changes.

Although they focus on the contribution of innovation to the transition, net zero missions are, therefore, hardly purely technical and neutral and are formed in a context where many elements of consensus on how to reach the national net zero commitments are still to be realised. Setting clear objectives at the outset is not limited to adopting "good project management practices". The goals – and when they exist, the targets that accompany them – enshrine the results of negotiations on the objectives. They also reflect hypotheses regarding the evolution of sometimes uncertain variables (e.g. carbon and energy prices, availability of raw materials, geopolitics, capacity to overcome scientific and technological bottlenecks, evolution of users' perceptions and preferences) that influence these sociotechnical options, and their even more uncertain results on the state of the world. The framing of the possible solutions within a mission is therefore "*likely to be a very politically and normatively laden process in which different actors try to lead the innovation system's focus into the direction that they favour*" ((Hekkert et al., 2020[5]).

A mission is, therefore, not only a technological and economic partnership but a locus of debates, providing a platform for public-private, cross-ministerial and inter-sectoral negotiations. These dialogues become pivotal when decisions about long-term futures – ones that intimately impact people's well-being – are at stake. Narrowing the lens solely to the scientific and technological ambiguities would overlook the intricate socio-political dimension of missions and underestimate the underpinning power conflicts and disagreements, which are important drivers of their implementation (Wanzenböck et al., 2020[6]). While contemporary innovation systems offer many instances where these negotiations can take place (such as committees, industrial associations and unions), the specific added value of missions is that they make the results of the negotiations readily "actionable", since they are directly linked to decision and implementation structures.

Direct linkages between the orientation, co-ordination and implementation of STI activities represent significant changes relative to policy practices and processes of traditional fragmented innovation systems. The mission stakeholders in the negotiation can directly refer to the ensuing actions to strengthen their positions. Moreover, the government can tie its financial commitment to the fulfilment of the mission's objectives, ensuring that the selected path upholds certain societal values that might not always resonate with the singular objectives of corporations or other interest groups.

Strategic policy intelligence is essential to support the development of the mission objectives and strategic agenda

Developing objectives requires substantial information and knowledge to strengthen their underlying hypotheses. However, the absence of a dedicated budget for certain missions means they must lean heavily on the capacity and resources of specific participants during the mission definition stage. This can compromise the acceptability of these objectives, especially when controversial topics are at play.

Time is another critical resource in the development of objectives and targets. This condition is not always realised, since missions can be launched under high political pressure to start functioning as soon as possible. Budget and time not only ensure that the objectives are evidence-based, but also allow them to depart from conservative options driven by incumbents.

> *Net zero mission case*
>
> *▸ Clean hydrogen, France 2030 Acceleration Strategies, France. It took more than a year for the French authorities to develop the "clean hydrogen AS". This time was used to conduct preliminary studies to calibrate and strengthen the legitimacy of the targets; run extensive consultations to assess needs; and issue calls for expressions of interest to identify potential solutions and project partners and negotiate common objectives with them despite a wide diversity of views and interests. As a result, the mission deliberately includes some strong choices that exclude certain options. For example, the strategy focuses only on clean hydrogen for applications where battery storage technologies are ill-suited (hence mainly heavy vehicles), which would be produced with electrolysers plugged into the electricity network. The mission objectives also include clear choices regarding the type, capacity, and distance of the electrolysers to the application site.*

The absence of budgets for supporting the development of objectives (left to the poorly evidence-based political debate or to stakeholders themselves) also results in the limited use of dedicated forward-looking support tools. Only a handful of missions harness formal foresight techniques to support objective-setting, despite the advantages in addressing comprehensive sociotechnical challenges.[3] In most cases, a mission's strategic agenda is defined using technology road-mapping techniques rather than a full-fledged foresight exercise.[4] This, in part, reflects countries' limited experience using foresight in policy making. Another reason for the limited use of foresight is the narrow techno-centric scope of many net zero missions.

Some missions have used advanced methods to define their objectives in a forward-looking way, using various design approaches (Vinnova's pilot missions) or theory of changes (BMK[5] national missions).

> *Net zero mission cases*
>
> *▸ Vinnova's pilot missions, Sweden. Vinnova has prototyped two missions to develop, test and formalise a novel design process for missions. The initiative was led by a dedicated strategic design team (about 3 full time equivalent) including design and domain experts and two specific mission teams. The process was also supported by groups of academic researchers. The resulting process involved various top-down and bottom-up steps of consultations and engagement of the concerned ecosystems' actors (respectively around school food and mobility), from pupils to experts and ministers. Each stage of the design process resulted in an object (Angles, Missions, Prototypes, Demonstrators) and used different event moderation techniques and tools such as Systems Actors workshop, Design Workshops and System Canvas. The resulting process is described precisely in Hill (2022[7]).*

▸ Transition missions, Austria. The strategic agendas in the form of concrete Impact Pathways 2030 were designed for each of the four BMK national missions (climate-neutral city, energy transition, mobility transition and circular economy) collectively in workshops using electronic tools (such as Mural or Miro) in 2022. These pathways start with the problems to tackle and define the general goals that need to be achieved to tackle them. They are then translated into specific goals, operational STI goals. Respective activities and target groups have been identified to meet the goals as have in some cases expected results and outcomes, and expected impacts. The linkages between these different elements, including when it pertains to different problems areas, were also identified. Moreover, the governance structure needed to implement the impact pathways for the four missions has been set up and a monitoring system including indicators was developed. These Impact Pathways are a reference point for concrete annual STI funding and additional activities for each mission. Moreover, there is an annual review meeting, when each mission team reflects on the progress of the mission based on the defined indicators and additional qualitative information.

▸ CSIRO Missions, Australia. To support the mission definition stage that hinges upon consultations and consensus building among actors pertaining to different disciplines and sectors, CSIRO use dedicated tools, including 'mission design canvas' and 'mission theory of change'. The theory of change focuses mission teams on defining the timebound and specific mission objective and describing impact pathways, i.e., how the innovation system will need to function to achieve the objective. The Mission Design Canvas are used to define the work packages that will be needed to operationalise the impact pathways. They also include what resources and capability will be needed and the sequencing of activities. This framework also helps to 'surface any dependencies or trade-offs between or within interventions'. (CSIRO, 2023).

The mission-oriented strategic agendas act as collective action frameworks

In several cases, the objectives are not the starting point but rather a first result of the mission itself. Many missions start with broad objectives, priorities or "mission areas". The first step of the mission is to develop or refine the objectives, most often embedding them in a strategic agenda or road map. The five EU missions,[6] for instance, started with five broad mission areas and a mandate for groups of high-level specialists in each area (the mission boards) to first devise a strategy featuring objectives and targets (the mission board reports) then a plan (the implementation plans). These loose directional elements do not really aim to set a clear orientation, but rather incentivise and facilitate the formation of large partnerships, wherein public and private actors jointly set attainable objectives and develop a collective strategy to meet them. This is particularly true of ecosystem-based MOIPs, which start with a call for strategic agendas, followed by the selection and implementation of some of these agendas.

A mission's initial objectives and targets are almost always accompanied by a strategic agenda to ensure the directionality and consistency of its different activities. These agendas (under different denominations and formats) are key to the expression of top-down and bottom-up dynamics. While governments still play a strong role at the political stage of setting the mission's objectives and targets, it is almost always the stakeholders who develop the strategic agenda which maps the different pathways towards fulfilling these objectives. What differentiates these mission-oriented strategic agendas from traditional strategies is that they are developed, implemented and monitored in an integrated way, allowing the strategic agenda to become the authoritative framework for action. In several missions, some components of the strategic agendas are directly used to develop the call for proposals; they can also be used on a regular basis to monitor progress on the different activities against the road map and identify gaps in the mission.

Net zero mission cases

▸ Carbon-free Built Environment', Mission-driven Top Sectors and Innovation Policy, The Netherlands. The implementation of the Dutch "Carbon-free Built Environment" mission is guided by four multiannual mission innovation programmes (MMIPs) covering different sub-areas. The MMIPs include not only the activities to be performed but also the map of public financial resources deployed across the entire innovation chain by different identified actors, from fundamental and applied research to pilots and demonstrators. The call for

proposals for the implementation of the mission are directly based on these MMIPs (some calls include copy-pasted text from the initial mission document). Since all the 25 top sectors' missions have developed such MMIPs, they are also used to identify and strengthen synergies among them.

▸ The EU Climate-Neutral and Smart Cities mission, Horizon Europe Missions, EU. The mission, officially launched in 2021, aims to 'support, promote and showcase 100 European cities in their systemic transformation towards climate neutrality by 2030 and turn these cities into innovation hubs for all cities, benefiting quality of life and sustainability in Europe by 2050.' Like for the other four EU missions, the objectives of the EU 'Cities mission were developed by a Mission Board that was formed in 2019 to help specify and design the mission, and start its implementation. The Mission Boards undertook multiples consultations of stakeholders, citizens as well as national, regional, and local authorities, listening to their expectations and needs through a series of events across EU countries. The Commission together with partners also held citizen engagement events to collect proposals from the public for the five EU missions. Two sessions per mission were organised with 10 different European countries. Citizens could also upload their ideas on a digital platform. As a result of this process, the experts issued their Mission Board report in September 2020. This report provides details on the mission objectives, the different mission's axes and ways to achieve them. It was complemented in September 2021 by a Mission Board Implementation Plan which provides precise information on the ways to achieve the mission's objectives. According to interviewees, the mission represents a significant change with regards to other EU Framework Programmes. Firstly, the mission has clear objectives and targets regarding the impact to be achieved by a certain date transcending the Framework Program, while traditionally the programmes are more exploratory, open-ended and limited to a seven-year timeframe. This focus on the expected impacts by 2030 and 2050 results in 'reverse calendar' practices, whereby the whole mission is planned backward from these deadlines. Secondly, the mission agenda was developed in an inclusive manner by the Mission Board with significant stakeholder engagement, while traditionally the European Commission sets the objectives with consultations done through official channels (programme committees with EU Member representatives).

▸ CSIRO Missions, Australia. CSIRO missions are developed collectively following an iterative co-design process. Following the internal preparation of the process during about 4 weeks, the first critical stage is called the 'initial sprint' and lasts about 6 to 8 weeks. This stage aims to 'facilitates consensus building among internal stakeholders, validates the mission idea for initial investment and accelerates the mission idea toward launch readiness.' It includes several steps notably 'problem exploration' based on a first brief, 'system discovery' to map the system's key areas, 'stakeholder engagement' to improve the problem definition, 'reframe and refocus' bases on what has been learned and ensure linkages to CSIRO priorities, 'mission projects' and 'mission roadmap' to define and prioritise projects, and insert them in pathways to address the problem. This stage ends with the presentation of a mission proposal to CSIRO senior management. (CSIRO, 2023).

▸ INNO-CCUS, Innomissions, Denmark. Following broadly the approach used by Sweden to select its Strategic Innovation Programmes, the Danish Innomissions started with a 'Call for roadmaps' thought which all relevant stakeholders are encouraged to come together to contribute their expertise and propose a realistic and robust strategy to achieve the objectives of broadly define challenges. Roadmaps describe challenges and gaps within the mission, strongholds and potential and sketch key activities and relevant work stream themes for future partnerships. They develop a holistic perspective, covering the entire value chain and all components of the innovation system (from research to investment, education, legislations, etc.). They define expected short-, mid- and long-term impacts. As a result of this call, the Innovation Fund Denmark's Board of Directors selected six roadmaps out of the 12 that were submitted. The roadmaps were developed by wide range of actors. The Carbon Capture, Utilisation and Storage (CCUS) roadmap for instance was the result of a collaborative effort between six universities, three Research & Technology Organisations (RTOs), clusters and other stakeholders including regulatory authorities, industry, and non-governmental organisations. These roadmaps were then used to guide applications to the 'Call for partnerships'. Consortia were asked to submit action plans to realise the roadmaps.

▸ The Alchemist, Korea. The programme sets themes and supports a series of projects under each theme through a stage-gated approach – starting with six projects in year one of a theme, three projects in year two. The Alchemist has set 19 themes so far. To set the themes, KEIT conducts desk research on the current state of technologies, and then what the future societal challenges will be. It also uses its big data platform to explore quantitative trends behind technologies, and a public platform where citizens can submit their ideas. In addition, KEIT conducts a survey of top industry leaders and academics from the National Academy of Engineering, and other academics. This work culminates in 20-30 draft themes. These draft themes are presented to the

Alchemist Programme's Grand Challenge Committee, which consists of experts from science and technology, as well as humanities and social sciences, like science fiction writers, to help embed some futures thinking into the programme. Thematic working groups are created for each candidate theme to inform this work. The Grand Challenges Committee then selects 10-20 themes. Once the challenge themes are selected, a working group of industry and academic experts then oversees each theme and decides what projects to fund. Each theme has an accompanying brief that provides directionality by identifying several priority technology areas, and then how it envisions the innovations developed will improve society in the future. For instance, the Sustainable Beyond Plastics theme identifies bioplastics, new organic/inorganic materials, recycled plastic, and recycling technology as some related technologies. It then sets out its vision for the future as a "post-oil sustainable plastic economy and society, improving the functions of existing plastics. A society where material circulation of new plastics and composite materials based on innovative alternative renewable resources is possible". The briefs for each theme also include more technical analysis with regards to technical limitations, the innovativeness of the theme, prospects for creating new markets, expected timelines for the innovations to have societal impact, the global competitiveness in the technology areas, how Korea can secure global leadership in the field, the potential social impact, and technological differentiation (OECD, Forthcoming[8]).

While strategic agendas are never binding and there is no "stick", peer pressure among the mission partners in the broad governance bodies can exert a significant influence on possible opportunistic behaviours by the different partners.

An underlying condition for the effectiveness and legitimacy of strategic agendas is that they should be both directional and flexible. They must be a "living document" that evolves regularly to adapt to new internal and external conditions. In this regard, some missions, such as the Danish Green CCSU mission or the Japanese Moonshots, have established procedures to revise their strategic agendas annually.

Missions' net zero objectives interact with a broader set of objectives

The objective of combatting climate change in net zero missions is always intertwined with other objectives, most often environmental and economic objectives and, in some specific cases, health or security goals (Table 4.4).

Table 4.4. Selected examples of net zero missions by type of objective

Type of objective	Definition	Example of net zero missions
Climate change	All missions, by virtue of the selection for inclusion in this study, had addressed climate change. This objective relates to all factors associated with mitigating or adapting to climate change.	Germany's High-tech Strategy 2025 mission to address climate change through achieving substantial greenhouse gas (GHG) neutrality in industry and use research and innovation funding (research, development, demonstration and market launch) of new technologies to enable industry to contribute to the long-term goal of achieving substantial GHG neutrality by 2045.
Economic impacts	Economic impacts encompass any explicit aim to develop markets/technologies/applications/outputs that had tangible commercial benefits and/or were able to position the country as a market leader or stimulate job creation.	Korea's Alchemist's mission on low-cost CO_2-free hydrogen production facilities aims to address climate change by making energy alternatives, such as CO_2-free hydrogen production facilities, more readily available and attractive by developing fundamental technologies and processes for mass producing cost-effective and eco-friendly hydrogen. In so doing, it seeks to position Korea as a leader in the global market in hydrogen car production and energy production.

Environment	Environment relates to reducing the negative effects on the natural environment, as distinct from mitigating or adapting to climate change per se.	Australia's Commonwealth Scientific & Industrial Research Organisation's mission to end plastic waste aims to address climate change by reducing dependence on GHG emission-intensive industries such as plastic by reinventing the way plastic is made, processed and recycled to reduce the amount of plastic entering the environment.
Food security	Food security encompasses missions that focus on the availability of food and on ensuring populations have access to it.	The UK Research and Innovation Industrial Strategy Challenge Fund's mission to transform food production seeks to address climate change by supporting new ways to produce food that reduce emissions and pollution and contribute to feeding a growing world population in a sustainable and secure way.
Health	Health encompasses missions that in some way relate to physical and mental health and well-being.	Sweden's Vinnova's Pilot Mission on healthy sustainable food addresses climate change through a focus on reforming the food system, so that is centred more around health and sustainability. It uses the "school meal" as a lever.
Social justice and inclusiveness	Social justice and inclusiveness encompass missions that include a focus on ensuring that a broad spectrum of people is able to participate in and contribute to all aspects of a society and that there is an equal spread of economic, political and social rights and opportunities.	Sweden's Innovation Partnership Program's mission on skills supply and lifelong learning aims to address climate change by better preparing for climate change and digitalisation by stimulating the requisite skills development and lifelong learning.
Sovereignty	This mission explicitly stated an objective to reduce dependence on foreign sources of energy/ technologies/applications and achieve autonomy by generating their own comparable outputs.	Spain's Centre for the Development of Industrial Technology mission to strengthen technological capabilities for safe and sustainable energy autonomy addresses climate change by developing alternate, clean energy sources that, in turn, create a system where energy sovereignty is possible.

Source: OECD *Net Zero Mission Database*.

By definition, all net zero missions aim to tackle climate change by reducing GHG emissions. In addition to mitigating climate change, 70% of them have economic objectives (e.g. creating jobs) and 55% wider environmental objectives (Figure 4.1).

Figure 4.1 Breakdown of net zero missions analysed in this study by objective groups

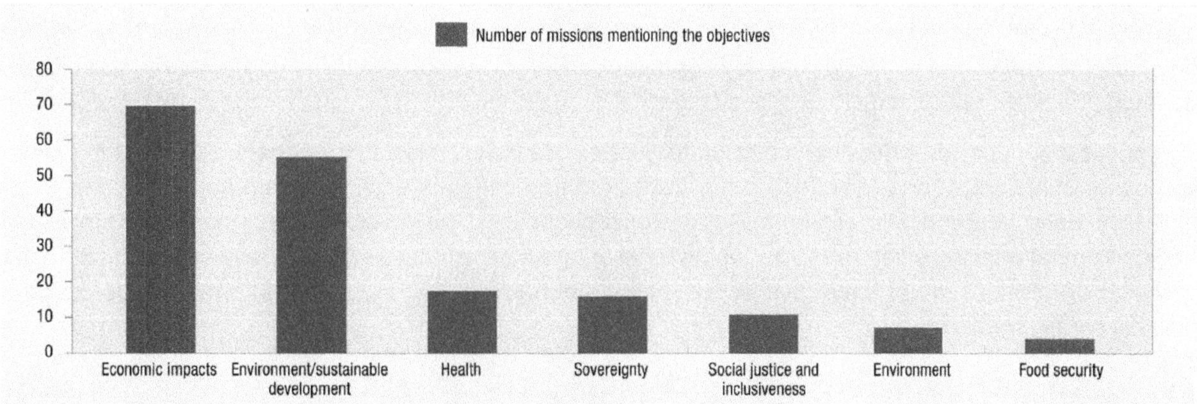

Note: Each net zero mission can be relevant to multiple objective groups.
Source: OECD *Net Zero Mission Database*.

As shown in Annex C, some missions have translated their economic objectives into targets. Furthermore, while not always officially emphasised, strengthening national competitiveness and creating new jobs always feature among the missions' objectives, if only informally.

Net zero mission cases

- *Develop safe, networked and clean mobility, High-Tech Strategy 2025, Germany. During the 2017-21 legislative period the mission aimed to "Make Germany into the leading supplier and market for electromobility".*
- *Low-cost carbon dioxide (CO2)-free hydrogen production facilities, The Alchemist, Korea. The mission that aims to "develop fundamental technologies and processes for mass-producing cost-effective and eco-friendly hydrogen in order to secure the leading position of Korea in global market in hydrogen car production and energy production.*
- *Clean Hydrogen mission, France 2030 Acceleration Strategies, France. Beside its target in terms of installed electrolysis capacity, the French Clean Hydrogen mission added the goal to 'build an industrial sector that creates jobs and guarantees our technological mastery, in particular by creating 50,000 to 150,000 jobs in the country'.*

These diverse objectives primarily reflect the multifaceted and systemic nature of societal challenges. This diversity is also intrinsically linked to the mission process. To encompass a broader spectrum of policy sectors, early mission advocates must negotiate and evolve the mission objectives, incorporating additional goals and targets. As argued in Chapter 2, one of the intrinsic "how-to conundrums" of missions consists in balancing a broad range of partners on one side and directionality and consistency on the other. The resulting bargaining between different policy sectors creates a risk of diluting the mission by adding multiple objectives or making these objectives wide and vague to accommodate all partners' interests.

Missions often lack high-level political support

The "inspirational" nature of their missions, as well as their potential societal impact, can, in principle, justify and attract higher level support in the political and administrative sphere. It is often claimed that missions are political, due to their directional nature. First, their normative goals, which in principle have more to do with societal ends than means and therefore have a stronger impact on people's life and well-being, are *de facto* political. Second, these goals raise a higher level of social contestation and can, therefore, be contested by some actors, which facilitates a *politicisation* of MOIPs compared to traditional policies (Wittmann et al., 2021[9]).

The political dimension of missions originates primarily from their direct connection to societal impacts and, therefore, citizens and politicians' mandates. In a sense, the mission makes explicit the link between citizens' lives and the needed research and innovation activities and the policies that support them. As explained by an interviewee, "*the mission framework makes the activities, even when they involve advanced scientific and technological developments, much more accessible to policy maker and citizen, as their objectives talk directly to people's issues*".

The political support for a mission is difficult to assess. However, mission managers claim that it is often too low or only declaratory, not effective nor translated into concrete acts. They are hardly referred to by high-level politicians and policy makers. Notable exceptions exist, however, such as Austria's EU missions and certain national transition missions, which receive direct ministerial support. These cases illustrate the potential of missions when they have active, high-level backing that translates into real resources and political commitment.

Alignment and holistic monitoring of various actors' plans

Reducing GHG emissions, like other intricate societal challenges, requires extensive cross-sectoral co-ordination. Policy fragmentation greatly hinders innovation systems' capacity to respond adequately to wicked societal challenges, such as those included in the 2030 Agenda for Sustainable Development (OECD, 2019[10]). Against this backdrop, net zero missions ensure the cross-sectoral alignment of policy makers' plans.

Missions gather a broader range of policy sectors around common objectives but cross-government coordination beyond the STI policy area remains difficult

In-depth fieldwork for 17 net zero mission case studies shows that almost all involved a significantly expanded scope of co-ordination between different public policy actors. These missions gather around the table not only public authorities in charge of research and business innovation, but also relevant sectoral ministries and agencies with authority on the relevant needed reforms, demand support policies and other essential framework conditions for the transition. This allows taking more informed and holistic decisions.

This co-ordination primarily takes place in dedicated governance bodies with various advisory, decision-making or monitoring roles. In the larger MOIP initiatives, these groups are replicated at different levels (political, strategic and operational).[7]

> *Net zero mission case*
>
> *▸ EU Climate-Neutral and Smart Cities mission, Horizon Europe Missions, EU. The five EU Horizon Europe missions have introduced new coordination practices within the European Commission. At the highest level, there is a Project Group of Commissioners that meet two or three times per year to supervise and discuss the execution of the five missions. Each mission is led by two high level managers from the Directorate-General for Research and Innovation (DG RTD) and another Directorate-General of the European Commission. The EU Climate-Neutral and Smart Cities mission (Cities Mission) is co-led by two high-level managers from the Directorate-General for Environment and the Directorate-General for Research and Innovation. Besides the leadership, several groups and committees – notably the" mission owners' groups" at working and director levels – co-ordinate actions between the twelve Directorates-General more or less directly involved in the mission. This is said to have significantly reduced the number of overlaps between different directorates' activities related to cities. The mission's mode of governance is new, as climate neutrality has traditionally been addressed by different parts of the European Commission (transport, energy, urban planning, etc.). The Cities Mission provides a legitimate authority at the systemic level (a "climate neutrality interlocutor"). The mission also supports a cross-sectoral approach within each of the selected 112 cities, which are asked to co-develop a "Climate City Contract" (CCC) with the different stakeholders. These contracts include an overall net-zero transition plan across all sectors (energy, buildings, waste management, transport, industry and AFOLU), together with related investment plans. This holistic approach is an essential component of the common guidelines and requirements that cities must follow in developing these contracts. The CCCs embed and officialise the systemic dimension for each city participating in the mission.*

STI public authorities in charge of research or business innovation policy have initiated the bulk of the MOIP initiatives with net zero missions and act as the "champions" of mission-oriented policies in their respective national systems.

Out of the 30 MOIP initiatives included in this study, 21 are directly led by public bodies with authorities on research and innovation policies (Figure 4.2). They are also essential in the missions that are co-led by STI and sectoral authorities, such as the Federal Ministry for Climate Action, Environment, Energy, Mobility, Innovation and Technology's transition missions in Austria. Within the "super ministry" in charge of climate, environment, energy, mobility, innovation and technology, the department in charge of innovation leads and supports the four missions, with the involvement of the relevant sectoral departments (e.g., energy). Out of the three MOIP initiatives led by central government organisations, two are under the responsibility of the Japanese high-level committee in charge of the STI policies (the Council for Science, Technology and Innovation). The remaining initiative (the French acceleration strategies) are led by a dedicated institution under the Prime Minister Office in charge of France 2030, the large investment and recovery plan that "aims to transform the national economy through innovation".[8]

Figure 4.2. Breakdown of net zero missions analysed in this study by main responsible authority

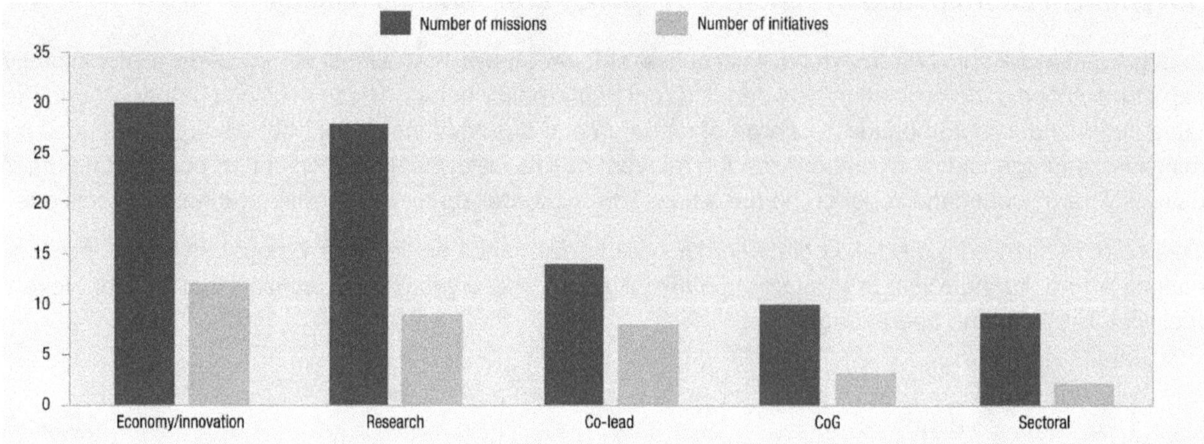

Note: COG: centre of government.
Source: OECD *Net Zero Mission Database*.

Cross-sectoral co-ordination faces many costs and challenges

Holistic co-ordination has been acknowledged as a key weakness of national innovation systems for decades. All OECD Reviews of Innovation Policy point to the core issue of co-ordination between public authorities in charge of research and those responsible for business innovation. The upswing in societal challenges has made this issue even more acute, as the scope of the needed co-ordination includes other sectoral policy and regulatory administrations with closely related mandates (the "challenge owners").

While MOIP is seen as a possible response to this new imperative, in many countries it occurs in a context where previous challenges related to the functioning of the innovation system and economic growth remain unresolved. As emphasised by Whitman et al. (2021) and Arnold et al. (2018[11]) traditional unsolved challenges of co-ordination and political leadership that have been debated for decades are still relevant in the context of MOIPs.

This study shows that cross-sectoral co-ordination is not only one of the main expected added values of MOIPs, but also one of the main practical challenges. This is confirmed by a recent survey of mission practitioners and stakeholders, who rank "silo effects" as the highest risk for a mission's success (OECD and DDC, 2022[12]).

Managing broad missions demands numerous meetings to take collective decisions involving a wide set of actors in different parts of the government on a diverse set of issues. It is, therefore, necessary to strike a "sustainable" balance between the benefits of co-ordination on the one hand and transaction costs on the other. Although most net zero missions are still recent, some have already readjusted this balance based on experience.

Net zero mission case

- *Mission-driven Top Sectors and Innovation Policy, The Netherlands. The Dutch 25 missions are characterised for their detailed governance, coordinating various actors across different challenge areas and levels (high-level/political and operational), in several governance bodies (e.g. mission teams, top sector teams, programme advisory groups to support MMIPs and transversal teams across several missions) (Janssen, 2020[13]). Several actors involved in this policy have pointed to a growing "mission fatigue" owing to the high number of meetings of these bodies. The policy is now being reformed to simplify this governance structure and increase its efficiency.*

In cross-sectoral co-ordination, getting diverse actors to the negotiation table is just the beginning. The subsequent challenge is ensuring each representative – particularly those from sectoral departments – actively participates, disseminates information, and potentially commits interventions and funding for the mission. Missions compete for time and resources in administrations that would not normally be involved in such activities, as they are not traditionally considered central to their sectoral mandate. Some of these actors, who act not only as contact points but also as "ambassadors" for the mission within their administration, struggle to engage the leaders of related programmes and activities in the mission and convince them to commit resources.

Policy mix integration and portfolio management are still underdeveloped.

Missions combine different types of public interventions but fall short of supporting scale-up and deployment

As shown in Figure 4.2, a mission involves a portfolio of policy and regulatory measures which, in almost all cases, predate it. The mission integrates existing interventions in a coherent bundle to meet specific objectives. The different interventions can be categorised into six different types (Figure 4.4).

Figure 4.3. Different types of public interventions to support the transition towards net zero

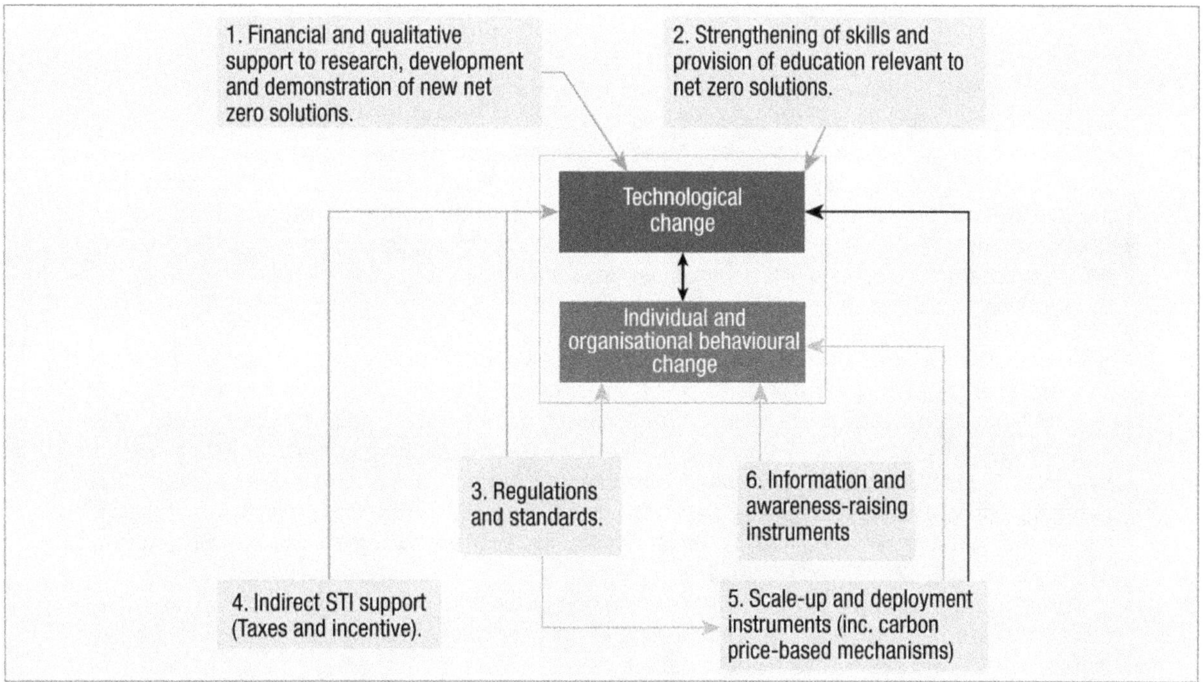

Note: STI: science, technology and innovation.

Although net zero missions vary greatly in terms of scale and scope, they always combine several of these interventions under a common strategic and governance framework. Grants for research and innovation activities remain one of the main policy instruments for channelling mission funding to project partners. They are, however, accompanied by a wealth of other measures designed to support (among others) specific projects, competence or excellence centres, regulatory reforms, competitions and prizes, demonstration sites, training or communication, and awareness-raising activities. For example, the UK industry decarbonisation missions dedicate specific actions to skill strengthening. The Danish

CCSU mission performs studies to better understand and shape public acceptance of these technologies. Several missions, such as the Finnish Growth Engine "Green E2", support the emergence of new ecosystems around the mission, which constitute "interest groups" that help promote the necessary regulatory reforms.

An important rationale for integrating complementary instruments is to provide continuous support across the different stages of the innovation chain, from R&D to market deployment.

Net zero mission cases

- *Pilot E, Norway. In Pilot-E, the three agencies in charge of research and research-based innovation (Research Council of Norway), innovation and demonstration (Innovation Norway), and early-market deployment of energy technologies (Enova) have teamed up to provide a one-stop-shop for sustainable energy projects, such as green ships. Each of them mobilises its interventions to support the projects that are jointly selected to deliver the needed solutions, notably in the area of net zero or low carbon maritime transportation. The main instruments are the Research Council of Norway's Innovation Projects to support R&D, Innovation Norway's Environmental Technology Scheme to test solutions before commercialisation and Enova's implementation grants to support market deployment (including via public procurement for innovation).*

The external evaluation of Pilot-E performed in 2020 concluded that this combination of instruments along the innovation chain using a funnel approach is a 'relevant solution to respond to the need for better coordination of measures aimed at energy and environmental technology'. This improved coordination scheme 'has good potential for fulfilling the scheme's objective of getting new solutions onto the market faster', which is line with the expected results of this type 'acceleration mission' (Larrue, 2021[14]; Menon Economics, 2020[15]).

- *Moonshot R&D Programme, Japan. In each of its seven Moonshot goals, the Moonshot R&D Programme implements a portfolio approach to manage the high risk of failure of projects. The main idea is to create an R&D portfolio system as a package of projects for each Moonshot Goal and evaluate the possibility of achieving a goal at the level of this package, not at the level of each individual project. Between 3 and 13 projects were selected for each of the seven goals. This strategy is reflected in the design of the programme. A Programme Director is appointed specifically at the level of each of the Moonshot goal and is tasked with the development and implementation of a Portfolio Plan. Programme Directors are asked to choose projects that try out different paths and methods to meet their respective Moonshot goals.*

- *Viable Cities, SIP, Sweden. The Viable Cities Strategic Innovation Programme (SIP) adopted a portfolio approach to achieve a systems view of the climate transition and help steer all needed innovation activities towards the common goal of climate neutrality. The portfolio is co-developed by each of the nine Member cities and their external partners. It not conceptualised as a mere list of projects but includes everything seen as relevant to the mission and also specific the challenges, needs, barriers or future options. Further aspects may feature investment plans, learning and people. Viable Cities defines seven dimensions of portfolios that portfolio managers should consider: 1/ Portfolio (co)-ownership: who oversees and owns the overall portfolio as well as its component parts. 2/ Portfolio logic: what drives portfolio activities. 3/Portfolio elements: what activities are part of the portfolio. 4/ Nature of relations between elements: how objectives, teams, and activities are linked. 5/ Leverage mechanisms: how objectives, teams, or activities in the portfolio can be strengthened or transitioned. 6/ Categories of impact: what outcomes the portfolio approach targets (e.g., a greater number of innovation activities, or better alignment between efforts). 7/ Portfolio-building practices: how better portfolio coordination and collaboration can be supported (Hanson and Bleckenwegner, 9 June 2021[16]; OECD, 2022[17]).*

Although they integrate a broader set of policy instruments, very few missions currently include instruments to support the mass deployment of the newly developed solutions. The French Clean Hydrogen Acceleration Strategy is an exception in that respect. In most other initiatives, the scale-up and deployment support instruments are located outside the mission and are, therefore, not systematically co-ordinated with other interventions, notably STI instruments.

Net zero mission case

▸ Clean Hydrogen mission, France 2030 Acceleration Strategies, France. The French Clean Hydrogen Acceleration Strategy (AS) launched in 2020 has a budget of 3.4 billion euros for the period 2020-2023, with a further 7 billion euros planned up to 2030. With such a significant budget (the highest of all net zero missions in the database), the mission covers all aspects of setting up a hydrogen value chain (Technology readiness level [TRL] 1 to 9), from research to production, skills infrastructure, and markets. SA also aims to develop key technologies and key components through pilot projects for different types of uses and markets. An essential and unique added value of AS is that it also integrates scale-up instruments in the form of price-based deployment support mechanisms designed to compensate for the extra cost of decarbonized hydrogen compared with conventional hydrogen. To coordinate and manage this wide portfolio, the Clean Hydrogen AS – like all other ASs – has its own interministerial governance structure and a central coordinator attached to a public body under the Prime Minister Office. The coordinator's role is to support the coordination between the community of public and private mission partners and monitor all actions implemented against the collectively developed 10-year strategic agenda (Larrue, 2023[18]).

Another insightful case is DOE's energy Earthshots™. While these missions aim to achieve science and technology breakthroughs, several of them are co-ordinated with deployment targets and support mechanisms anchored 'outside' the formal scope of the mission.

▸ Energy Earthshots™, United States. The Earthshots™ offer an extensive policy mix that ranges from fundamental research to development and demonstration. A range of support schemes and funding sources are mobilised, such as Energy Earthshot Research Centers, a variety of challenge prize approaches as well as diverse type of technical assistance, such as capacity building through educational resources, training, and on-call assistance from technical experts and researchers at the DOE's national labs. Despite this broad policy mix, these missions remain focused on science and technology bottlenecks, as shown by their target formalised in terms of technical or costs performance. However, there are several examples of how the Energy Earthshots™ are complemented by related deployment targets. For example, the Clean Fuels and Products Shot is bolstered by the Sustainable Aviation Fuel Grand Challenge's deployment target. Floating Offshore Wind Shot has a second target led by the US Department of the Interior – it is a specific deployment target. The Earthshots™ also work closely with the other organisations responsible for delivering funding under the Bipartisan Infrastructure Law, the CHIPS and Science Act, and the Inflation Reduction Act, which offer additional support for deployment and infrastructure investments. For instance, the Hydrogen Shot has complementary programmes through the Bipartisan Infrastructure Law (Hydrogen Hubs and Hydrogen Demand Side Programs). The Inflation Reduction Act also creates a new Hydrogen Production Tax Credit to incentivise the domestic production of clean hydrogen, which will make this emerging low-carbon fuel source more cost-competitive. These initiatives all will advance the Hydrogen Shot and help bring the technologies it develops to market.

An important distinction between missions is not only the range of these instruments but their level of integration, i.e., the extent to which decisions regarding their implementation follow the commonly developed strategic agenda and are collectively monitored. Some missions can be loosely integrated, with the mission acting as a common heading for all relevant activities under its remit. As shown in Figure 2.4, this was the case for the missions under the former German "High-tech" Strategy (2009-21), which Wittman et al. (2020[19]) categorised as "umbrella missions".

Monitoring and evaluation frameworks have yet to be adapted to mission-oriented innovation policies

It is clear from interviews and a dedicated study commissioned by the Mission Action Lab to an external consultant (Arnold, 2022[20]) that in most mission cases there is still an important mismatch between the specificity of the mission approach and existing monitoring and evaluation rules and practices. Even in agencies having developed an innovative approach that differs significantly from traditional programmes, monitoring and evaluation remains traditional, paying little attention to the directional and systemic dimension of missions. There is a widely shared perception that new methodologies, processes and practices are needed to evaluate these policies, but no clear idea yet as to what these should be.

As mentioned above, a key task of evaluating missions should be – in addition to traditional STI policy evaluation at the level of each instrument – assessing its "second-order additionality" (see *Missions combine different types of public interventions but fall short of supporting scale-up and deployment*). This additionality depends on different types of systemic effects, in particular focusing effects, alignment effects and integration effects (Box 4.1).

Box 4.1. What are the main systemic effects expected from mission-oriented innovation policies?

To consider the specificities of missions in their evaluation, it is necessary to define their (expected) systemic effects. In essence, the systemic effects of missions pertain to three main groups of effects in relation to the three building blocks of mission-oriented innovation policies (MOIPs): 1) orientation; 2) co-ordination; and 3) integration.

Focusing effects: missions focus different actors, programmes and activities on the same objectives, more or less following the same strategic agendas they have collectively developed. These focusing effects can result in:

- greater legitimacy and higher visibility of the collective efforts
- greater scale (including critical mass effect) and scope (broader coverage of the problem-solution space)
- a higher level of engagement (due to risk sharing, mission inspiration and legitimacy, a more inclusive approach, etc.)
- higher ambition (more ambitious goals associated with collective action).

Alignment effects: These effects correspond to the benefits drawn from the co-ordination of the plans of the different public and private actors across administrative mandates and (industry and service) sectors to reach the common objectives they have defined. This alignment allows reaping different system benefits:

- reduction of unnecessary overlaps and duplications
- budget scale effects
- gathering of skills, strategic policy intelligence and information
- a better connection between public and private actors, leading to a higher leverage effects and greater effectiveness of public action.

Integration effects: Missions allow the integration of different activities and policy interventions (in a broad sense, i.e. including supply and demand-side instruments, financial and technical support, and reforms) to pursue the common objectives. This integration brings different system benefits:

- greater range and higher performance of solutions due to the combination of different components of a systems innovation (e.g. from charging infrastructure or the provision of green energy supply to the vehicle and the battery in the case of electric vehicles)
- more effective and efficient public support relying on the exploitation of synergies between different instruments and the reduction of conflicts and overlaps
- acceleration of solution development when the mission co-ordinates the policy interventions across the different stages of the innovation chain
- more thorough scanning and testing of different potential options (co-ordinated exploration of the problem-solution space).

Source: (Larrue, Tõnurist and Jonason, 2024[21])

To date, very few MOIPs have been evaluated and they rely to a large extent on traditional evaluation frameworks which overlook the systemic effects in the implementation of missions. The directionality of missions is also most often neglected, as confirmed by Haddad, Wise and Arnold (2023[22]) when comparing three evaluations of Swedish programmes (including two featuring in the OECD *Net Zero Mission Database*: Challenge-Driven Innovation and strategic innovation programmes). The authors emphasise that the evaluation approach remains rather "neutral" and process-oriented and hardly accounts for the purposeful and goal-specific nature of missions. Several other MOIPs are approaching the evaluation stage and mission teams, academics and analysts in many organisations, including the OECD, are searching for new methods and processes to capture their added value. Yet, some evaluation questions and criteria speak to the systemic dimension of missions, and they already provide some interesting insights regarding the added value of this policy approach and challenges in its implementation.

Net zero mission cases

▸ Mission-driven Top Sectors and Innovation Policy, A carbon-free built environment by 2050', in the Net Zero Mission Database. There has been no evaluation of the policy nor of any of its 25 missions yet, but a study was commissioned to an academic expert in 2020 by the lead ministry two years after the launch of the MOIP. The so-called 'post-commencement analysis' focused notably on the governance of the policy. It relied on interviews and desk review, and an in-depth mission case study (Janssen, 2020[13]).

▸ Pilot-E, Norway. Pilot E have been evaluated in 2020 – hence four years after its launch – by external consultants. It uses using a traditional STI programme evaluation method and framework but investigate some more specific issues such as the presence of system failures (define as 'market failures that cannot be corrected by the underlying arrangements individually'), the need for a better coordination of measures across the innovation chain to support commercialisation and whether the initiative has led to larger and more ambitious that the underlying schemes from the three agencies. The evaluation was informed by desk review, interviews and an online survey of beneficiaries (Menon Economics, 2020).

▸ UKRI Challenge Funds, UK. The National Audit Office performed an audit of the Challenge Fund in 2021. This exercise is at the level of the MOIP initiative (Challenge Fund) not at the level of the missions (the 23 Challenges). The audit put the emphasis on the management of the initiative and did not address coordination issues. It examines the overarching question of whether it has been set up in a way likely to optimise value for money. It relied on interviews and desk review. The National Audit Office also organised 'discovery and design' sessions with UKRI and the Department for Business, Energy & Industrial Strategy to build an early understanding of the challenges faced in implementing the initiative. This audit will be complemented by baseline, interim and final impact evaluation of each of the 23 challenges (NAO, 2020).

▸ SIP, Sweden. The 17 SIPs (missions) have been evaluated every three years according to a stage-gate approach. The six-year evaluation is the most recent and complete. It comprised several components undertaken by an external consultancy company: an individual evaluation of each SIP in its sixth year (by

batches depending on their starting dates); Meta-evaluations of the evaluations undertaken in 2019, 2020 and 2021; A final meta-evaluation and policy learning review of the whole programme in 2023. All evaluations were informed by desk review and interviews, expert review of SIP activities, project portfolios, and sample project applications and a bibliometric analysis of the publications produced by the SIPs. The evaluation included a policy learning exercise using the transition conceptual framework. identified functions associated with creating Technological Innovation Systems plus a handful of other functions associated in the literature with transitions management and strategic niche management. It assessed the performance and potential of each SIP against a set of 15 functions associated with creating and transitioning Technological Innovation Systems. Although this was an exploratory and modest exercise, the consultants argue that it 'allowed the strengths, weaknesses, and potential of the SIP instrument in connection with future missions-like policies to be explored in ways that would have been impossible without it'. They conclude that 'it would have been useful to devote more effort to the systemic analysis' (Technopolis, 2022; Arnold, 2022).

- *Horizon Europe missions, EU. A first assessment of the EU mission initiative and its five missions were performed in 2023 by external consultants and complemented by a European Commission self-assessment. The consultants performed interviews (around 13 per mission), an online survey and mission-specific policy workshops. The mission evaluation components were traditional: goal and objectives; selection process of each EU Mission; governance structures and functioning arrangements; progress towards the fulfilment of the objectives; and budget and funding arrangements. However, the underpinning assessment criteria took into account several key dimensions of missions: the presence of measurable goals; the relevance of the mission strategic agenda (the Implementation Plan); the added value compared to existing EU initiatives in the mission areas; the buy-in and support of several DGs (with concrete evidence of this support notably in terms of budget and alignment of policies); the articulation of different funds and programmes (European Commission, 2023[23]; 2021[24]). In its Communication 'EU Missions two years on: assessment of progress and way forward' (COM(2023) 457 final), the Commission concluded that "Experience with two years of implementation of five EU Missions has confirmed that the mission-based approach as an instrument of Horizon Europe incentivises the engagement of broad and enthusiastic communities of stakeholders. Through its ability to promote experimentation, coordination and scaling of deployment, the EU Mission instrument can play a pivotal role in necessary societal transitions across multiple domains." It also states that "Nevertheless, experience has also shown that to fully deliver on its potential, the Mission instrument needs to address a few remaining challenges, notably regarding public awareness, governance and its ability to leverage other sources of funding, including private funding."*

A review of the five most valuable evaluations of MOIPs including net zero missions against the three types of effects presented above shows that missions did deliver some of their expected effects in terms of directionality, cross-sectoral scope and co-ordination, and a broader portfolio of instruments and activities. Even more important at this early pilot stage of the MOIP approach where the formative dimension of evaluations is essential are the limitations identified and options for learning and improvement provided by these exercises (see Table 4.5 and Annex E). Overall, they clearly illustrate the potential benefits and difficulties of complementing well-established organisational and sectoral dynamics by a mission framework that enables the steering, co-ordination and integration of activities across silos.

Table 4.5. Synthesis of the main results of five mission-oriented innovation policy evaluations against three types of expected systemic effects

Policy	Focus	Alignment	Integration
Mission-driven Top Sectors and Innovation Policy	Confusion due to the high number of interrelated missions The mission strategic agendas are a useful guide but are too broad Strong sectoral directions appear very strong relative to mission dynamics	Difficult for some of the mission teams to assert their mandate relatively to sectoral bodies Increasingly committed sectoral ministries but remain mission partners rather than mission leaders Overly complex governance structure	Broad portfolio of existing instruments and additional activities to realise the missions Positive experiment of a dedicated mission integrated instrument Higher financial commitments (to be confirmed)
Pilot-E	Significant emphasis on the demand in the calls' development and project selection, but users not sufficiently involved in selected consortia	Close co-ordination of three agencies in the initiative allows scale and scope effects, more ambitious projects, and more predictable funding Lean structure and low modest transaction costs (15%)	Better integration of the different support measures along the innovation chain Significant synergies between the different agencies' interventions Lack of a unified project management and monitoring system
UK Research and Innovation Challenge Funds	Strong challenge orientation of missions ("Challenges") Long process for selecting, legitimising and substantiating the missions Too many missions (24) Useful strategic agendas ("benefit maps") in all missions	Audit does not address co-ordination issues Lack of an impact-oriented monitoring and evaluation system	Key role of the Challenge Directors in each mission but difficult to hire due to their rare profiles
Strategic innovation programmes (SIP)	SIPs' orientations are long term and determined bottom-up by the ecosystems to address broadly defined societal challenges Each SIP defines its own theory of change with support from significant strategic intelligence, but is unevenly used in practice	Broad intersectoral scope of the SIPs The SIPs provided a platform for strategic dialogue among various system actors	Increased integration along the innovation chain Incremental innovations, no system change Lack of effects at mission level, focus remains too much at individual project level
Horizon Europe missions	The missions provide shared goals to various Directorate Generals as well as national and local authorities Wide co-creation of the missions' strategic agendas Lack of high-level political ownership	New forms of collaboration across European Commission services and levels of government (cross-sectoral steering and co-ordination bodies, co-lead of missions) Emergent co-ordination around missions at member state level; complex and heavy governance Lack of an appropriate mission monitoring system	Some level of interest from sources of funding beyond Horizon Europe but commitments remain limited Narrow portfolio of instruments mobilised and insufficient involvement of the private sector

Source: Annex D

Most of these evaluation exercises were conducted after only two or three years of implementation and were not fully fledged evaluations (apart from the Pilot-E and SIP ones). They mostly served as exploratory studies and early assessments. These results should, therefore, be taken as food for thought rather than definitive judgements. More and more elaborated evaluation cases will need to be developed in the coming years.

Significant efforts are ongoing to design evaluation frameworks suited to capture missions' specific design features and effects, led by academic and mission practitioners.[1] Elzinga et al. (2023[25]), for instance, propose several mission evaluation steps, including an assessment of the mission's contribution to a well-defined set of innovation system functions. These functions are drawn from earlier work on innovation systems and the transition literature.[2]

The OECD Mission Action Lab has developed a self-assessment framework based on the mission design principles framework (OECD, 2023[26]). This framework was applied in a pilot exercise conducted in Austria to support the co-ordination and implementation of EU missions in the country (Box 4.2).

Box 4.2. The Mission Action Lab mission-oriented innovation policy self-assessment framework

In co-operation with Austrian authorities, the mission design principles framework has been further developed into a self-assessment tool and tested in the national context. Austria provides one of the most elaborated efforts not only to mobilise and co-ordinate the relevant community of actors around the five European Union (EU) missions, but also to make them national missions in their own right (see Federal Ministry of Education, Science and Research, Austria (2022[27])). Besides the development and real-condition testing of the tool, this Mission Action Lab exercise aimed to provide Austrian actors involved in each mission with: a map to assess their current position – a self-assessment of their progress in the mission design and implementation "journey" using a framework developed specifically by the OECD to analyse missions; and a compass to show the way forward based on the identified gaps.

The tool consists of assessing the extent to which the different mission communities feel their mission complies with each design principle and what actions need to be taken to improve it in this particular dimension. For instance, the tool asks whether the mission is guided by clear and well-informed orientations, is legitimate, etc. A first step consisted in designing an assessment survey sent to the members of each of the five mission action groups and the "EU Missions Working Group" in charge of central support and monitoring. Each design principle is informed by a few questions. To better guide action, each question distinguished between the assessment (how the mission performs on the design principle?) and needs (what would need to be improved?) dimensions. The comparisons at design principles or building block level revealed marked profiles that were very effective to support informed discussions in subsequent workshops in each mission area (Figure 4.5). Discussions during these workshops focused on understanding the reasons for the contrasted results and building consensus on actions going forward in the concrete implementation of the mission. A final all-missions roundtable complemented the process. The conclusions of this self-assessment exercise were synthetised in a final report that included overarching and mission-specific recommendations.

Figure 4.4. Results of the questions informing the horizontal and vertical co-ordination design principles

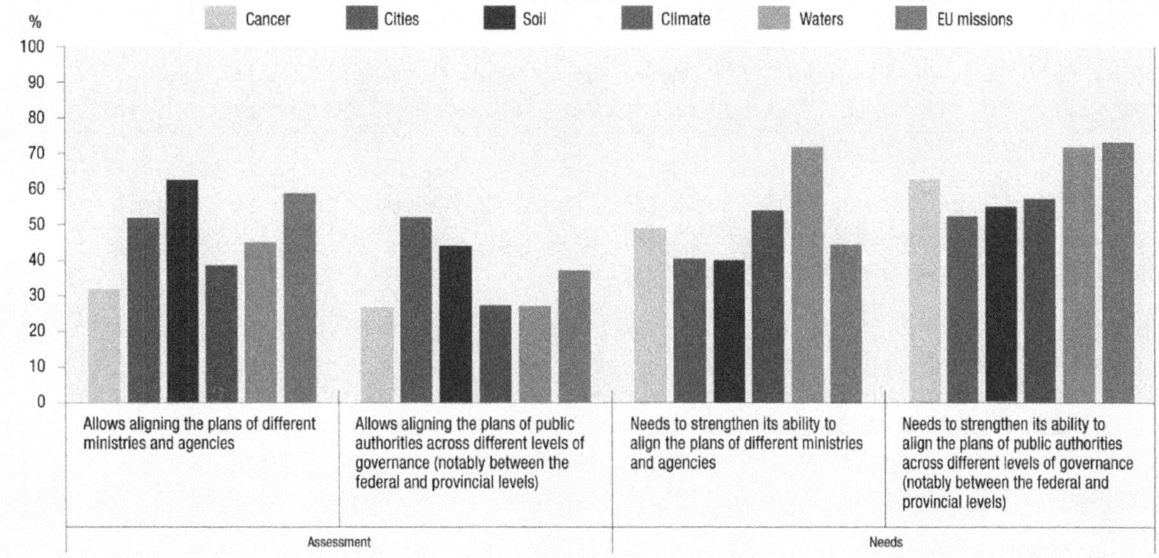

Notes: EU: European Union. Share of survey respondents that agree or strongly agree with the following statements regarding the mission.
Source: OECD (2023[26]).

References

Arnold, E. (2022), "How should we evaluate mission policies? Some lessons from theory and practice", Mission Action Lab, Technopolis, unpublished. [20]

Arnold, E. et al. (2018), *How Should We Evaluate Complex Programmes for Innovation and Socio-technical Transitions?*, Technopolis. [11]

Elzinga, R. et al. (2023), "Assessing mission-specific innovation systems: Towards an analytical framework", *Environmental Innovation and Societal Transitions*, Vol. 48, https://doi.org/10.1016/j.eist.2023.100745. [25]

European Commission (2023), *EU Missions Two Years On: Assessment of Progress and Way Forward*, COM(2023) 457 final, European Commission, Brussels, https://ec.europa.eu/transparency/documents-register/api/files/COM(2023)457?ersIds=090166e5fee45eb1. [23]

European Commission (2021), *Assessment Criteria for EU Missions*, European Commission, Brussels, https://research-and-innovation.ec.europa.eu/system/files/2021-03/ec_rtd_assessment-criteria-missions.pdf. [24]

European Commission (2021), "Foresight in support of the EU missions", https://research-and-innovation.ec.europa.eu/news/all-research-and-innovation-news/foresight-support-eu-missions-2021-10-21_en (accessed on 8 October 2022). [28]

Federal Ministry of Education, Science and Research, Austria (2022), *Implementation Framework for the EU Horizon Europe Missions in Austria*, Federal Ministry of Education, Science and Research, Vienna, https://era.gv.at/public/documents/4882/Implementation_framework_EU_missions_in_AT.pdf. [27]

Haddad, C., E. Wise and E. Arnold (2023), *When Theory Meets Practice in Transformative Innovation Policy Evaluation: Experiences from Sweden*, EU-SPRI 2023 Conference, 14-16 June, Brighton, United Kingdom. [22]

Hanson, A. and C. Bleckenwegner (9 June 2021), "Stewarding innovation portfolios for collective system change: Examples from practice", *OPSI Blog*, https://oecd-opsi.org/blog/stewarding-innovation-portfolios-for-collective-system-change. [16]

Hekkert, M. et al. (2020), "Mission-oriented innovation systems", *Environmental Innovation and Societal Transitions*, Vol. 34, pp. 76-79, https://doi.org/10.1016/j.eist.2019.11.011. [5]

Hill, D. (2022), *Designing Missions: Mission-oriented Innovation in Sweden: A Practice Guide by Vinnova*, Vinnova, https://www.vinnova.se/en/publikationer/mission-oriented-innovation---a-handbook-from-vinnova. [7]

Janssen, M. (2020), *Post-commencement Analysis of the Dutch 'Mission-oriented Topsector and Innovation Policy' Strategy*, Utrecht University, Utrecht, Netherlands, https://www.uu.nl/sites/default/files/Post-commencement%20analysis%20of%20the%20Dutch%20Mission-oriented%20Topsector%20and%20Innovation%20Policy.pdf. [13]

Larrue, P. (2023), *Répondre aux défis sociétaux: Le retour en grâce des politiques orientées mission?*, Les Docs de la Fabrique de l'Industrie, https://www.la-fabrique.fr/fr/publication/repondre-aux-defis-societaux-le-retour-en-grace-des-politiques-orient. [18]

Larrue, P. (2021), "Mission-oriented innovation policy in Japan: Challenges, opportunities and future options", *OECD Science, Technology and Industry Policy Papers*, No. 106, OECD Publishing, Paris, https://doi.org/10.1787/a93ac4d4-en. [1]

Larrue, P. (2021), "Mission-oriented innovation policy in Norway: Challenges, opportunities and future options", *OECD Science, Technology and Industry Policy Papers*, No. 104, OECD Publishing, Paris, https://doi.org/10.1787/2e7c30ff-en. [14]

Larrue, P., P. Tõnurist and D. Jonason (2024), "Monitoring and evaluation of mission-oriented innovation policies: From theory to practice", *OECD Science, Technology and Industry Working Papers*, Vol. No. 2024/09, https://doi.org/10.1787/5e4c3204-en. [21]

Mazzucato, M. (2018), "Mission-oriented innovation policies: Challenges and opportunities", *Industrial and Corporate Change*, Vol. 27/5, pp. 803-815, https://doi.org/10.1093/icc/dty034. [3]

Mazzucato, M. (2016), "From market fixing to market-creating: A new framework for innovation policy", *Industry and Innovation*, Vol. 23/2, pp. 140-156, https://doi.org/10.1080/13662716.2016.1146124. [4]

Menon Economics (2020), *Evaluation of Pilot-E*, Menon Publication 147 [in Norwegian], Menon Economics, https://www.menon.no/wp-content/uploads/2020-147-Evaluering-av-PILOT-E.pdf. [15]

National Audit Office, United Kingdom (2021), *UK Research and Innovation's Management of the Industrial Strategy Challenge Fund*, National Audit Office, London, https://www.nao.org.uk/wp-content/uploads/2021/02/UK-Research-and-Innovations-management-of-the-Industrial-Strategy-Challenge-Fund.pdf. [2]

OECD (2023), *Leveraging EU Missions in Austria*, Mission Action Lab, www.trami5missions.eu/sites/default/files/2023-11/OECD%20Mission%20Action%20Lab%20-%20Final%20report%20231116.pdf. [26]

OECD (2022), *Tackling Policy Challenges Through Public Sector Innovation: A Strategic Portfolio Approach*, OECD Public Governance Reviews, OECD Publishing, Paris, https://doi.org/10.1787/052b06b7-en. [17]

OECD (2019), *Governance as an SDG Accelerator: Country Experiences and Tools*, OECD Publishing, Paris, https://doi.org/10.1787/0666b085-en. [10]

OECD (Forthcoming), "Mission-oriented innovation policy in Korea: Challenges, opportunities and future options", *OECD Science, Technology and Industry Policy Papers*. [8]

OECD and DDC (2022), *Mission-oriented Innovation Needs Assessment Survey*, OECD and Danish Design Center, https://ddc.dk/wp-content/uploads/2021/10/REPORT-mission-needs-assessment-survey-110222-.pdf. [12]

Pietrobelli, C. and F. Puppato (2016), "Technology foresight and industrial strategy", *Technological Forecasting and Social Change*, Vol. 110, pp. 117-125, https://doi.org/10.1016/j.techfore.2015.10.021. [30]

Wanzenböck, I. et al. (2020), "A framework for mission-oriented innovation policy: Alternative pathways through the problem-solution space", *Science and Public Policy*, Vol. 47/4, pp. 474-489, https://doi.org/10.1093/scipol/scaa027. [6]

Wittman, F. et al. (2020), "Developing a typology for mission-oriented innovation policies", *Fraunhofer ISI Discussion Papers Innovation Systems and Policy Analysis*, No. 64, https://www.isi.fraunhofer.de/content/dam/isi/dokumente/cci/innovation-systems-policy-analysis/2020/discussionpaper_64_2020.pdf. [19]

Wittmann, F. et al. (2021), "From mission definition to implementation: Conceptualizing mission-oriented policies as a multi-stage translation process", *Fraunhofer ISI Discussion Papers Innovation Systems and Policy Analysis*, No. 71, https://www.isi.fraunhofer.de/content/dam/isi/dokumente/cci/innovation-systems-policy-analysis/2021/discussionpaper_71_2021.pdf. [9]

Wittmann, F., M. Yorulmaz and M. Hufnagl (2021), "Impact assessment of mission-oriented policies: Challenges and overview of selected existing approaches", *Fraunhofer ISI Working Papers*, https://www.isi.fraunhofer.de/content/dam/isi/dokumente/ccp/2021/HTF-Begleitforschung_Literaturbericht-Wirkungsmessung_2021.pdf. [29]

Endnotes

[1] Many objectives in the *Net Zero Mission Database* are extracts or reconstructions based on this type of text available in official documents and on official websites.

[2] See Annex C for a complete list of net zero mission targets.

[3] For instance, the European Commission engaged in a multi-year foresight analysis in five mission areas to strengthen reflexivity in the policy preparation process of the EU mission (European Commission, 2021[28]).

[4] Technological roadmapping is a normative tool that makes detailed projections about future technological developments and their socio-economic impacts. On the other hand, foresight is a "systemic" exercise that analyses the long-term impacts of STI developments to contribute to "better-informed policy decisions" (Pietrobelli and Puppato, 2016[30]).

[5] Federal Ministry for Climate Action, Environment, Energy, Mobility, Innovation and Technology (Austria).

[6] "Adaptation to Climate Change": support at least 150 European regions and communities to become climate-resilient by 2030; "Cancer": work with Europe's "Beating Cancer Plan" to improve the lives of more than 3 million people by 2030 through prevention, cure and solutions to live longer and better; "Restore Our Ocean and Waters by 2030"; "100 Climate-Neutral and Smart Cities by 2030"; "A Soil Deal for Europe: 100 living labs and lighthouses to lead the transition towards healthy soils by 2030".

[7] See Larrue (2021) for an analysis of the different mission co-ordination structures.

[8] See: https://www.gouvernement.fr/france-2030.

[1] For a review of some of the tools and framework development for mission evaluation see Wittmann, Yorulmaz and Hufnagl (2021[29]).

[2] The so-called mission-specific innovation system functions are: programming functions (providing problem directionality, providing solution directionality, co-ordinating the transition), innovation performance functions (knowledge development and diffusion, etc.) and destabilisation performance functions (unlearning, market destabilisation, etc.).

5 What are the outcomes of net zero missions?

This chapter presents the results of the assessment of net zero mission outcomes, which is the second layer of systemic effects. These outcomes relate to the scope and ambitions of the missions, the investment from public and private partners in mission activities, and the systemic dimension of missions.

Mission-oriented innovation policies (MOIP) are expected to build upon their three main outputs discussed in Chapter 4 (strategic agenda, governance structure and policy package) to essentially "aim higher", benefit from more resources and engagement from all partners, and explore more systemic solutions. This chapter assesses the extent to which net zero missions contribute to these three outcomes. Table 5.1 provides a synthesis of the main outcomes of net zero missions.

Table 5.1. Synthesis of the main outcomes of net zero missions

Expected effects	Main outcomes
A) Scope and level of ambitions in missions	
Broader set of potential solutions considered	The scope of the mission is a matter of important debate to strike a balance between the benefits of "open" missions (characterised by neutrality and exploration) and more narrowly defined missions (characterised by directionality and integration between different mission activities). Few missions are open, and some are evolving towards more narrowly defined and directional missions.
More ambitious and long-term objectives	Most missions have set objectives for 2030 and 2050. The differences in different missions' levels of ambition are difficult to assess.
B) Resources and engagement in net zero missions	
More and longer-term funding	Missions generally benefit from longer term funding compared to traditional research and innovation schemes. Funding is only informally earmarked for missions in the long run, but public funding announcements tend to generate some pressure for public authorities to commit the promised resources. Net zero mission budgets mainly originate from science, technology and innovation public authorities. Few sectoral public authorities have committed additional funding to achieve the missions. There is limited financial innovation in leveraging public funding to attract private funding (through blended finance, equity funding, etc.)
Stronger buy-in and commitment from private actors and stakeholders	There is strong stakeholder engagement in developing the strategic agenda. There is insufficient information on private sector financial contributions to conclude on mission leverage effect.
C) Systemic innovation in net zero missions	
Better integration of the demand and impact dimensions	Connection to needs and demands is one of the aspects most frequently raised as a novelty of net zero missions. Net zero missions provide various means to articulate demands at different stages of the mission life cycle, from mission definition to mission evaluation.
More comprehensive and consistent range of activities	Net zero missions allow a wider and more consistent range of activities, from basic research to demonstration and, in some cases, deployment, capacity building, communication and advocacy. Proactive portfolio management practices in missions are necessary to reap their systemic benefits but require significant resources, new skills, and new rules and procedures in ministries and agencies.

Scope and level of ambition of net zero missions

Missions have a broader scope and higher level of ambitions than comparable initiatives in traditional strategic and policy frameworks.

Net zero missions belong to broader portfolios of missions

In a large number of cases, net zero missions are presented in a bundle along with other missions that aim to tackle other or similar societal challenges.[1] Figure 5.1 shows that 65% of the identified mission-oriented innovation policy (MOIP) initiatives include more than one mission tackling different challenges beside climate change ("general multi-mission MOIP"). Examples include Horizon Europe missions, Germany's High-tech Strategy 2025 and the Swedish strategic innovation programmes. Ireland's National Challenge Fund initiative groups its eight missions into two main themes: 1) green transition; and 2) digital translation.

The remaining 35% of the MOIP initiatives only have "green missions", either several ones ("green multi-mission MOIP", 19%) or a unique one ("green mono mission MOIP", 16%). For instance, the Danish Inno mission initiative includes respectively four missions that all directly relate to climate change. Stand-alone green missions are often the evolution of a programme or a strategy that became a first mission-oriented pilot initiative, such as Chile's Green Hydrogen mission and Colombia's Bioeconomy mission.

Figure 5.1. Breakdown of net zero mission-oriented innovation policy initiatives analysed in this study by mission portfolio

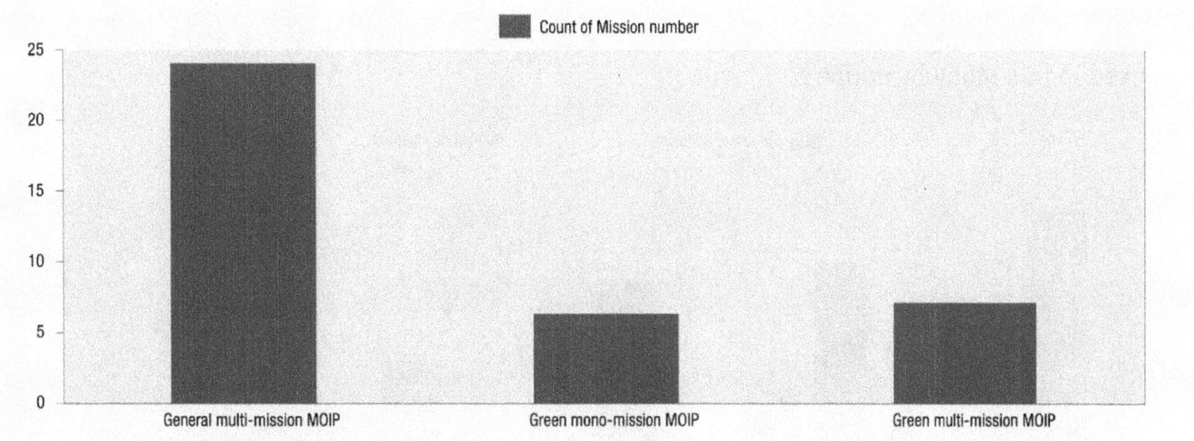

Note: MOIP: mission-oriented innovation policy.
Source: OECD *Net Zero Mission Database*.

The scope of a mission must be negotiated and aligned with its available resources and anchored in its innovation system

The issue of the scope of the mission is one of the most difficult to apprehend conceptually and handle in practice. One of the reasons for this can be found in the apparent paradox that lies at the core of the mission principle: a mission must be open to all potential solutions for any given challenge, but the selection and scoping of the challenge *de facto* limits the range of potential solutions. As the famous saying from Mazzucato goes "missions pick problems, not solutions". However, picking problems is far from neutral. A broader mission scope increases the range of potential solutions, which increases the likelihood of finding an adequate solution but reduces the potential synergies between the different solutions that will be actually investigated.

In theory, the only goal of a net zero mission that does not restrict the range of potential solutions is simply to "achieve net zero" by a certain milestone, without any mention of any sectors of emissions or technology that could limit the range of options. Technology neutrality is maintained best at high levels of aggregation, as explained by Boon and Bakker (2016[1]), and "the further one goes down the staircase" in offering support to a specific problem, the more likely alterations are possible to the "level playing field". The final milestone for the realisation of the mission also has implications for the breadth of the "problem space". A close deadline will focus efforts on mature solutions to the detriment of the exploration of new – possibly more transformative – ones.

A critical variable in this trade-off between the benefits of a large exploration space and a consistent portfolio of options is the level of financial resources and capabilities available for the mission. A small innovation system will be in a difficult position to pursue a net zero mission of the necessary scale and scope to cover a wide mission scope. It will not be able to support enough projects to cover such a wide problem space and its underpinning research innovation actors will not have the corresponding capabilities in all the relevant domains. In such a case, a more focused scope will be more sustainable and effective.

Interviews and desk research confirms that, in principle, a great deal of attention is placed on the "solution neutrality" of the missions. In the most interesting cases, the multi-mission MOIPs have been experimenting with various scopes of missions. However, very few have set widely open net zero missions. Most missions have set "solution-neutral objectives" within the confines of a technological area, an ecosystem or a sector (most often an application sector, hence leaving open the choice of the potential solutions to fulfil the objectives).

Figure 5.2. Breakdown of net zero mission-oriented innovation policy initiatives and missions analysed in this study by scope and focus

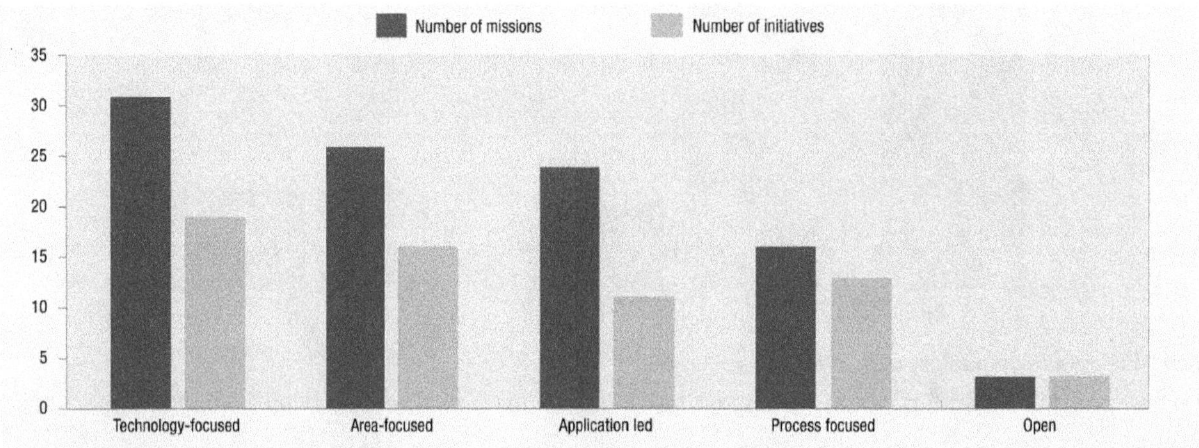

Source: OECD *Net Zero Mission Database*.

The technological focus associated with the missions can be directly included in the mission objectives or mentioned in the text that accompanies the description of the mission. In some cases, it is difficult to assess whether these technologies marked the boundaries of the problem space *ex ante* or were the result of the mission co-ordination and implementation. However, despite this caveat, Figure 5.3 provides some good indications as to what technologies the net zero missions focus on. Energy technologies come first, in accordance with their current level of emissions and their potential to reduce emissions in many sectors. The circular economy, which requires the close co-ordination of numerous actors along products' value chain, is also considered in a significant number of missions.

Figure 5.3. Breakdown of net zero missions analysed in this study by technological focus

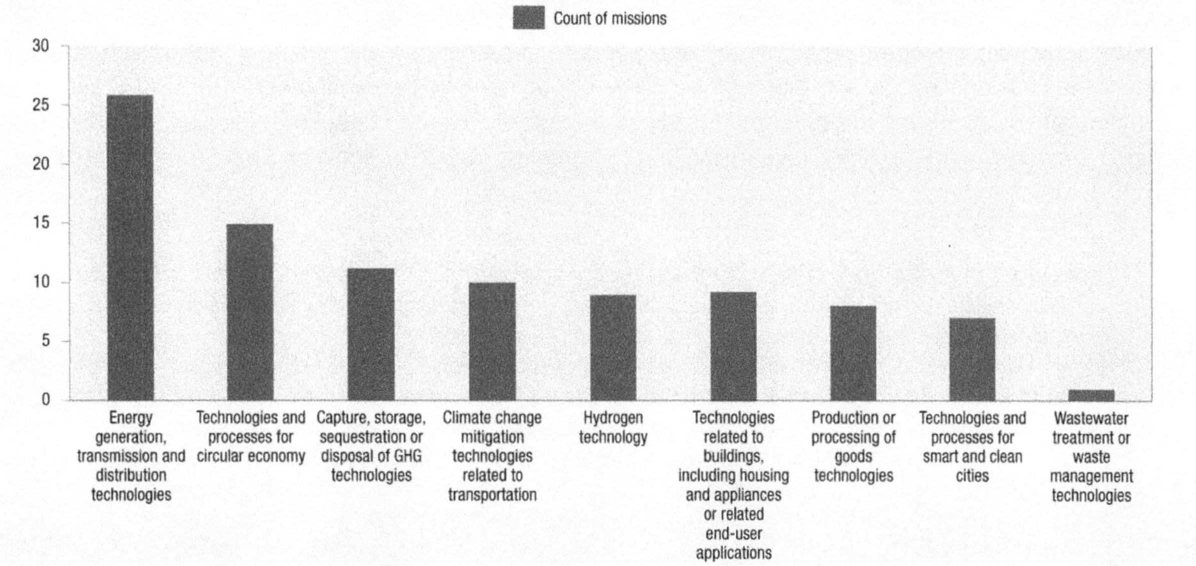

Note: GHG: greenhouse gas.
Source: OECD *Net Zero Mission Database*.

> ▸ *Net zero mission case*
>
> *Zero Emission Challenge, Research Ireland Challenge Research Programmes, Ireland. Determining the 'right' scope of the missions has been debated within Research Ireland (formerly Science Foundation Ireland - SFI) when they initiated their Challenge Research Programmes. The agency has deliberately launched missions with different degree of openness to draw lessons on this key issue. The Zero Emissions Challenge for instance was very open, aiming to 'Support interdisciplinary teams to develop disruptive solutions that accelerate progress towards net-zero greenhouse gas emissions in Ireland by 2050'. It attracted a project to create a carbon neutral resilient dairy farm ('Farm Zero C', the winning project at the end of the competition), as well as projects on the recycling of lithium cobalt batteries or new solar panel technologies. Others were more narrowly defined such as the Food Challenge, the Plastics Challenge, or the AI for Societal Good Challenge. Some further specifications permitted to fine-tune the balance between openness and strategic pre-orientation: the Zero Emissions Challenge was open to all solutions to reduce GHG emissions, but a specific 'bonus' of 1 million euros was announced for projects that would succeed in developing Carbon dioxide removal (CDR) technologies (this bonus was not awarded).*

A carefully managed interface with exploratory research allows mission renewal

Missions often include parallel activities on different generations of technologies to fulfil staged objectives, often related directly or indirectly to national GHG reduction commitments for different time horizons (2030 and 2050 in most cases). Mission co-ordinators usually try to remain more open and flexible regarding the scope of solutions under investigation for future technologies, as they require more exploratory research.

While such an approach can appear to be in line with the "common wisdom" of research management, it has implications on the design of the mission. Since the directed and integrated features of missions are less suited for exploratory research, upstream research activities may be better placed either outside the mission or in a specific sub-programme with their own operating principles and governance, although still directed towards mission goals. In both cases, it is essential to set up institutionalised linkages between these upstream activities and the mission's "core" development, demonstration and deployment activities.

Concretely, this can be done through mutual representation in the governance bodies of the missions and the exploratory research programme, and periodical progress reviews of basic research promising advances, common events with presentations of results and challenges on both sides. This "controlled interface" maintains the strategic autonomy and freedom of research while ensuring that researchers are aware of the mission's needs and that their progress will be reviewed against these needs. In France and the United States, specific basic research initiatives are attached to one or several missions without being formally embedded in them. They have their own operating principles, budgets and governance structures.

> ▸ *Net zero mission cases*
>
> *Acceleration Strategies, France. Within the French acceleration strategies, exploratory research is conducted in Priority research programs and equipment (programmes et équipements prioritaires de recherche, PEPRs) which are attached to one or several AS to support them. As of mid-2023, 43 PEPR had been launched to support about 20 ASs. They are used either to support ASs ('acceleration PEPRs') or to structure new scientific communities around emerging research areas ('exploration PEPRs') which could become, if deemed relevant and promising, ASs in their own right. The average support given to each of these PEPRs ranges between 20 and 120 million euros. Acceleration PEPRs, such as the "Carbon-free Hydrogen" PEPR, have their own strategic agenda. They are led by a designated scientific coordinator, possibly with a co-leader from another higher education or research institution. Although operationally and financially autonomous from the ASs, they are formally linked to the SAs they support by an interface enabling two-way connections: from the PEPR to ASs, some PEPR funds are dedicated to the transfer of new technological options within the strategic agendas of the relevant ASs; from the ASs to the PEPRs, the ASs can issue some specific calls for proposals for premature and mature technologies to explore the potential of new basic research progress and mobilise them to achieve their specific objectives. The linkages between Sas and PEPRs are also ensure by mutual presence in their respective governance bodies. The PEPR « Supporting innovation to develop new, largely carbon-free industrial processes » for instance is attached to the Industry Decarbonisation AS, covering the TRL 1-4 via breakthrough research on, for instance, CCSU research. This programme has a budget of 70-80m Euros (compared to 610m Euros for the AS).*
>
> ▸ *Energy Earthshots™, US. The U.S. Department of Energy's (DOE) Energy Earthshots™ Initiative sets specific cost and performance targets across clean energy technologies. The Energy Earthshots™ focus is on having technology meeting the cost and performance targets ready to be deployed at scale within a decade. Reaching these targets will require major RD&D breakthroughs to solve significant technology barriers that exist today, and will make major impacts on some of the largest emitting sectors of the energy economy. Energy Earthshots™ drive integrated program development across DOE's Office of Science and its Applied Energy Offices, and integrate into the innovation and deployment strategies of the Department as a whole. The Energy Earthshots™ mobilise basic research through specific activities of the Office of Science, that address the fundamental science challenges for each of the Energy Earthshots™ as identified by subject matter experts in the basic and applied research, development, and demonstration space via different initiatives. 1) The Energy Earthshot Research Centres (EERCs) are multi-disciplinary, multi-institutional teams led by DOE laboratories. USD100 million were allocated to these centres in 2023. They focus on key research challenges at the interface of basic and applied R&D in support of Energy Earthshots™. Each EERC focuses on one Energy Earthshot mission (e.g. Hydrogen Shot™, to achieve $1 for 1 kilogram of hydrogen by 2031), and thus becomes a center of innovation that can catalyze and connect with applied work and foundational science. 2) DOE also created Scientific Foundations for Energy Earthshots (SFEE): Small group awards led by academic or private sector institutions focused on use-inspired fundamental research addressing knowledge gaps limiting the achievement of Earthshot goals. SFEEs research goals are applicable to multiple Energy Earthshots™. Applied Energy Offices within DOE support technology development, applied R&D, through early demonstration. This is through specific funding opportunities targeted toward key technologies critical to achieving one or more Energy Earthshots™, as well as through consortia engaging industry, national labs, and universities that are aligned with specific mission targets. One example is the H2NEW consortium launched and managed by the Hydrogen and Fuel Cell Technologies Office within DOE's Office of Energy Efficiency and Renewable Energy. H2NEW is a cohesive, coordinated effort on "Hydrogen for the Next Generation of Electrolysis from Water." Funding for H2NEW is planned at approximately $150 million over five years. Additional funding is provided through competitive funding opportunity announcements, such as $470 million in specific electrolyzer development and manufacturing-related topics in March 2023.*

Resources and engagement in net zero missions

Net zero missions have yet to attract funding commensurate with their level of ambition, scope and time horizon.

Missions have a longer term horizon and provide more longer term funding

Most net zero missions have set ultimate target dates for either 2030 or 2050, consistent with their country's global CO_2 reduction pledges. While the administrative budgeting processes and political cycles do not allow securing budget allocations until these target dates, the analysis reveals that these missions generally benefit from more longer term funding than traditional research and innovation initiatives. Specifically, among the net zero missions with available data, 61% have funding durations exceeding four years, with 38% spanning beyond six years. For purposes of comparison, OECD findings on competitive research funding indicate that the majority of research grants are provided for three to five years. However, there is a growing trend toward longer grant durations in newer schemes. Financial support exceeding seven years is primarily channelled to "centres of excellence" with fewer grant applications or is tied to institutional funding (OECD, 2018[2]). Further comparison with EC-OECD STIP Compass data affirms this: approximately 45% of public research grants and 34% of business research and development (R&D) grants extend beyond three years.[2]

Since many funding organisations (ministries, agencies) are still subject to an annual budget cycle, multi-year funding is most often only announced (or at best, earmarked), but not appropriated. However, even if non-binding, it is announced publicly, and therefore usually represents fairly reliable budget commitments that reduce the level of uncertainty of the partners and stakeholders involved in the mission, allowing them to plan ahead and set more ambitious and long-term objectives. Missions are too recent to allow for an assessment of whether they can withstand several budgetary restrictions, such as those experienced after the 2008 financial crisis. The tightening of budgets after the COVID-19 pandemic is the first mission robustness test.

Most missions' budgets remain in the range of large-scale climate R&D programmes, but are better integrated

Most missions with available budget information[3] have budgets in the EUR 1-20 million and EUR 20-200 million (each range representing 35% of missions) (Figure 5.4).

Figure 5.4. Breakdown of net zero missions analysed in this study by annual budget range

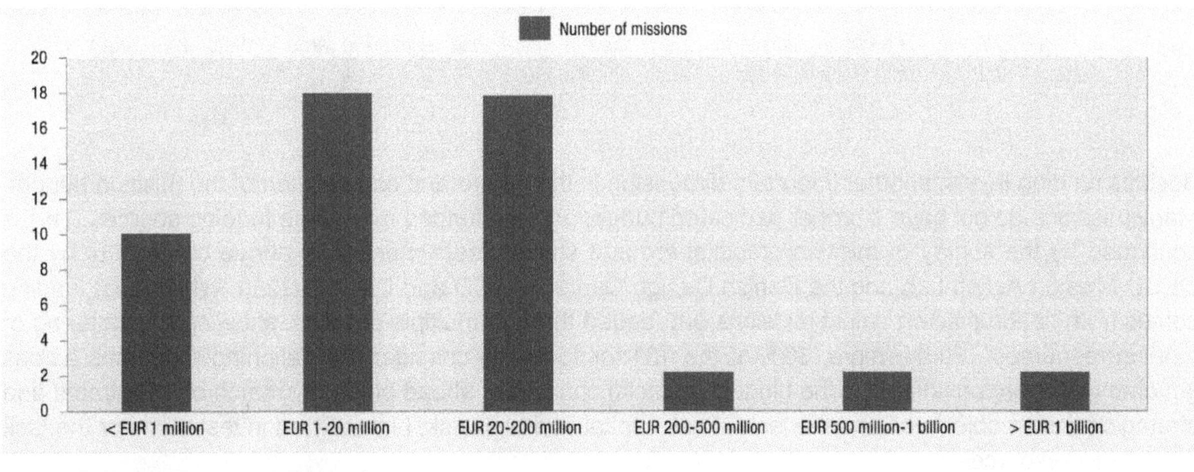

Source: OECD *Net Zero Mission Database.*

As for other policies, many variations in mission budgets predominantly reflect the general disparities in the size and development stage of a country's science, technology and innovation (STI) budgets. The scope of the mission is another crucial determinant of its budgetary allocation. Broad, systemic missions, especially those encompassed within a comprehensive mission-oriented strategic framework, often comprise numerous relevant programmes. However, as previously mentioned, these budget figures should not be taken at face value since these large missions are often loosely integrated and only aggregate *ex post* policies and programmes that remain, for the most part, independent from each other. A prime example is the former German HTS mission, "Achieve Substantial Greenhouse Gas Neutrality in Industry", which operated with an annual budget of EUR 6.25 billion.

A mission's budget envelope correlates with its content. Notably, the few missions that also support the market deployment of new solutions generally require far greater budgets than missions focusing on research. As mentioned in Chapter 4, this is the case for France's "Clean Hydrogen" Acceleration Strategy, whose more than EUR 1 billion annual budget is allocated to provide price-based incentives for adopting new (more costly) technologies. On the other end of the spectrum, the Irish "Zero Emissions Challenge" research programme, which aims to include the demand dimension in its research activities but remains focused on R&D, has an annual budget of EUR 1.5 million.

Although imperfect, a comparison with some selected examples of climate change-related research and innovation "programmes" provides some meaningful orders of magnitude. It shows that ("non-mission oriented") thematic programmes in renewable energy; carbon capture, utilisation and storage; or sustainable transport technologies have budgets in the range of EUR 5-100 million, as is the case for most missions. These comparisons, therefore, tend to suggest that the funding envelopes available to net zero remains, while significant, somewhat in the order of magnitude of more traditional large climate-related R&D programmes, apart from some large umbrella missions and some more systemic missions which include scale-up and investment support.

At the project level, some cases such as Pilot-E and Mission-driven Top Sectors and Innovation Policy (Netherlands) suggest that the joined up approach enables public bodies to award larger grants to larger consortia performing a wider range of activities.

> *Net zero mission cases*
>
> ▸ *Mission-driven Top Sectors and Innovation Policy, The Netherlands. The Mission-oriented research, development, and innovation (MOOI) scheme in the Carbon-built environment mission is an integrated instrument specifically developed for this mission. It provides support to multidisciplinary consortia that develop proposals that combine various technological and non-technological sub-solutions, including also activities concerning the commercialisation and societal acceptance of the projects (Janssen, 2020).*
>
> ▸ *Pilot-E, Norway. The cooperation of three agencies in Pilot-E has resulted in larger projects with larger budgets than those traditionally awarded by the agencies alone.*

Besides funding levels, another important dimension is the nature and composition of the mission budget. Many missions do not have a proper dedicated budget and are funded by diverse funding sources. This is confirmed by the survey of mission practitioners and stakeholders mentioned above carried out by the OECD Mission Action Lab and the Danish Design Center (OECD and DDC, 2022[3]). While most funding comes from national actors, most missions are funded through multiple sources, showing a "scattering of funding resources". Furthermore, 36% of the 131 respondents consider that "aligning resources across government or organisations" is the biggest financial challenge, ahead of the mismatch of investment and strategic mission objectives and the lack of risk capital and high-risk, high-reward investments or the lack of targeted resources.

The uncertainty with regards to the unfolding of the net zero pathways and the consequent development of the mission strategic agenda or road map as a "living document" in many missions requires some degree of flexibility on the budgetary side as well. There must be firm financial commitments from public authorities over the long term while preserving a significant margin for changes to adapt to new internal and external developments. Striving to do this, missions can face difficulties due to existing rigid public budgetary and accounting rules. One way to get around those is to commit a portion of the announced funding and earmark another portion which might be awarded under certain conditions regarding the performance of the funding, notably its ability to form a wide and solid partnership that gathers the necessary capabilities and resources to meet the mission's objectives. Another more widespread mean in the world of missions (and increasingly in other STI support programmes) is to use a gated funding model, where projects have to go through pre-determined assessment milestones to progress to the next phase and receive the associated instalment.

> *Net zero mission case*
>
> *INNO-CCUS, Innomissions, Denmark. When the Danish CCUS INNOmission was initiated, it was granted DKK 200 million, including DKK 100 million awarded to 20 projects. These 20 projects were referred to as the "pool 1 projects". Forty per cent of this amount (DKK 80 million) was reserved for subsequent "pool 2 projects", where projects could be added to the mission. Elaborating this more flexible process was considered cumbersome because the implementation of this new funding mechanism involved legal changes.*

Missions need a dedicated process and support to leverage their initial funding and mobilise additional partners

The funding of a mission should thus be considered in a dynamic perspective. A mission's success depends in the end on the funding that it can attract using the governance and policy frameworks built with its initial budget. However, the academic literature rarely addresses the mission's leverage effect. Several interviewees described the initial budget of their mission, in almost all cases originating from the leading STI authorities, as "seed money". Given the transformational objectives of the net zero missions, the necessary financial amounts to bring the developed sociotechnical solutions to scale are several orders of magnitudes higher than their endowment at the outset. Others have invested in developing a "map" of potential funding sources that could be mobilised, in line with the unfolding of the mission strategic agenda. Some initiatives, such as CSIRO's missions, have embedded this leverage imperative into their mission approach.

> *Net zero mission case*
>
> *CSIRO Missions, Australia. The title of the Mission Playbook developed by CSIRO – "Convening missions" – clearly conveys the organisation's strategic approach to missions. The CSIRO Missions Program was launched in 2019 as an internal endeavour, integrating the capabilities of several internal departments and business units, and joining forces with a limited number of external public and private partners. The success of the mission then depends on the ability to build upon this initial impetus to attract new partners with their own capabilities and resources. The CSIRO mission theory of change translates the progress of the mission through the gradual broadening of the range of partners involved: it goes from the 'institution (CSIRO) outcomes' to the 'network outcomes', 'system outcomes and finally meet the 'mission objective'. The convening dimension of CSIRO missions is therefore double: 1/ it is about convening various internal resources of this large interdisciplinary research organisation (6,000 staff members); 2/ to succeed the missions need to convene partners well beyond the initial 'coalition of the willing'. CSIRO refers to an 'agency convened' model of missions. This 'model seeks to accelerate the diffusion of solutions by 'crowding in' existing and new policy*

initiatives, investment, research activities and innovation system actors around a shared objective'. To trigger this snowball effect CSIRO invests internally over EUR 30 million per year of 'seed funding' and expect to crowd in about EUR 120 million per year. The CSIRO's mission office supports all missions in the convening process and fund raising (CSIRO, 2023).

Some missions benefit from a label effect that support the leveraging of their funding. In the case of EU missions, this labelling is formal. In other cases (Research Ireland Challenge Research Programmes, Pilot -E) it is only informal, building upon reputation effects. At the project level, several mission leaders report cases where the selected projects have benefitted from significant additional or follow-up funding from other programmes, benefitting from their embeddedness in a particular mission. This is particularly the case for the mission-oriented schemes that take the form of a challenge-led "prize competition", as they involve a fair degree of competition. As mentioned above, the public authorities in charge of the mission, as part of their more hands-on project management, can support projects with dedicated commercialisation and entrepreneurship training, connections to users and investors.

Net zero mission cases

- *Horizon Europe missions, EU. The Cities Mission has set up an innovative procedure to labellise cities that comply with some criteria established collectively at the level of the mission, to ease their access to complementary funding. The initial mission budget (EUR 360 million over 2021-23) originates only from Horizon Europe. To date, there is little fund committed to or earmarked for the mission by other programmes. This initial budget is mainly dedicated to setting up the overall framework for developing and normalising the process to be followed by the 112 cities to become 'smart and climate neutral' and supporting the cities in implementing this process through the Mission Platform. The latter enables direct exchange and networking between participating cities and provides them with the necessary expertise and assistance for developing and implementing their Climate City Contracts (CCCs), as well as financial and technical advisory services to develop their tailor-made investment plan to access public and private funding. In particular, a key component of the mission leverage effect consists in awarding a 'Mission label' by the Mission Manager to selected cities having completed a CCC that has been positively reviewed. This label aims to 'unlock synergies with other programmes' by facilitating access to other funding and financing opportunities (not least the EIB and the European Regional Development Fund (ERDF)). Cities are invited to make explicit reference to their Mission Label in their award procedures (calls for proposals, prizes etc.). It is also expected that in the second phase of the mission which started in 2023, when the vast majority of CCCs are in place, linkages will be established to calls for proposals under other funding programmes at EU, national or regional level. Labellised cities could for example receive additional "points" in the award criteria under these calls' evaluation process.' The Council of the EU, in its 'Conclusions on European missions' adopted in June 2022, proposed that this labelling procedure be used for the other EU missions in the context of calls for proposal outside Horizon Europe in order 'to facilitate the construction of missions' portfolios, to increase the visibility of the related initiatives and to gather their results (Council of the European Union, 2022[4]).*

- *Net Zero challenge, Research Ireland Challenge Research Programmes, Ireland. In Ireland, the Zero Farm project that won the Research Ireland Net Zero challenge received 1.2 million euros from Research Ireland and 10 million euros from the EU and Enterprise Ireland. According to the mission leader the Prize helped raising additional funds.*

- *Pilot-E, Norway. In Norway, the evaluation of Pilot-E concluded that there is broad agreement among beneficiaries that having been selected as part of this scheme is 'a stamp of quality for the project' (Menon Economics, 2020)*

Most mission funding almost only draws in STI budgets

To date, few missions have been able to secure significant financial commitments beside the initial STI funding. This is notably one of the results of the first assessment of EU missions (see Table 4.5 and Annex E), which concluded that the level of resources mobilised beside Horizon Europe remains lower than expectations.

Although it is difficult to collect systematic data on this matter, the question was asked in all interviews and the results firmly confirm this argument.

This has two major consequences. First, at the outset, many missions only receive seed funding and depend on their ability to attract partners and leverage additional funds to reach their objectives. Their success is thus compromised at this stage. Second, the difficulty of missions to raise funds beyond the STI budget creates a mismatch with the mission scope. In other terms, several missions end up supporting non-STI activities with STI funding which, in some cases, has raised criticisms and generated tensions. This has been pointed out in other case studies and assessments. For example, the 12 missions of the German former High-Tech Strategy were clearly addressing societal problems, but they still strongly relied on STI policy means, which made "effective integration with sectoral policies … rather patchy" (Roth et al., 2022[5]).

Systemic innovation in net zero missions

Needs and demands related to the mission are articulated throughout its life cycle

Although different types of STI policies have made progress in the way they identify the needs and demands to be addressed, and how they use these to calibrate their objectives and design, the demand conditions are still not given full consideration when designing the policies to support missions (Boon and Bakker, 2016[1]). The systematic review of net zero missions in this chapter draws a less negative picture of missions. It finds that, in many cases, the missions tend to be effective platforms for demand articulation in the specific context of systemic and complex societal challenges.

The mission's demand-driven nature is one of the aspects the most frequently highlighted as a novelty of the mission-oriented policy approach. There are various means to articulate demands in missions at different stages of their life cycle, from mission definition to mission evaluation (Figure 5.5).

During their early stages of definition, missions use different ways (e.g., consultation workshops and platforms, committees, and studies) to determine and integrate the interests of society and various stakeholders' views. Through these various channels, the demand and use dimensions are embedded by design into the mission's objectives and targets. While the mission targets can sometimes be politically driven (as for the 25 missions of the Dutch Mission-driven Top Sectors and Innovation Policy), in many missions, the development of the strategic agenda is the main channel for integrating the demand and use dimensions. This is especially true for ecosystem-based MOIPs. In these initiatives, large communities of actors coalesce to develop an agenda that is consensual enough to reconcile the interests of the broadest part of the ecosystem and ambitious enough to maximise its chances of being selected by public authorities for implementation.

The governance of the mission can also serve as a channel to connect more continuously to the potential user community and various interest parties. Although these co-ordination structures most often involve representatives from various public authorities, the presence of sectoral ministries or agencies can help integrate the use dimension into missions. Again, ecosystem-based MOIPs are an exception, as their governance structure features large representation from the ecosystem itself. Some of the largest overarching mission schemes can also have a dedicated advisory body comprised of stakeholders and experts with strong consultation mandates.

Figure 5.5. Integration of the demand dimension into net zero missions at different stages of the mission's life cycle

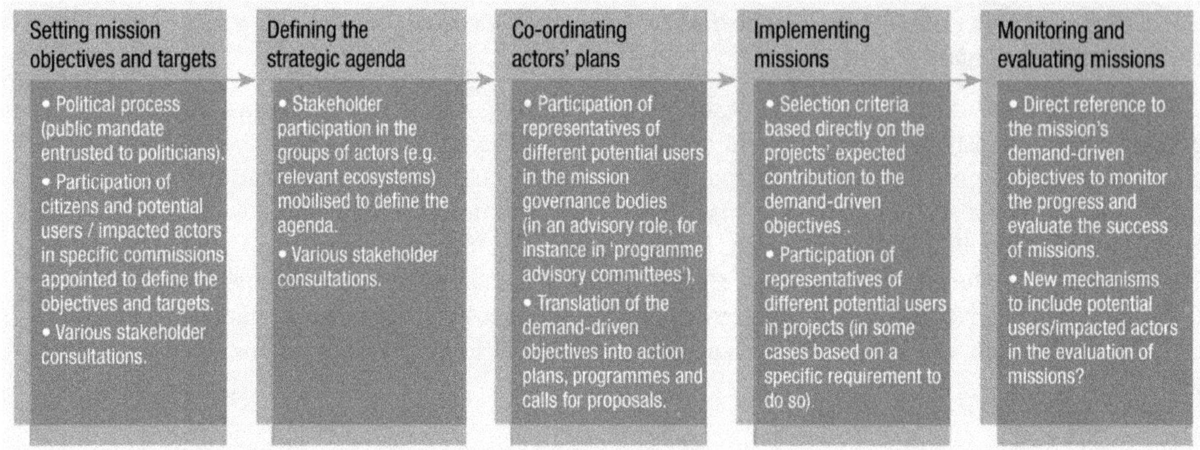

During implementation, some missions – even the most research-intensive ones – have included specific mechanisms to engage users and other actors related to the demand side (e.g. regulatory authorities) at the project level.

Net zero mission cases

▸ Net Zero challenge, Research Ireland Challenge Research Programmes, Ireland In the Irish Challenge Research programmes, including those targeted at zero emissions, project applicants are strongly encouraged to include stakeholders and end-users in the proposal. Even during the so-called "concept phase" (first phase in the programme's stage-gate funding), Research Ireland promotes interactions between the "challenge teams" and potential "solution beneficiaries" so that they can test whether their ambitions are realistic, and also navigate non-technical issues relating to challenges (e.g., stakeholder engagement) and solutions (e.g., barrier identification). A "societal impact champion" is nominated for each project, to provide a strong societal perspective for team members as they develop their solutions and build relationships between scientific researchers and their stakeholders and beneficiaries. In addition, Research Ireland strives to identify and map the "impact actors" related (in a broad sense) to the various applications and use of the technologies being developed, and support connections between the researchers involved in the mission and these organisations. Research Ireland strongly encourages the mission teams to engage with these actors so that they better understand the challenges and start building connections. This has a significant acceleration effect, bringing projects closer to the market and impact. Research Ireland also organises "meet and greet" events with investors, to familiarise researchers with their way of thinking.

▸ Energy Earthshots™, United States

The Earthshots™ use a variety of approaches to ensure potential users and regulatory authorities are involved in the initiative. This is done for instance through calls for proposal at a rather early stage. For instance, the Hydrogen Shot has issued Small Business Innovation Research and Small Business Technology Transfer (SBIR/STTR) challenges for innovators to respond to, and these could result in procurement from government if innovators are successful. The Hydrogen Shot also used an Incubator Prize to foster innovative concepts for producing clean hydrogen, and hosted a "Pitch Day" for the winners to present to potential investors and commercial partners. Also, as part of its support for the Carbon Negative Shot, the DOE has created a market for carbon off-sets through its Carbon Dioxide Removal Purchase Pilot Prize. Under this scheme, companies are competing for the opportunity to deliver carbon dioxide removal credits directly to DOE. This is the first example of the US government agreeing to purchase these sorts of credits. It aims to help catalyse the development of the carbon dioxide removal market through rigorous monitoring, measurement, reporting, and verification practices through third-party scientific validation. The DOE has developed a leader board for companies to make companion purchases of these high credible carbon credits. Some companies have already made pledges to purchase these credits once the credits are verified by the DOE. In addition, regulators are included in the governance of the initiatives, which helps ensure they align their regulations with the novel technologies developed by DOE. In the case of the Floating Offshore Wind Shot, the Department of Transport is providing priority permitting approvals to the speciality vessels that will deploy offshore wind technologies.

Missions support a more comprehensive and consistent range of activities but remain too confined to science and technology development

Depending on a mission's objectives, its tailor-made policy mix supports a wide range of activities, from basic research to deployment, capacity building, communication and advocacy.

Net zero mission case

▸ *Atmosphere and Climate Competence Centre, Flagship Programme, Finland. The Atmosphere and Climate Competence Centre (ACCC) is a Finnish flagship programme that aims to mitigate climate change by increasing forest and soil carbon sequestration and improve global air quality. The ACCC consortium brings together three universities and one research institute, and over 40 key stakeholders. The mission sustains a diverse array of activities, which range from education, research and impact programmes to engagement and citizen science, and solution development and prototyping. Among these activities, the Verified Climate Safety initiative verifies climate neutrality based on observation systems; the GlobalSMEAR initiative integrates 1 000 atmospheric-earth system stations to provide data from various ecosystems around the world; the Citizen Science Initiative allows the general public to contribute to problem definition, data collection and analysis in climate science; the Initiative for "Safer Climate" works at the intersection between civil society, academia and art; the Climate University develops climate change and sustainability education in higher education; and ACCC Impact Week promotes dialogue between earth system scientists and society stakeholders interested in the co-creation of science-based solutions for climate change and air quality.*

Most (if not all) net zero missions illustrate the additionality of the mission approach, compared to traditionally more fragmented policies, when it comes to designing and directing a consistent pool of activities towards a shared goal. It is, therefore, worth delving further into the subject and attempting to debunk this notion of portfolio consistency. A first step consists in identifying the main dimensions that allow making sense of a portfolio of activities. In principle, a portfolio can be composed of projects and activities that:

- pertain to different solutions (or combinations thereof) or pathways
- span different components of each of these potential solutions (from knowledge and innovation to skills, infrastructure, etc.)
- pertain to different generations of these solutions, each of them being at any point in time at different stages of maturity (from basic research to market deployment) (Figure 5.6).

Managing and monitoring a mission portfolio therefore requires being able to map the different projects and activities along these dimensions and link this portfolio to the mission's strategic agenda to identify gaps and progress made.

Figure 5.6. The three main dimensions of a mission portfolio

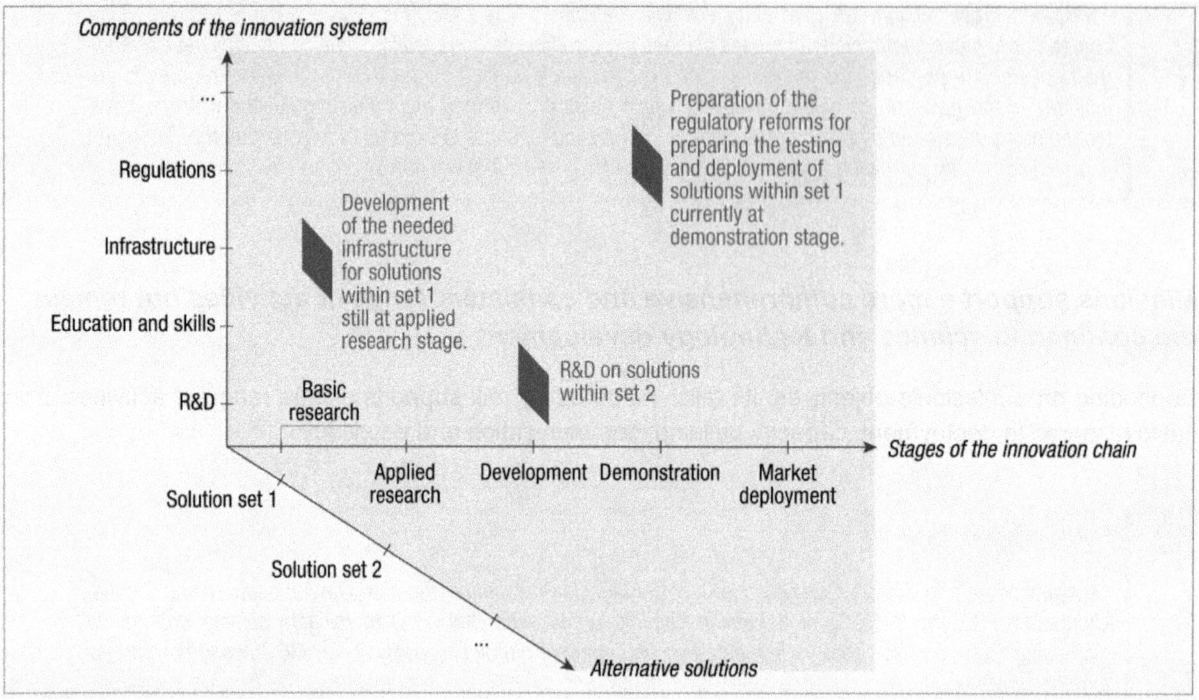

Note: R&D: research and development.

However, the added value of the mission approach not only resides in the diversity of the activities it covers, as more traditional initiatives like large-scale programmes or clusters may also cover a wide spectrum of activities. Rather, the mission should enable greater consistency in the pool of projects and activities. A critical challenge for net zero missions is that these different project and activities are most often under the authority of different public bodies.

A second step involves determining what type of complementarities and synergies are expected between the different activities and projects in a mission portfolio. Figure 5.6 provides such an analysis, using an *ad hoc* typology of the announced rationales for integrating activities within missions.[4]

Figure 5.7. Breakdown of net zero missions by type of rationale in missions

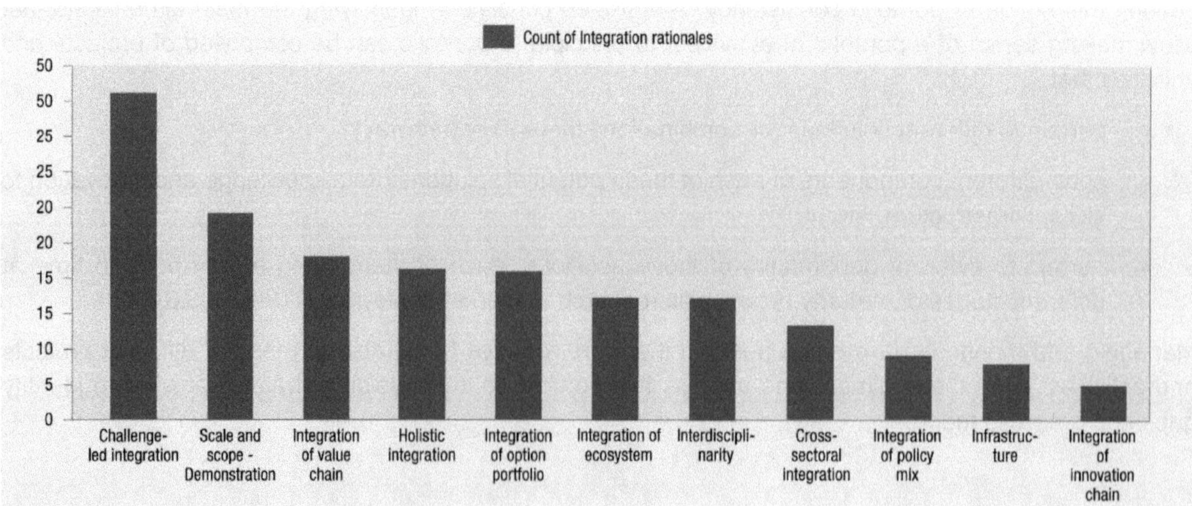

Source: OECD *Net Zero Mission Database*.

As the label "mission-oriented" suggests, one of the main expected benefits of MOIPs are the common focus of a diversity of actors towards a common challenge. Challenge-led integration is, therefore, often put forward in policy documents de scribing the different initiatives. The second most frequent "pro-mission" argument is scale and scope effects, notably to finance demonstration and scale-up. This shows that the net zero missions' scope extends beyond R&D and seeks to better bridge the demonstration or scale-up stages, ensuring continuity. Holistic integration comes in third position. It translates the fact that missions are implemented to cover consistently several dimensions of an innovation system (scientific, technological, social, legal, behavioural, educational) to solve a particular challenge.

However, the limits in the scope of missions' policy mixes are reflected in their range of activities: few missions directly include in their "sphere of influence" activities related to the scale-up and deployment of the solutions developed and demonstrated as part of the mission. Most activities supported by missions relate directly or indirectly to science and technology development.

Hands-on portfolio management practices are slowly emerging

Effective portfolio management is essential to integrate the different policies and activities. As defined by the United Nations Development Programme, a portfolio-based approach is a methodology that seeks to develop, test, learn and scale a suite of interventions that are complementary and can shift complex systems by focusing on multiple intervention points at a given time (UNDP, 2022[6]). Partly inspired by their use in the financial sector, these practices have been used in traditional STI policies, notably for spreading the risks of investments in uncertain projects, and valuable tools and models exist to promote their use in the public sector (OECD, 2022[7]). Closer to missions, they are also being used by DARPA (Defense Advanced Research Projects Agency) and DARPA-like agencies (Bonvillian, Van Atta and Windham, 2019[8]).

Yet, as revealed in interviews with mission leaders, they are only emergent in other types of broader and more systemic missions. The barriers hindering their effective and widespread use are numerous and significant: lack of effective methodology and criteria to enhance synergies between instruments (not only reduce risk), lack of staff both in terms of quantity and necessary skills for hands-on and proactive management, conflicting staff and organisation incentives (still focused on individual project performance and limited to the mandate of specific organisations), inadequate bureaucratic rules and regulations (favouring competitive mechanisms to ensure a level playing field over more effective and purposive direct interventions) (Box 5.1).

Box 5.1. What is mission portfolio management?

Mission portfolio management (MPM) is the practice that consists in selecting, steering and monitoring a group of consistent activities in a systemic way to more effectively meet within the set deadline the objectives that have been collectively developed. This approach starkly contrasts with traditional practices.

Table 5.2. Differences between the mission portfolio approach and the traditional approach

	Traditional project management	Mission portfolio management
Selection and management of projects/activities	*Project level* Selection based on the individual characteristics of projects, limited interactions and exchanges between projects	*Project and portfolio levels* Holistic/systemic approach, design and management of a coherent set of activities
Logic for designing the portfolio	*Linear approach/knowledge-push* The portfolio is the *ex-post* result of the selection of activities based on their expected performance as judged from application (excellence, relevance, etc.)	*Result-led* The portfolio is designed *ex-ante* based on the identified activities needed to obtain certain end results

MPM raises specific challenges which are still, to a large extent, unresolved:

- Which criteria should be used to select activities and design the portfolio? MPM relies on traditional criteria such as excellence and relevance but adds an essential new family of criteria at portfolio level: the coherence of the portfolio relative to the mission's objectives, i.e., how each project contributes to the mission's objectives as part of a consistent set of projects and activities.
- How to proactively design the portfolio while still preserving a sufficient level of competition between projects/activities and ensuring the sound and equitable treatment of project proposals? Hands on MPM approaches are less suited than a "distant" call for proposals to ensure a level playing field between different candidates and keep the process accountable. In many countries, public administrations can only allocate funding using competitive mechanisms.
- How to promote exchanges between different projects/activities while preserving the confidentiality of certain knowledge and information? Project participants – especially in private firms and research and technology organisations – can be reluctant to exchange with other companies by fear of disclosing proprietary information.
- How to manage strategically the portfolio of interventions? This requires some skills and knowledge that can be in limited supply in many public administrations, notably deep and broad knowledge of specific technological and industrial areas to be able to plan and assess the portfolio's progress towards the objectives, identify arising needs, and terminate some activities.
- How to manage the portfolio at a reasonable cost? MPM hands-on and strategic practices require more and more costly human resources.

Source: (OECD, Forthcoming[9]).

The implementation of such portfolio approaches calls for a change in established practices; first regarding the criteria to select projects and, as a result, to constitute the portfolio. In most cases, these criteria are not yet formalised in net zero missions. As stated by one interviewee, the selection panel pays great attention to ensure that each project is a building block of the mission. However, this new approach is still in its infancy and there are few precise comparative studies on the different ways to assess the "mission portfolio fitness" of a given project.

Net zero mission cases

▸ Horizon Europe missions, EU. The five EU missions represent a step change in the way the projects are selected in Framework Programme. The Horizon Europe Implementation Strategy planned specific procedure designed to allow for the selection of a coherent portfolio of projects (European Commission, 2020[10]). It was envisaged to proceed via two-stage calls: firstly, an evaluation of the intrinsic quality of each individual proposal submitted; and secondly, the identification of high-quality proposals that go together in a way that maximises the expected impact of the portfolio as a whole. The evaluation committees would be provided more flexibility to adapt to a mission-oriented approach. For instance, the art 26 of the Regulation stipulated that the 'evaluation committee may rank the proposals having passed the applicable thresholds according to their contribution to the achievement of specific policy objectives and may also propose any substantial adjustments to the proposals in as far as needed for the consistency of the portfolio'. Actions were also encouraged before a call with a view to support the building of a consistent portfolio, for example using an expression of interest mechanism. Another novelty was found in the necessary tailor-made approach due the inherent specificity of each mission: the chosen approach to the selection of projects was expected to vary from mission to mission. While it is not clear whether such procedures have been implemented, the European Commission has launched

some 'sense-making' initiatives to understand portfolio of activities relevant to missions. Such portfolio analysis found a portfolio of 841 past and present EU projects that contribute to the objectives of the Ocean and Waters missions. The analysis of the results of these projects and of the remaining gaps compared to what is needed to realise the mission by 2030 is expected to inform the mission activities. It also provides indication in terms of needed synergies with other EU programmes, including regional and cross-regional development programmes (European Commission, 2023[11]).

- *Strategic Innovation Areas, Wallonia, Belgium. As part of its Smart Specialisation Strategy 2021-2027 Wallonia defined five Strategic Innovation Areas (SIA) as a coherent and ambitious portfolio of innovative activities, of regional scope, with strong economic impact and societal contribution. The objective is to maximize cross-fertilisation between actors across policy fields, technologies and disciplines. The processes started in each SIA with the development of 'Co-constructed Roadmaps' to serve as the main reference for the selection of projects and the concentration of resources in the SIA. To implement these roadmaps and move beyond individual projects, 19 'Strategic Innovation Initiatives' or Integrated portfolio of projects have been selected via a dedicated call. Each portfolio proposal was required to gather a critical mass of stakeholders representing the quadruple helix and to show the various proposed activities, distinguishing their technological and economic maturity levels (Technology Readiness Levels [TRLs] and Market Readiness Levels [MRLs]), identify the necessary 'bricks', the needed public support arrangements, the cross-sectoral and multidisciplinary interactions among portfolio activities.*

In the course of implementing a mission, the proactive and strategic management of the portfolio of projects and complementary activities also challenge existing structures (e.g. incentive structures) and skills. As documented by a voluminous body of research, portfolio management in these agencies is greatly predicated not only on the rare combinations of competencies among the programme staff, but also on the conditions offered to them within their agencies (notably in terms of support resources, empowerment and autonomy) to allow them to perform active project management.

While it is difficult to quantify, several mission managers emphasised that proactive portfolio management calls for significantly greater resources than traditional practices. They also mentioned that these practices are often hindered (or in some cases made impossible) by organisational procedures – and in Europe, by R&D state aid rules that prioritise the fair treatment of project applicants to ensure a level playing field among potential beneficiaries.

Missions support ecosystem structuring

The systemic dimension of missions often goes beyond the portfolio of projects and activities it directly supports, expanding toward the entire "mission area" or ecosystem. The objectives of a significant number of missions, in particular those pertaining to ecosystem-based MOIPs (39% of net zero missions, in 37% of MOIPs) directly relate to strengthening the relevant ecosystem. In some cases, the mission aims to create a new ecosystem in a new area, gathering disciplines and sectors that had barely met before.

Several MOIP initiatives adopt such proactive practices and engage in frequent interactions with mission partners, including during the calls for proposals. This is particularly the case of ecosystem-based MOIPs, whose success depends on the co-operation of a wide range of ecosystem partners in the framework of a co-developed strategic agenda. In these missions, such as the Finnish Growth Engine "Green E2", significant funding (sometimes the entire budget) is dedicated to supporting the formation and structuring of the ecosystem partnership and providing resources for its "orchestration".

Net zero mission case

- *GreenE2, Growth Engines, Finland. The objective of the GreenE2 Growth Engine is to create a cross-sectoral network for global business in Finland that focuses on green hydrogen, technologies and 'e-products' (chemicals, fuels) and, based on this ecosystem, contributes to making Finland climate neutral by 2035. Growth Engines work by administering funding in two-year periods (for a maximum of ten years) to either 'platform companies' or 'orchestrators' to form a network of operators around selected 'business spearheads'. In the case of the Flexens Growth Engine, which aim to 'Bring together all the actors to create the solutions needed to build a 100% renewable energy system', the selected 'platform company' is financed during the preparation stage through an equity loan (interest rate of 1%, loan is limited to EUR 400 000). Once the platform company and its network are established, it can apply to a Business Finland's Competitive bidding on Growth Engines which can allocate capital loan typically in the range of EUR 2-10 M€ through a tendering by public procurement procedure. The Platform companies (small and medium-sized enterprises under 5 years of age) are tasked with tasked with 'promoting the development of the competitiveness and new innovations of the companies involved in the Growth Engine ecosystem'. These can for instance be data providers, developing an ecosystem among their partners and value chain suppliers and clients towards a common goal. In the second case, the 'orchestrator', is financed via a grant covering a maximum of 50% of the costs of supported 'orchestration' activities. The funding is intended for the goal-oriented development of innovation cooperation in a business-driven ecosystem. Growth engines aim to create an innovative ecosystem (which can be expressed variously as joint visions/ research/ pilot/ demo projects, business models, activities etc.) geared toward developing new business initiatives that have 'global market potential amounting to at least 1 billion euros in new exports'. The objectives are therefore primarily economic but Growth Engines were 'particularly welcome' on data economy, circular economy and low carbon economy themes. Some Growth Engines have objectives directly related to the reduction of GHG emissions, such as GreenE2, Flexens or the Compensate Platform company that aim to 'establish an ecosystem that enables the compensation of carbon dioxide emissions easier in international scale, while creating business opportunities for Finnish companies'.*

The systemic nature of societal challenges requires that mission co-ordinators and "ecosystem orchestrators" have not only a broad range of competencies, but also adopt different perspectives, more holistic and proactive ones, i.e. involving different sectors and disciplines at the same time, and not only responding to their respective needs and demands as service providers. As research and technology organisations (RTOs) are hybrid organisations in many regards (interdisciplinary and cross-sectoral scope, public-private status, involved in science and industrial development, providing services to industry and administrations), they appear well-suited to perform this function in many cases. In one OECD study on the contribution of RTOs to solving societal challenges (Larrue and Strauka, 2022[12]), interviewees used different labels to describe the emerging role of RTOs: "system intermediaries", "orchestrators", "transition architects", "innovation system hub"', "virtual OEM", "system platforms", "system translator", etc. (Box 5.2).

Box 5.2. What is the role of research and technology organisations in missions and of missions in research and technology organisations?

Research and technology organisations (RTOs) play an active role in many ecosystem-based missions. This role calls for new capabilities such as the "convening capacity" (Olsen-Boyd et al., 2023[13]), in addition to new forms of technological knowledge and expertise. In Europe, participation in large European-funded projects, from FP6's Integrated Projects to the various European Partnerships, have been instrumental in helping European RTOs further develop these capabilities. Evaluations of the strategic innovation programmes provide evidence that these initiatives have had significant systematic impacts, by gradually achieving a national joining of forces and mobilisation, both across traditional sectoral boundaries and along value chains. RTOs (notably the RISE institutes) have significantly contributed to this "by fulfilling a system integrating function, especially with regard to industry" (Åström, Arnold and Olsson, 2021[14]).

A Finnish impact study analysing in detail several ecosystems using network graphs showed the role that the Finnish RTO VTT played in several of them as a link between different actors (Zegel et al., 2021[15]). VTT was even one of the key actors in 2015-16 to think and help design the national ecosystem approach with public authorities. While VTT is not the only actor to play this role (some universities and large companies are also network "nodes"), it is non-equivocally the one that ensures this bridging function in the greatest number of ecosystems and appears more central in ecosystem network graphs. VTT also leads and formally acts as the formal co-ordinator of several of these ecosystems (such as Smart Otaniemi in smart energy solutions or BATCircle in battery materials and component development). VTT has created a position of "co-creation managers" who oversee specific eco-systems. Several other RTOs play advisory or co-ordinating roles to support mission-oriented policies, for instance in Austria (Austrian Institute of Technology, Joaennum), Germany (Fraunhofer) and France (Alternative Energies and Atomic Energy Commission).

Some of the largest RTOs, especially when their functions expand beyond research implementation toward agency activities, have launched missions within their organisation to foster internal collaboration between their various centres and departments and build ecosystem-wide partnerships with external partners to achieve clear goals. In Australia, the Commonwealth Scientific & Industrial Research Organisation (CSIRO) launched its Mission Programme in August 2020. Missions represent significant five to seven years partnerships that harness the power of science and technology to create meaningful outcomes that cannot be attained by a single organisation alone. These missions are designed to mobilise science, technology and innovation with the aim of tackling well-defined goals associated with one or multiple national challenges. CSIRO has launched eight missions: 1) drought resilience; 2) ending plastic waste; 3) future protein; 4) hydrogen industry; 5) trusted agrifood exports; 6) towards net zero; 7) minimising antimicrobial resistance; and 8) AquaWatch Australia. CSIRO mostly initiates missions internally first, then engages partnership with government and industry stakeholders across Australia to co-develop and crowd-in the missions, gathering the resources and competencies needed to implement them. These include government bodies, academic institutions, industry partners and the broader community. Missions at CSIRO are supported by a dedicated Mission Office. All missions have a unique mission co-ordinator and a dedicated governance structure, including an advisory group composed of representatives of public and private organisations involved in the mission.

In Canada, the National Research Council launched internal Challenge Programmes in 2019. These programmes bring together for up to 7 years, researchers and facilities across the National Research Council's 14 research centres, with academic and industrial partners to advance transformative, high-risk, high-reward research that addresses Canadian priorities. In 2022, there were nine National Research Council programmes. For instance, the Materials for Clean Fuels Challenge aims to develop transformative technologies to sustainably transition Canada's energy and chemical industries to a low-carbon economy through materials innovation (including the Materials for Clean Fuels Programme). The mission has received about EUR 40 million in funding for the seven-year period (2019-26). It follows a funnel approach whereby the number of projects in the programme decreases and the amount of investment per project increases over time.

Source: (Larrue and Strauka, 2022[16]); OECD MOIP Online Toolkit, https://stip.oecd.org/moip.

References

Åström, T., E. Arnold and J. Olsson (2021), *Meta-evaluation of the Third Round of Strategic Innovation Programmes After Six Years*, Technopolis, https://www.vinnova.se/contentassets/e9aafdfe5f67491ab2f7016758458ac5/metautvardering-av-andra-omgangen-strategiska-innovationsprogram-efter-sex-ar.pdf?cb=20201215174117. [14]

Bonvillian, W., R. Van Atta and P. Windham (2019), *The DARPA Model for Transformative Technologies: Perspectives on the US Defense Advanced Research Projects Agency*, Open Book Publishers, Cambridge, United Kingdom, https://doi.org/10.11647/OBP.0184. [8]

Boon, W. and S. Bakker (2016), "Learning to shield: Policy learning in socio-technical transitions", *Environmental Innovation and Societal Transitions*, Vol. 18, pp. 181-200, https://doi.org/10.1016/j.eist.2015.06.003. [1]

Council of the European Union (2022), *Council Conclusions on European Missions (Adopted on 10 June 2022)*, Brussels, https://www.consilium.europa.eu/media/56954/st10124-en22.pdf. [4]

European Commission (2023), *Portfolio Analysis EU Mission "Restore Our Ocean and Waters by 2030": Analysis of a Portfolio of Projects Financed by Sixteen EU Programmes Contributing to the Objectives of the Mission Ocean and Waters*, Directorate-General for Research and Innovation, European Commission, https://data.europa.eu/doi/10.2777/683. [11]

European Commission (2020), *Implementation Strategy for Horizon Europe – Version 1.0*, Directorate-General for Research and Innovation, European Commission, https://research-and-innovation.ec.europa.eu/system/files/2020-04/ec_rtd_implementation-strategy_he.pdf. [10]

Larrue, P. and O. Strauka (2022), "The contribution of research and technology organisations (RTOs) to socio-economic recovery, resilience and transitions", *OECD Science, Technology and Industry Policy Papers*, No. 129, OECD, Publishing, Paris, https://doi.org/10.1787/ae93dc1d-en. [12]

Larrue, P. and O. Strauka (2022), "The contribution of RTOs to socio-economic recovery, resilience and transitions", *OECD Science, Technology and Industry Policy Papers*, No. 129, OECD Publishing, Paris, https://doi.org/10.1787/ae93dc1d-en. [16]

OECD (2022), *Tackling Policy Challenges Through Public Sector Innovation: A Strategic Portfolio Approach*, OECD Public Governance Reviews, OECD Publishing, Paris, https://doi.org/10.1787/052b06b7-en. [7]

OECD (2018), "Effective operation of competitive research funding systems", *OECD Science, Technology and Industry Policy Papers*, No. 57, OECD Publishing, Paris, https://doi.org/10.1787/2ae8c0dc-en. [2]

OECD (Forthcoming), "Mission portfolio management: towards a dynamic practice", *OECD Science, Technology and Innovation Working Papers*. [9]

OECD and DDC (2022), *Mission-oriented Innovation Needs Assessment Survey: Highlights & Insights on Mission Work*, OECD and Danish Design Center, https://ddc.dk/wp-content/uploads/2021/10/REPORT-mission-needs-assessment-survey-110222-.pdf. [3]

Olsen-Boyd, A. et al. (2023), *Convening Missions: A Playbook for Collective Implementation of Mission-oriented Innovation*, CSIRO, Brisbane, Australia, https://www.csiro.au/-/media/Missions/CSIRO_MissionPlaybook.pdf. [13]

Roth, F. et al. (2022), "Putting mission-oriented innovation policies to work: A case study of the German High-Tech Strategy 2025", *Fraunhofer ISI Discussion Papers Innovation Systems and Policy Analysis*, No. 75, https://www.isi.fraunhofer.de/content/dam/isi/dokumente/cci/innovation-systems-policy-analysis/2022/discussionpaper_75_2022.pdf. [5]

UNDP (2022), *System Change: A Guidebook for Adopting Portfolio Approaches*, United Nations Development Programme, Bangkok, https://www.undp.org/sites/g/files/zskgke326/files/2022-03/UNDP-RBAP-System-Change-A-Guidebook-for-Adopting-Portfolio-Approaches-2022.pdf. [6]

Zegel, S. et al. (2021), *World-class Ecosystems in the Finnish Economy: Impact Study*, Business Finland, https://www.businessfinland.fi/4a702b/globalassets/julkaisut/World-class-Ecosystems-in-the-Finnish-Economy-2-2021.pdf. [15]

Endnotes

[1] Climate change is the most frequent challenge tackled by MOIP initiatives identified to date, followed by health and healthcare issues.

[2] Team calculation based on data retrieved on 20 September 2022 for 289 policy instruments with replies to the grant duration question in the *STIP Compass database*, in the same countries with net zero missions covered in the OECD study (https://stip.oecd.org/stip).

[3] About 50% of missions. In some cases, budgets per year were calculated based on overall budgets divided by the number of funding years.

[4] This analysis is based on the authors' appreciation of missions' rationales presented in available mission documents. It should be considered tentative at this stage.

6 Stepping up net zero missions

This chapter draws implications of the study results in the form of three main policy traps missions should "escape" and lays out two scenarios for the future of missions. It then provides specific recommendations for mission practitioners, policy makers and their partners.

This report provides a comprehensive analysis of the additionality of mission-oriented innovation policies (MOIPs) *vis-à-vis* more traditional science, technology and innovation (STI) governance and policy frameworks to help countries meet their greenhouse gas (GHG) emissions reduction pledges. Building on work conducted by the Committee for Scientific and Technological Policy on MOIPs since 2019, the report uses a theory of action to assess missions' systemic effects. For this purpose, the analysis mobilised a purpose-built database and in-depth case studies of net zero missions and identifies key strengths and weaknesses as well as possible future evolutions of net zero missions.

The three mission-oriented innovation policy traps

The analysis shows that most net zero missions produce many of the effects presented in their theory of action. In most cases, they represent a marked improvement over traditional STI policy mixes. They allow the collective development of common objectives and strategic agendas; broader co-ordination of policy plans across administrative, sectoral and disciplinary silos; and higher integration of various support instruments across the different stages of the innovation chain. The practices to achieve these results significantly vary among missions, as they adapt to the specificities of the challenge they tackle and to the national institutional setting in which they are embedded.

However, these achievements will not be sufficient to scale-up and deploy these innovations on a massive scale. At the still early stage of this policy approach, net zero missions remain too focused on technological innovation (the "STI trap"), fall short of having an actual influence on policy beside providing directionality (the "orientation trap") and are not yet sufficiently leveraging resources apart from the public budget (the "policy trap"):

- The STI trap: net zero missions remain led by STI authorities, relying almost exclusively on STI policy interventions and budgets. While sectoral policy and regulatory authorities have a hand in the mission structure of governance, and can share information – and to some extent, influence decisions – they have not yet contributed their own resources and programmes to the mission. To bring about the transformative changes needed to achieve net zero (as opposed to simply reducing overlaps and speeding up technological innovation), net zero missions will require investments of a far greater scale and scope, including by drawing upon the large transition or climate funds available in an increasing number of countries. They will also need to balance, align and accompany the mass deployment of these innovations with solutions to promote social and behavioural changes, which is prerequisite for reducing GHG emissions rapidly and significantly.
- The orientation trap: most missions have been successful in setting legitimate and powerful objectives and targets, as well as a widely shared systemic strategic agenda to fulfil their objectives. However, the strategic agenda influence on collective decision making regarding budget allocation and policy implementation is less clear. Because of these difficulties, missions are generally less integrated at the implementation level than at the orientation and co-ordination levels. Several missions have co-constructed shared strategic agendas which are then implemented by the different partners, with only minimal common monitoring and exchange of information.
- The policy trap:[1] as argued in this report, missions are essentially an extra layer of orientation, co-ordination and – in the best case – integration on top of pre-existing interventions. The bulk of efforts appear in many of them directed at creating policy consistency on these three dimensions, which tend to make them confined to the public sector. However, their implementation will also depend on their ability to mobilise the private sector's funding and capabilities, as investors, technology providers and users. For the most part, the private sector's contribution to missions is made via the traditional co-funding of activities at the project level. To succeed in leveraging the

level of necessary funds, missions will also need to innovate in the way they are funded, using, for instance, new forms of public-private partnerships, blended finance options and equity financing.

Toward third-generation mission-oriented innovation policies

Using the well-known distinction between the first generation of missions focused on technological challenges (e.g., Apollo in the 1960s) and the second generation of missions addressing complex societal challenges, the net zero missions scrutinised in this report clearly belong to the second category. However, they fall short of having the design, notably in terms of ambition, scope and resources, that would enable them to be transformative. The second generation as it appears in this study is mostly populated by missions that have concentrated efforts on some shared agendas, accelerated changes and avoided costly overlaps. The results of this study support a call for a third generation of missions that address the three traps laid out above: they need to enlist public actors and policies beyond the STI realm, deliver and effect changes via joint implementation, and crowd in the missions with private actors' resources and capabilities (Figure 6.1).

Figure 6.1. Toward third-generation mission-oriented innovation policies

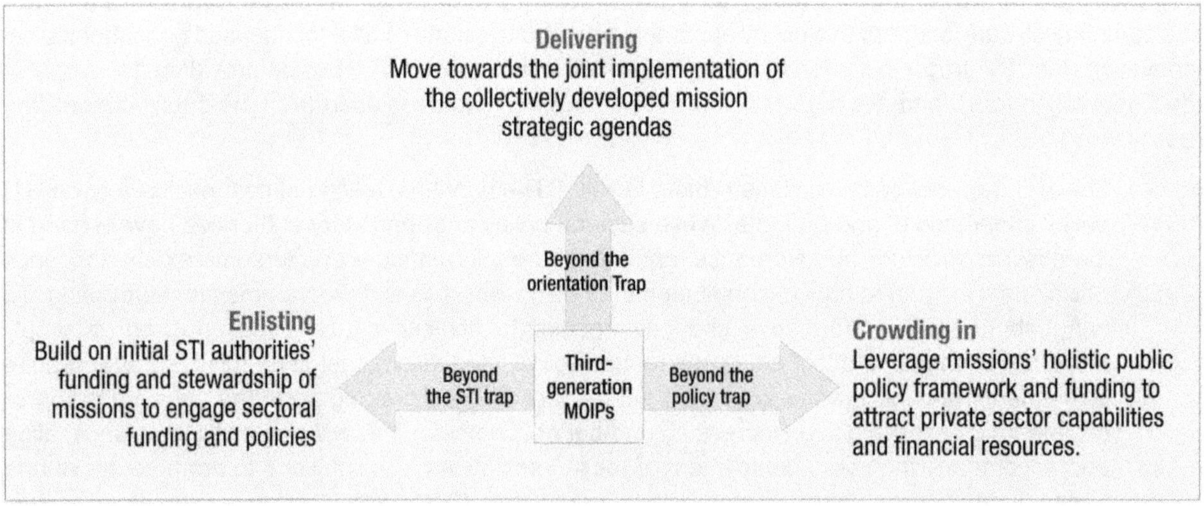

Note: MOIP: mission-oriented innovation policy; STI: science, technology and innovation.

The first major step concerns the overall design of the missions to overcome the important mismatch between their broad scope of objectives and the narrow policy mix for action. Building on initial STI authorities' funding and stewardship, missions should secure commitments from sectoral funding and policies; this step involves setting clear, measurable and realistic targets and gathering a policy mix of interventions suited to realise these goals, using the mission strategic agenda or theory of change to identify the needed actions (Figure 6.2).

Figure 6.2. Turning the mission pyramid upside down: Design of the third-generation missions

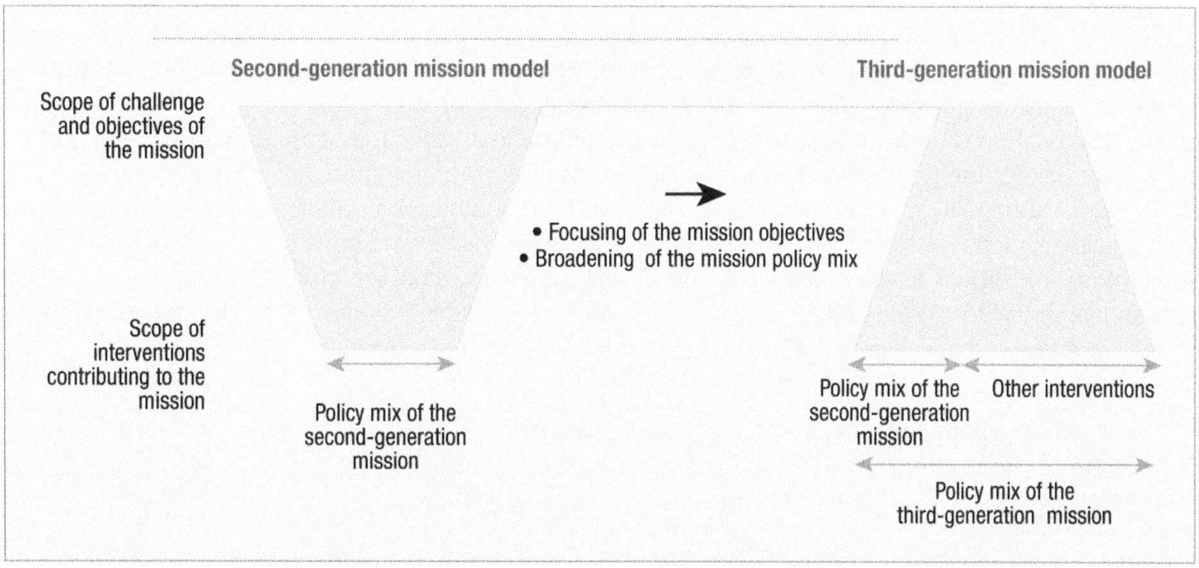

This joint implementation will require sectoral ministries and various public authorities in charge of scaling up and deployment (including ministries of industry, economy and finance) to factor research and innovation more prominently into their agendas. It will also demand that STI public authorities who championed the missions accept to share (and sometimes lose) the leadership of these missions.

In no way should these three observed limitations be considered an argument against this policy approach. The vast majority of missions have been launched recently (95% of net zero missions in the database have been created since 2018) and moved toward implementation at least a year later. The long and iterative work of persuasion and enlisting of new public and private actors beyond the initial "coalition of committed partners" has barely started. At this early stage, as argued in the growing literature on the evaluation of missions and other transformative policies, the results from studies and evaluations are to be used primarily for learning and driving improvements, not for accountability purposes. The mission traps are not a judgement against MOIPs, simply a "waypoint" in their policy trajectory which shows directions for change.

There are already some interesting examples of changes building upon the experience of recent years' mission pilots. In Germany, the missions of the former High-Tech Strategy 2025, which were criticised for their weak directionality and loose co-ordination, will be followed by the "Future Research and Innovation Strategy". This new strategy is meant to feature dedicated governance structures which would materialise the mission-specific goals, establish milestones and assess their achievement through continuous monitoring, as requested by the advisory High-Tech Forum prior to its dissolution. In Austria, the mission-oriented thematic programmes "Building of Tomorrow", "Mobility of the Future" and "City of Tomorrow" are the basis upon which four national "Transformative missions" and significant efforts towards European Union missions develop. In Ireland, the Research Ireland's Challenge Research programmes will benefit from the funding and institutional dynamics of the Irish Recovery and Resilience Plan, expanding and "deepening" their mission-oriented approach within the newly created "National Challenge Fund". This is expected to be characterised by greater directionality to allow a more consistent and interrelated project portfolio. The Dutch Mission-driven and Top Sectors Policy are also entering a new cycle, following reform to render it more strategic and efficient.

Two possible pathways for the future of missions

This raises the fundamental question of where to anchor third-generation missions aiming to transform sociotechnical systems to achieve net zero in government structures. How far can MOIPs go in building on the leadership of STI authorities? Have the net zero missions led by STI authorities reached their "glass ceiling"? Should the "I" in MOIPs be dropped to switch from "innovation missions" to "transition missions"? Two scenarios for the future of missions can be distinguished: (i) a scenario of gradual improvement of missions, incrementally enlisting new actors, building trust, learning and attracting higher commitments from public authorities outside the STI realm and higher investments from private actors (Figure 6.3). (ii) A scenario of transfer of mission leadership, from STI actors towards sectoral ministries who 'own' the challenges, directly included in their mandate, and have essential intervention tools, resources and legal powers to address them (Figure 6.4).

Figure 6.3. The gradual improvement of missions scenario

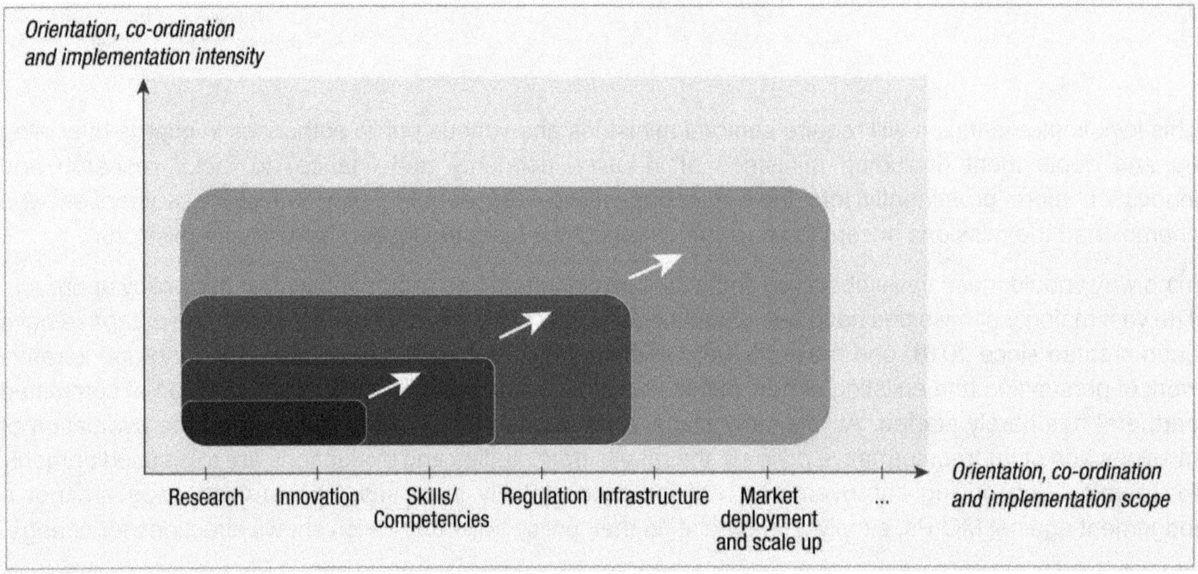

Figure 6.4. The transfer of mission leadership scenario

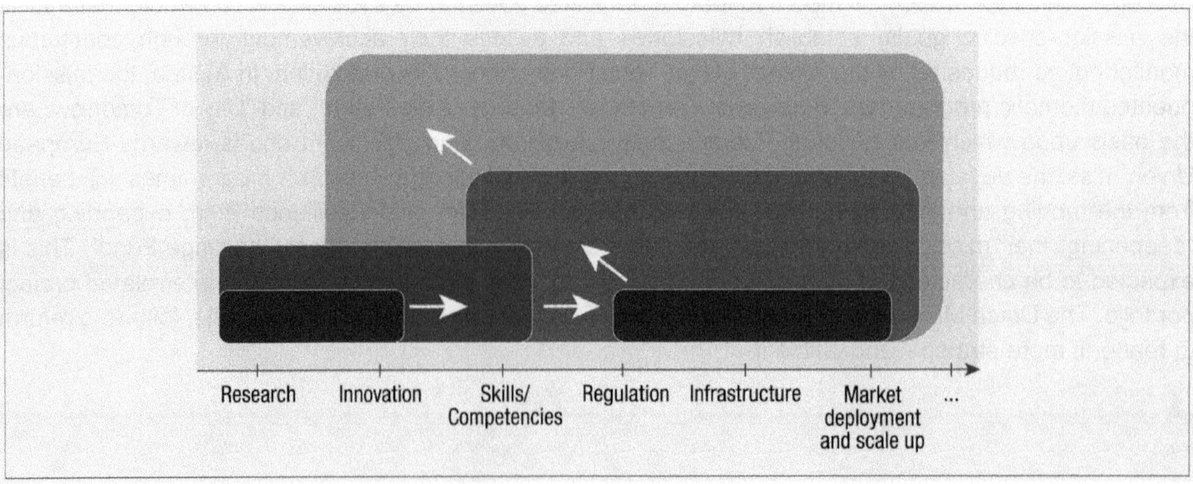

Other options include central institutions or cross-ministerial platforms taking responsibility of the missions, based on their broader remit and stronger systemic responsibilities across the government structure, a dedicated agency linked to several ministries, a large public-private partnership/platform or an autonomous organisation with foundation status. These may call for institutional innovations. Novel options to steer, govern and possibly manage large systemic missions still need to be designed and experimented on different levels across government structures (Box 6.1).

Box 6.1. Where should missions be anchored in national innovation systems?

The net zero mission "STI trap" raises questions of where missions aiming to transform sociotechnical systems to achieve net zero should be anchored in government structures. As a study of the German High-Tech strategy's missions concluded: "governance structures need to reflect the considerable coordination requirements of the mission-oriented approach, especially in regard to cross-ministerial cooperation. This may imply to move mission responsibility to higher political levels or, alternatively, to delegate the responsibility for missions to one or several agencies" (Roth et al., 2022[1]).

Although this does not apply to all national institutional settings, positioning the mission-oriented innovation policy leadership "above ministries" seems relevant for transformative missions to raise their level of ambition and broaden their systemic scope beyond science, technology and innovation (STI) authorities. For instance, in the European Union "Soil" mission, programmes and stakeholders need to be mobilised far beyond the scope of STI, which raises the question of whether the Horizon Europe research and innovation framework programme is the best location to "host" such ambitious objectives. This option is also more compatible with integrated multiannual budgets originating from different sources (including centralised budgets and "common pots") across policy fields. It is also important to strengthen high-level political buy-in and citizen ownership of ambitious net zero missions. A few countries with greater experience with this policy approach – such as Sweden, where missions lie within the research and innovation agencies – have tried to "elevate" missions to a higher and broader level of governance, although with mixed results. The French missions (the acceleration strategies), which are led by an autonomous agency attached to the Prime Minister's Office, with strong support from the president and a dedicated budget covering a broad systemic portfolio of actions over different generations of sociotechnical solutions, offer a different model of institutionalised missions.

An OECD study to support the development of the Norwegian Long-term Plan for Higher Education and Research explored the different options for anchoring national missions, building upon the experience gained in agency-level missions such as Pilot-E (Larrue and Santos, 2022[2]). The options envisaged and debated in the report included: a centre-of-government body, for instance the Prime Minister's Office or the Cabinet Office, attached to a high-level committee (like the Moonshot Program in Japan, led by the Council for Science, Technology and Innovation, headed by the prime minister and supported by a powerful Cabinet Office); the research ministry (Ministry of Education) with a stronger co-ordination role, as is the case in Korea, where the powerful Innovation Office within the Ministry of Science and ICT is tasked with STI co-ordination and budgetary negotiations across the government; the Ministry of Trade, Industry and Fisheries, since this ministry controls many of the policy and regulatory instruments key to achieving a large net zero mission; a large mission-oriented cross-ministerial programme, directly supervised by ministries in a dedicated governance body; a dedicated "mission" agency or a virtual cross-agency platform with some dedicated management and governance bodies that would rely on the staff from the different participating agencies; some large public-private partnerships/consortia to lead and manage some industry-led missions, possibly drawing on existing industry collaborative platforms (the "21 platforms").

Recommendations for mission governance

Make deployment actors, interventions and mechanisms integral to the mission

The issue

This study has provided evidence of the many challenges missions face to enlist actors and raise commitments beyond STI authorities and funding. This "glass ceiling" of missions hinders the missions' ability to realise their objectives, which in all cases requires much more than R&D. While most missions include market and use considerations more prominently in research and innovation than is the case with traditional STI policies, missions are often too loosely connected to the large pockets of money available for sustainability transitions, for instance in national transition or climate funds. Only a few examples of missions encompass in their scope of co-ordination and sphere of influence the policy instruments and incentives that support scale-up and deployment. This is the case of some of the French acceleration strategies as part of the France 2030 national plan and some US Earthshots that are formally connected to the fund available via the Bipartisan Infrastructure Law, CHIPS and Science Act, and the Inflation Reduction Act. As a result, missions are well-equipped to develop knowledge and innovations that could realise their objectives but lack the interventions to support them in "shaping markets" and going the critical "last mile" of the innovation process.

Possible ways forward

Enabling missions requires engaging the public authorities whose actions are necessary for the diffusion and deployment of new solutions. These include notably the ministries of industry, economy and finance as well as the sectoral ministries in charge of, for instance, energy, environment, transport or health, depending on the competencies under their portfolio. The role of regulatory authorities can also be determinant in setting the adequate framework conditions. Finally, local authorities are also important, be it for setting the environment for demonstrating and testing new solutions, raising public awareness and acceptance, or as first buyers.

Some actions to help missions exit the STI trap are:

- Involve the public authorities necessary for the scale-up and deployment of the new solutions from the outset as key partners.
- Embed in the missions or formally connect the mission to the support mechanisms and incentives for scaling up and deployment.
- Provide missions with high-level political backup and anchor them as key implementation tools in the national agenda and governance framework, such as the net zero agenda and other national whole-of-government transition strategies and plans.

Connect the missions to the broader and higher level national strategic and governance frameworks that are relevant in their challenge area

The issue

In many countries there is a disconnect between MOIP initiatives and the broader national strategic and governance frameworks relevant to their challenge areas. For instance, net zero missions often focus heavily on research and innovation, while national frameworks (sometimes funded through large "transition funds") prioritise the deployment of existing solutions to achieve short- and medium-term impacts. This disconnect can hinder co-ordinated efforts to scale-up solutions over time and prevent the full exploitation of synergies across different generations of solutions.

Possible ways forward

To bridge this gap, missions should be better integrated – and when possible embedded – into the national strategic and governance frameworks with the support of high-level political authorities, including central governments and treasuries. Some countries that have legislated their net zero targets have already established dedicated governance structures to oversee progress, co-ordinate actions and advise on national strategy in a holistic manner. These frameworks should more explicitly recognise the crucial contributions of relevant missions to ensure mutual benefits and enhance overall coherence. Missions can provide valuable insights on the progress of different approaches, which can inform broader national strategies. At the same time, national priorities should be reflected in the strategic agendas of missions to align them with overarching goals and tap into funding opportunities, particularly in the later stages of development and deployment.

Recommendations for mission implementation and evaluation

Ensure that missions are supported by strong and well-resourced dedicated teams both at the level of the MOIP initiative and individual missions

The issue

Designing, governing, implementing and learning from missions require specific skills, mindsets, tools and processes that differ in many respects from those found in many public and private organisations. This calls for a dedicated team to manage and accompany this process of change and generate and accumulate some of the needed resources. Several of the cases studied in this report have such team, office or secretariat both at the MOIP level (especially the multi-mission MOIPs) or at the individual mission level (especially the large systemic ones). However, this is not yet systematically the case; these offices might be under-resourced (no dedicated full-time staff) and lack power (to counterbalance the "vertical/thematic/departmental" logics); or the type of skills needed is not yet clearly established, hence the difficulty to appoint the right people.

The various partners, who are most often also involved in other initiatives, cannot be left alone to lead.

Possible ways forward

The missions should be supported by strong, legitimate and well-resourced teams both at the level of the MOIP initiative (a "central secretariat") and individual mission level (a "mission secretariat"). The tasks these teams should accomplish are manifold:

- support mission design, co-ordination and implementation
- formalisation and institutionalisation of the mission processes, across missions and over time
- develop methodological and management guidelines and tools
- support learning and all reflexive activities, including monitoring and evaluation
- train mission partners, explain and promote the mission approach
- perform proactive and hands-on portfolio management
- execute the dedicated mission funding (strategic direction activities)
- build and maintain linkages to higher level strategic and governance frameworks.

Mission partners should explore and test new modes of implementation to strategically steer, manage and monitor ambitious systemic missions

The issue

Dealing proactively with systemic missions – especially large ones – proves beyond the capacity of any organisation regardless of the resources and capabilities of the support teams. As a result, missions might end up being either too broad but under a loose co-ordination umbrella where activities are managed at an arm's length or narrowly focused technological missions. In either case, the expected systemic effects – which are the essence of missions – will be limited.

Possible ways forward

New modes of implementation relying on effective partnerships can be instrumental in proactively managing large systemic missions. A mission portfolio can be divided into a consistent group of activities (e.g. thematic or local sub-portfolio) managed by platforms or other types of decentralised support structures. These platforms can manage their respective set of activities, promoting the expected synergies within their portfolio and ensuring their consistency with and contribution to the overall mission. This type of relay structure helps combine flexibility and integration.

Missions should be granted enhanced flexibility to take decisions, fund activities and take actions as needed to realise their objectives

The issue

Although most missions are pilots in practice, their experimental status is not formally acknowledged. They are therefore not granted any specific conditions to operate. In the vast majority of cases, missions operate in unchanged framework conditions and mobilise existing funding instruments. The specific modes of co-ordination and implementation that govern the mission build upon and must comply with the established administrative rules and mechanisms that frame traditional STI policies. These conditions have been designed to provide the best environment for interventions that are neutral (non-directional or simply thematic) and fragmented. However, they are quite remote from what is needed for missions to co-construct objectives and strategic agendas, set the collective decision-making rules and processes for the needed policy coherence, and jointly implement and monitor a diverse mix of interventions to realise the common objectives.

Possible ways forward

Missions need strategic flexibility to operate as required to realise their strategic agenda. This should apply notably to the way they allocate funding. New options must be developed and tested as alternatives to the sole recourse to competitive-based instruments such as calls for proposals managed at arm's length. These are not adapted to the directionality of missions, which can require direct intervention and longer term partnership between the funder and some public or private organisations with specific capabilities, resources or infrastructure (or able to develop them). Flexibility is also needed with regards to the funding time frame (multiannual needed), size (for larger, multi-partner projects) and scope (combined funding of different activities, beyond R&D), administrative rules (allowing risk-taking and, hence, failure) and reporting obligations (based on trust and less static, permitting changes of direction). These selected features are at the core of the mission approach, yet traditional support schemes fall short of offering them. In certain cases, creating these conditions will require creating new instruments rather than mere adjustments to existing ones. Yet only a few missions have led to the creation of new instruments. One example is the case of the Dutch Mission-Driven and Top Sector Policy, which led to the creation of a specific funding instrument (MOOI, for mission-oriented research, development and innovation), which encourages multidisciplinary consortia to create proposals that combine various technological and non-technological sub-solutions (rather than focusing on individual technologies as is usually the case), including also activities concerning the commercialisation and societal acceptance of the projects (Janssen, 2020[3]).

Establish dedicated multiannual funding for missions to strategically support them from design to implementation and evaluation

The issue

The analysis of many MOIP initiatives has revealed that numerous missions lack dedicated public funding and rely almost entirely on funds committed by each participating public authority, sometimes on an annual basis. This reliance makes any common mission activity contingent on the agreement and goodwill of these partners, leading to uncertainties, rigidities and increased bureaucratic burden, including for those performing research and innovation. Additionally, decentralised funding of the mission diminishes the mission teams' or offices' legitimacy and power. Most importantly, it increases the fragmentation of the portfolio, hence reducing the possibility of reaping the systemic effects of the mission (for instance, preventing management at the level of the entire portfolio). Several mission managers have reported difficulties overcoming the vertical forces within departments and organisations that drive partners' decisions. Even committed partners tend to prioritise their own organisation's incentives, mandates and decision-making mechanisms, which may not always align with the mission's common goals.

Possible ways forward

In addition to the resources committed by mission partners, a central, multiannual funding stream specifically attached to the mission is crucial. Such funding can incentivise partners to allocate resources to specific mission activities, help persuade internal stakeholders (not least the hierarchy of the persons directly involved in the mission) and attract additional resources, including co-funding.

These mission funds are also important to fill potential portfolio gaps and directly fund some strategic activities in the portfolio that are beyond (or in between) the partners' areas of interest. This implies that the mission funds should not only cover the operational costs of a mission team but also allow direct intervention and support of external activities (e.g. commissioning specific research and studies; issuing a call for proposals). Finally, dedicated mission funding is critical to allow reflexive activities and enable learning and improvement.

Design and experiment new innovative funding mechanisms to increase private engagement in and commitment to the missions

The issue

The analysis conducted for this report has shown that very few innovative financial models and funding instruments have been used in net zero missions and that, in most cases, private funding is raised via classic project cost-sharing rules. As missions progress and their focus moves toward deployment and scale-up, crowding in investment from outside of government and securing private sector engagement will become increasingly important. This evolution requires more buy-in from the private sector, since reaching many mission goals requires companies to adopt the MOIP-generated solutions or change their behaviours.

Possible ways forward

New funding models should be experimented with, such as different types of public-private partnerships, blended finance options and equity financing for "mission corporation". Given the wide scope of many missions, specific funding agreements could be secured directly with the relevant sectors. This has been done notably in the context of the Dutch Mission-Driven and Top Sector Policy. The Knowledge and Innovation Covenant in the health and care area described precisely the financial commitments of all health and care public and private partners to the five missions in this area and the expected deliverables in return, as specified in the mission-specific agenda.[2] In the United Kingdom, the Sector Deals set the financial commitment of the different missions related to specific Industrial Strategy Challenge Funds. For instance, the Aerospace Sector Deal passed in 2019 included a commitment of the government and the sector to provide up to GBP 125 million each to support R&D conducted in the Future Flight Challenge Fund.[3] This agreement included several other mutual commitments (including, for instance, on gender issues) and was managed and reviewed by an Aerospace Growth Partnership which met twice a year.

Mission partners should invest in the development of the needed capabilities, tools and methods for the proactive management of the portfolio of mission activities

The issue

Investigations of missions have shown that most missions barely undertake portfolio management. They either manage individual projects and activities selected using the sole traditional criteria of relevance and effectiveness or use static portfolio management practices, involving (*ex post*) tagging and mapping of existing relevant activities. This prevents them from reaping the benefits of mission systemic effects. The reasons for this situation are manifold:

- mission portfolio management requires acquiring a different set of skills than those present in many research and innovation agencies which have for decades placed the priority on the efficient disbursement of funds
- mission portfolio management also demands more human resources, dedicating more time to support the various teams
- most agencies' structures, rules and support instruments have been fine-tuned to manage on a project basis with limited consideration for the overall portfolio.

Notably, a number of missions still rely uniquely on competitive calls for proposal for designing their portfolio. While the mission's strategic agenda might be used to develop the terms of reference of the call for proposals, this approach is not sufficient to steer applicants in the direction needed to realise the mission. The portfolio design involves a number of iterative interactions to align what is "needed and feasible" and a certain power of the mission manager to push in certain directions that may be less desirable by applicants (notably in the case of more uncertain and risky activities, different from the existing portfolio, which is precisely what the mission might require).

Possible ways forward

Organisations involved in missions, notably agencies, should progressively implement (*ex ante*) proactive mission portfolio management practices to drive key decisions concerning what activities to select, initiate, mobilise, fund, reorient, monitor or terminate in relation to the objectives of the mission (and the associated mission strategic agenda, theory of change, impact pathway or roadmap). Another key dimension of proactive mission portfolio management consists of promoting interlinkages and exchanges between the different complementary projects and activities within the portfolio. These organisations must therefore engage in significant reforms involving:

- The acquisition of new skills. The portfolio managers must be more proactive, outcome-focused and strategic, with deep and broad knowledge of their thematic areas.
- Additional resources dedicated to developing new tools (including portfolio visualisation software)
- A change in the funding rules, including, for instance, the development of new criteria for selecting activities, accounting for the portfolio consistency fit of any project).
- Change of instruments (or addition of new ones) to increase the strategic flexibility of mission managers, for instance providing them with the possibility of direct funding and commissioning of certain activities, and more interactions with potential applicants ahead of and during calls for proposals.

For a more detailed discussion and recommendations on mission portfolio management, see OECD (2024 MPM).

Develop new methods and processes for monitoring and evaluating missions based on a clear theory of action and a developmental approach

The issue

The few monitoring and evaluation activities around missions have been carried out using traditional approaches. MOIPs have several features that make these traditional approaches unfit for evaluating them. First, missions are systemic initiatives. While the need for a systemic approach to public policy evaluation is well acknowledged (OECD, 2022), established methodologies and practices fall short of capturing the comprehensive benefits these missions are expected to offer at system level, which stem from integrating diverse knowledge, skills, interventions and funding streams across sectors. Capturing these "systemic effects", which is critical for doing justice to missions at a critical moment of the life cycle of this policy approach, requires the development of new processes, methodologies and tools (Wise et al., 2022). The most promising initiatives in this respect can be found in academic work, but these remain rather conceptual and have not yet been applied in real evaluation cases. Second, missions are evolving entities, with unclear and evolving boundaries. They typically start with broad goals that are gradually refined through negotiations, increasing trust among partners and the involvement of new stakeholders. This ongoing evolution makes evaluation challenging, as both the objectives and structure of the mission change over time. Evaluators need to assess not only the outcomes but also the mission's evolution in terms of design, governance and implementation processes.

Possible ways forward

This requires a developmental evaluation approach that tracks alignment with the mission's purpose, emphasising adaptation and learning among policy makers and partners. The specificity of missions involves a developmental approach which is adapted for the evaluation of complex and dynamic systems. In such approaches, evaluators do not operate at arm's length from the mission they evaluate but instead act alongside the missions and provide tools for supporting their effective design and implementation, in particular during the pilot stage. They are engaged ("embedded") in the intervention to be evaluated on a more continuous and longer term basis, participating through continuous interactions with the mission partners in the collection of data, framing of issues, testing of options and provision of feedback for the mission design and implementation. An important part of their assessment should be the extent to which and how the mission becomes a "real" mission as it deploys its activities and learns (i.e. the process by which the "mission-readiness level" increases). The evaluation should, therefore, consider not only the effects of the mission but also how it evolves in terms of design, governance and processes (objective-setting, funding, portfolio management, etc.); and whether these observed evolutions are relevant to what was expected and motivated the adoption of a mission approach, as well as the reasons for any observed gap. As missions progress, summative evaluations can be added to measure progress toward final goals.

A crucial tool for such developmental evaluation is the "mission theory of action". This tool is specifically developed to track the specific mission processes and the systemic effects they are expected to generate to tackle a specific challenge. It describes how the mission is designed and set up to achieve the mission. It maps the chains of causality that connect the way missions are designed and governed to the impact they are expected to produce. Rather than only focusing on the substantive dimension of missions (is the mission being realised and the selected challenge solved?), mission theories of action track the key processes that lie at the heart of the MOIP approach and allow assessing whether they unfold as expected and produce their "systemic effects" (i.e. is the adopted approach effective to tackle the selected challenge?). For a more detailed discussion of mission monitoring and evaluation and more detailed recommendations see OECD (2024 M&E).

Overall, there is a need to better recognise the current pilot nature of missions and their need for reflexive learning. This implies increased efforts in the mapping and sharing of good practices and challenges, supported by conceptual and action-research tools (such as the mission theory of action). This involves the mission partners working closely with researchers to develop new methods and tools.[4] This reflects more generally the new type of iterative and continuous linkages needed between policy makers and knowledge providers involved in transformative innovation policies, including missions (EuSPRI, 2024[4]).

Recommendations for mission design

Mission partners should dedicate significant time and effort to the earlier stage of the mission, notably the preparation stage

The issue

Missions are often rushed through to be launched as soon as possible, in a context of urgency and under high political and administrative pressure due to their visibility, sensitivity and the importance of the challenges they are tackling. The difficulty of, and therefore the time needed for, setting a mission in institutional and organisations' conditions often ill-suited for this policy approach is underestimated, resulting hence in a lack of time as well as human and financial resources during that period. However, this period is certainly the most crucial for the success of the mission. Experience clearly shows that the design stage is essential and requires time, notably to build consensus, convince, build trust, consult stakeholders, explore options (including ones that are not obvious) and substantiate them with robust strategic policy intelligence (including foresight if needed), set the governance structure, and secure partners' early commitments.

Possible ways forward

It is essential to institutionalise the mission preparatory stage and dedicate the necessary time and resources to perform a number of essential tasks:

- make explicit and align the respective expectations and strategies of the committed partners around a common challenge
- scan the existing environment and rally new actors with necessary complementary assets (policy interventions, authority and mandate, skills) around this challenge

- engage in problem framing and, if possible at this stage, develop a mission statement or objectives that reflect the most ambitious commitments possible, in consultation with a wide array of experts and stakeholders
- partners should design the mission (scope, governance, funding mechanisms, division of leadership and labour, etc.) in direct relation to the challenge at stake.

These co-design activities require building a certain level of trust between the partners, which cannot be hastened.

Investing the necessary time and resources in the preparation of these initiatives is particularly difficult. These are not yet missions at this stage and remain in "stealth mode". Furthermore, there are only few committed partners enrolled at this early stage to commit resources. A possible solution is to institutionalise the process for the definition, selection and final endorsement of missions, using a stage-gate approach for a gradual and increased investment as the soon-to-be mission passes pre-defined "mission-readiness milestones" and progresses through the steps. Such a process can be designed as part of an existing MOIP initiative to launch new missions as is the case for CSIRO missions. Outside an existing initiative, like in Norway, this process can be commissioned by a high-level political or policy authority to a mandated group (Box 6.2).

Box 6.2. Institutionalising a dedicated process for mission preparation

An organisation like Australia's Commonwealth Scientific and Industrial Research Organisation (CSIRO) has formalised a co-design process prior to officially launching a mission. This process can take one to two years depending on the level of complexity and consensus around a particular challenge. It involves several steps, including at the core a "Sprint process" that involves problem exploration, system mapping, early stakeholder engagement to inform preliminary problem framing, direct interactions for iterative problem reframing and focusing, identifying and defining projects addressing key areas and, finally, the development of a roadmap including implementation pathways. The resulting mission proposal is submitted to CSIRO's top decision makers.

Figure 6.5. CSIRO mission design process with a focus on the "Sprint' step

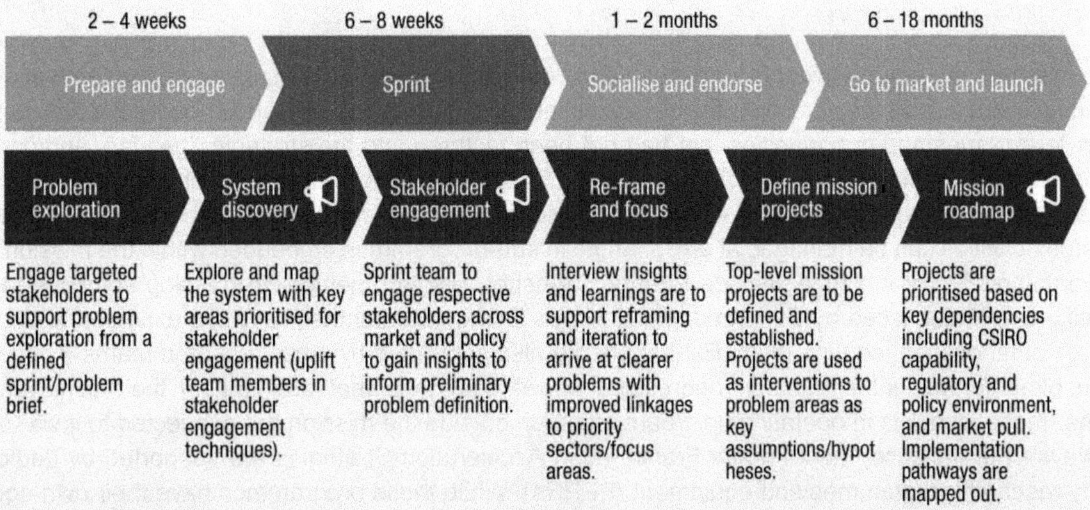

Norway has appointed a cross-sectoral "operational group" to develop each of the two national missions announced in the Long-term Plan for Research and Higher Education 2023-2032 endorsed by parliament in February 2023. Both groups had a mandate with a clear calendar. For instance, the operational group in charge of preparing the mission on the social inclusion of children and young people was composed of representatives of nine organisations (mainly agencies) which had to work against the following ten-month timeline during the so-called "design phase":

- June 2023: Propose a plan to increase the involvement, mobilisation and sense of ownership of all relevant sectors and actors (including children and young people) to concretise the mission and increase commitment and legitimacy. Consult with all relevant stakeholders (via various meetings and through an online portal). Co-ordinate this process with the concurrent development of a related higher level strategic document ("white paper") on social welfare policy by an interdepartmental group of ministries.
- November 2023: Perform a stocktaking of knowledge and experiences relevant to the mission and identify knowledge gaps. Map the set of existing programmes and instruments that are relevant to the mission, outline a possible process for combining these in new ways to achieve the mission's goals and lay out the budgetary implications.
- February 2024: Propose time-bound goals, sub-goals and scoping of the mission; propose the design, governance and modes of implementation of the mission after the design phase.

The final proposal was approved by the government in March 2024.

Source: CSIRO (2023[5]).

Establish formal and flexible linkages between missions and relevant upstream research programmes to ensure that the mission is aware of and open to relevant new scientific advances and breakthrough innovations

The issue

Due to their directional character, in public debates missions are still too often seen as opposed to and competing with upstream ("free", "investigator-led") research. The focus is, therefore, too often on striking the right balance between both rather than on establishing linkages to maximise their complementarities.

Possible ways forward

While missions are geared towards innovation and deployment, linkages with upstream research activities (including in social sciences and humanities) are essential to generate and explore novel solutions, unravel longer term issues and opportunities that had not been factored into the strategic agendas, and conduct advanced measurements and metrology services. Smart and agile connections should be established between upstream research and missions. To preserve their exploratory character, relevant upstream research activities can be managed at arm's length in sub-programmes embedded within the mission. The US Earthshots™, for instance, include Energy Earthshot research centers to develop solutions for the scientific challenges faced by Department of Energy's Energy Earthshots™ and are expected to become "centres of innovation" serving them. Earthshots are also supported by small research teams focused on use-inspired fundamental research addressing knowledge gaps that are limiting their achievement. Another model consists in operating upstream research outside the mission but connected to it via "smart gateways". For instance, most French France 2030 Acceleration Strategies are supported by dedicated priority research programmes and equipment (PEPRs). While these programmes have their own agenda and funding, they are formally linked to the Stratégies d'Accélération (SA) they support by an interface enabling mutual benefits from both the PEPR and the SA (see Section 5.1.3).

Make the missions more outcome-focused to combine high levels of ambition, effectiveness and efficiency

The issue

Missions have been criticised for being too top-down and directive which would stifle the creativity and entrepreneurial spirit necessary for innovation. However, the analysis of missions demonstrates that most missions are still largely bottom-up. Their objectives are often broad; their target, if any, non-measurable; and their strategic agenda and roadmap remain indicative and are not systematically used to monitor the progress of their portfolio of activities. Starting with broad mission areas and developing strategic agendas that try to satisfy all demands from national and sectoral groups of interest in a bottom-up way has led to missions appearing to some key actors as overly complex, broad and intangible. The lack of directionality also significantly limits the systemic effects expected from missions and increases co-ordination costs. It is one of the main challenges in defining the mission goals and targets to set the appropriate levels of directionality (how precise, directive should the goals be?) and ambition (how high should the goals be relative to the current state of the art?).

Possible ways forward

The missions should be focused, targeted towards a limited set of concrete objectives with clear targets and timelines, including intermediate milestones. While missions should be broad enough to enable system change (not just single technological innovations), they cannot be "the tool for everything". They should remain strategically focused and not try to encompass all potential issues in a broad area. Also, missions are expected to make the transition actionable but are not an open-ended transition policy. They should be bounded in time and scope. It is essential to re-establish missions as an instrument with systemic and ambitious goals but on a forcibly limited and realistic scope. Importantly, it should be made clear that this does not imply a reduction in the societal ambitions of the missions, which calls for an important role for public authorities to ensure that a high level of transformative ambition is preserved despite possible attempts of "mission capture" by incumbents. Public authorities are also instrumental in setting an appropriate process composed of different stages of top-down and bottom-up inputs to the agenda setting.

Enhancing the pragmatism of missions also involves being able to secure quick wins while still aiming for the longer term and more comprehensive realisation of the final objectives. This is important to maintain momentum and rally new partners.

Finally, designing pragmatic, actionable missions requires balancing the expected costs and benefits of missions. While broad co-ordination along several dimensions (for instance, sectors and missions) can produce different types of systemic effects, it can also rapidly translate into significant transaction costs, complexity, rigidity and, hence, "mission fatigue". The broadest and strongest form of co-ordination is not adequate for all missions. Based on a shared understanding of the costs and benefits of each mission (in its particular national and challenge contexts), partners should fine-tune the different types and intensities of co-ordination. The use of a mission theory of action during the preparatory stage can prove instrumental to form this shared understanding.

Box 6.3. What are the remaining knowledge gaps related to missions?

Mission-oriented policy has gained interest in recent years, and there has been a lot of learning about its implementation in the last five years. However, there is still much to be understood to take net zero missions to the next level and overcome the three traps that have been identified. OECD work on mission-oriented innovation policies (MOIPs), along with a detailed review of the literature on missions, has highlighted several areas where knowledge gaps exist:

- *How to make missions truly systemic and expand beyond the realm of science, technology and innovation (STI) actors, policies and funding?* This issue encompasses questions such as where to anchor missions in national innovation systems, what kind of incentives could promote such joint endeavours involving STI and sectoral public authorities, and what should be the supporting mechanisms and processes (not least budgetary ones). This question is closely related to the key issue of the mission scope: while it is clear that a broad cross-sectoral collaborative approach is critical to achieve net zero, little is known about what the boundaries of net zero missions should be. The fundamental and somewhat provocative question raised by the STI trap is whether the "I" in MOIPs should, in some cases, be dropped and become "mission-oriented policy for the transition", irrespective of the innovation content. This is, to a large extent, a political question, but more research on mission dynamics and limitations is needed to inform this debate.
- *How to practically integrate various interventions in a mission?* It is essential to provide the pragmatic tools to make different interventions work synergistically while preserving the specificities that make them effective in performing their respective functions. This entails notably improving portfolio management and developing specific tools (including visualisation tools, collective design tools, etc.) and systems (including IT budgetary and reporting systems).
- *How to monitor and evaluate the specific costs and effects of missions?* As revealed by the review of existing mission evaluations, methods and processes for assessing these systemic policies are only emerging and there is still a lot of work ahead to further develop, test and harmonise them.
- *What changes in the public sector governance and capabilities do MOIPs require to be successful and can these changes be promoted?* The MOIP approach challenges public sector structures (e.g. governance, roles and responsibilities of different organisations), processes (e.g. budgetary, human resource management), skills (e.g. for portfolio project management) and mindsets (e.g. system thinking, impact-led, future orientation). Many organisations have engaged in this policy approach without having made any internal reforms, which limits the transformative potential of missions. Besides structure, skills can also be a significant limiting factor. It is currently not clear which skills are needed to operate missions, notably in the dedicated mission support teams/offices (at MOIP initiative and mission levels) and among mission partners. Some bodies of knowledge and practice seem relevant to mission practices, for instance on outcome-based management or system thinking, but there is still no integrated curricula to rely upon. This has yet to be developed and put into action in specific training modules.

What should the linkages be between net zero missions and the broad and high-level national governance and policy framework for net zero? Net zero missions cannot be all-encompassing and in most cases are focused on particular sources of emissions (agriculture, transport, etc.), technological domains (hydrogen; carbon capture, utilisation and storage) or geographical areas (e.g. cities). There is, therefore, a need to co-ordinate these missions among themselves and with all other activities relevant to achieving each country's net zero commitment. Several countries – in particular those which have translated their net zero targets into law – have set up a dedicated governance structure to lead the progress reporting and review processes and co-ordinate and/or advise on actions on a national and holistic level. A better understanding of how these frameworks operate and how they provide and use information from and for the net zero missions (especially the broad systemic ones) would be instrumental to understand the nested structure of systemic approaches contributing in a consistent way to the achievement of net zero objectives.

References

CSIRO (2023), "Mandate for operational group", web page, https://www.forskningsradet.no/forskningspolitikk-strategi/ltp/ungt-utanforskap/mandat-operativ-gruppe. [5]

EuSPRI (2024), *Towards New Types of Linkages Between Science Policy Researchers, Stakeholders and Policymakers*, European Forum for Studies of Policies for Research and Innovation, https://euspri-forum.eu/wp-content/uploads/2024/02/SAB-Note-January-2024.pdf. [4]

Janssen, M. (2020), *Post-commencement Analysis of the Dutch 'Mission-oriented Topsector and Innovation Policy' Strategy*, Utrecht University, Utrecht, Netherlands, https://www.uu.nl/sites/default/files/Post-commencement%20analysis%20of%20the%20Dutch%20Mission-oriented%20Topsector%20and%20Innovation%20Policy.pdf. [3]

Larrue, P. and R. Santos (2022), "Towards a new stage in Norway's science, technology and innovation system: Improving the long-term plan for research and higher education", *OECD Science, Technology and Industry Policy Papers*, No. 133, OECD Publishing, Paris, https://doi.org/10.1787/ce07b7c3-en. [2]

Roth, F. et al. (2022), "Putting mission-oriented innovation policies to work: A case study of the German High-Tech Strategy 2025", *Fraunhofer ISI Discussion Papers Innovation Systems and Policy Analysis*, No. 75, https://www.isi.fraunhofer.de/content/dam/isi/dokumente/cci/innovation-systems-policy-analysis/2022/discussionpaper_75_2022.pdf. [1]

Endnotes

[1] The argument of the missions' "policy trap" was first proposed by Matthias Weber (Head of Center for Innovation Systems & Policy at the Austrian Institute of Technology) at the first meeting of the European Mission Forum (EMIN) on 25 January 2023. EMIN was created as part of the EU-funded TRAnsnational cooperation on the MIssions approach project (see: https://www.trami5missions.eu).

[2] The Convenant 2023-2023 is available at: www.health-holland.com/sites/default/files/downloads/kennis-en-innovatieconvenant-2020-2023-gezondheid-en-zorg.pdf.

[3] The Aerospace Sector Deal is available at: https://assets.publishing.service.gov.uk/media/5c10e9a040f0b60c8d6019b0/aerospace-sector-deal-web.pdf.

[4] This is already happening in several mission initiatives. Vinnova is working with the University College London's Institute for Innovation and Public Purpose, the Transformative Innovation Policy Consortium, and the OECD Mission Action Lab. The Austrian EU missions have developed a mission monitoring demonstrator with the OECD Mission Action Lab; the German High-Tech Strategy 2025 with the Fraunhofer Institute for Systems and Innovation; and the Mission-Driven and Top Sectors Policy with Utrecht University's Copernicus Institute of Sustainable Development.

Annex A. Definitions of mission design principles and corresponding questions

Table A.1. Definitions of mission design principles and their corresponding questions

Design principles	Corresponding questions
Strategic orientation	
Legitimacy A large group of stakeholders (including citizens) is engaged in building consensus on the societal challenge(s) to be prioritised.	• What stakeholders have been involved in the initial consultations and how? • What roles have they played in the initial decisions regarding the orientations and design of the initiative? • What diagnosis and/or foresight studies or other sources of information on needs, trends and opportunities have been used to feed into debates and decisions? • What actions have been taken to achieve consensus and increase buy-in/ownership of the initiative? • What has been the political process in initiating and providing the orientations? • Is the initiative supported by high-level political or administrative officials? • Is the initiative embedded in government authoritative strategic documents and processes?
Directionality Clear orientation and strategic guidance for developing appropriate policy intervention are informed and selected.	• What challenges does the initiative address? • How are the orientations formalised? • What debates have surrounded the choices of the orientation of the initiative? • Have the orientations been contested?
Intentionality Specific and well-articulated goals, with a clear timeline and milestones, are derived from the broad objectives.	• Have the broad challenges and orientations been translated into clear and measurable objectives/targets? • How precise/granular are these targets? • Are the objectives set against a clear timeline? • How distant are the targets from the current performance? How ambitious/transformative are they?
Flexibility The targets and means of intervention to meet them can be revised at different stages of the process (predetermined milestones) based on feedback from monitoring and evaluation.	• What processes and information channels have been established for monitoring progress toward the goals? • What are the established process and rules for revising/updating goals? • What arrangements are in place to revise the objectives if needed?

Strategic co-ordination	
Horizontality Several policy bodies covering different policy fields (e.g. ministries, agencies) are involved in the governance of the initiative.	• What policy fields (sectors/thematic areas, stages of the innovation chain, represented by different bodies) are covered in the governance and decision making? • What governance structure supports horizontal co-ordination? • What are the main co-ordination bodies (with their functions)? • To what extent does the co-ordination process involve actors besides the policy arena? • What degree and form of co-ordination are there between the different policy actors (e.g. strong or weak co-ordination, binding or non-binding decisions, centralised or decentralised decision making, etc.)? • To what degree are the budgets integrated (e.g. common pot/integrated budget, earmarked decentralised budget, decentralised budget, etc.)?
Verticality Several policy bodies covering different levels of government are involved in the governance of the initiative.	• What is the governance structure to support vertical co-ordination? • What levels of government (national, regional, local) are involved in the governance and decision making, and how are they represented?
Exploratory/novelty Policy bodies and stakeholders co-ordinate their plans (e.g. via a portfolio approach) to cover a broader spectrum of alternative options/development paths, share associated risks, and learn from successes and failures.	• What is the range of (technological and non-technological) alternative options supported to achieve the initiative's objectives? • What arrangements are in place to scan/test different (technological or non-technological) options? • Is the initiative connected with relevant fundamental/breakthrough research and how? • Are there mechanisms or 'spaces' for experimentation within the initiative?
Demand-articulation Potential users (or related representatives of the demand side) and relevant regulatory authorities are involved in the initiatives from the beginning and participate in the decisions.	• Are potential users and/or relevant policy/regulatory authorities involved in the governance of the initiative and what role do they play? • Are there any formal plans for regulatory reforms and support to market deployment (e.g. public procurement)? • How are the demand and need dimensions embedded in the initiative?

Policy implementation	
Policy mix diversity A package of policy instruments supports a diverse set of activities mixing different disciplines, sectors and areas, across the whole space of the innovation spectrum from (oriented) basic research to demonstration and early market creation, as needed to meet the objectives.	• What modes of intervention/policy measures are mobilised to achieve the objectives? • What arrangements are in place to ensure operational consistency (i.e. reduce overlaps, enhance complementarities) of the different policy instruments/measures?
Leverage Public and private stakeholders involved in the different phases of the innovation process are mobilised to contribute to decision making and funding of the initiative.	• How are partners and beneficiaries (including the private sector, other public bodies and stakeholders) engaged in the initiative? • What incentives are in place to raise funds and ensure other types of contributions from partners and beneficiaries? • What factors are fostering or hindering the level of engagement of (potential or actual) partners?
Evaluability and reflexivity The policy is endowed with monitoring and evaluation methods and processes adapted to its systemic nature to assess its results and learn from its implementation in view of continuous improvement.	• What methods and processes measure the progress, outcomes and impact of the initiatives? • To what extent are these methods and processes adequate to capture the specific added value ("systemic effects") of the missions (relative to other traditional policies)? • What arrangements are in place to support learning and improvement of the initiative? • Do the policy bodies have the sufficient absorptive capacity to analyse the information stemming from monitoring and evaluation and translate this into action?

Annex B. List of MOIP initiatives and net zero missions

Table B.1. List of MOIP initiatives and net zero missions

Australia
CSIRO's missions https://stip.oecd.org/moip/case-studies/44
Drought Resilience mission
Ending Plastic Waste mission
Hydrogen Industry mission
Towards Net Zero
Austria
Austrian transition missions https://stip.oecd.org/moip/case-studies/34
Climate Neutral City mission
Mobility Transition mission
Circular Economy mission
Energy Transition mission
Austrian EU missions https://stip.oecd.org/moip/case-studies/33
Adaptation to Climate Change including Societal Transformation (ACC)
Climate-neutral and Smart Cities
Healthy Oceans, Seas, Coastal and Inland Waters
Soil Health and Food
Belgium
Smart Specialisation Strategy of Wallonia https://stip.oecd.org/moip/case-studies/35
Agri-food Chains of the Future and Innovative Environmental Management
Circular Materials
Energy Systems and Sustainable Housing
Circular Flanders https://stip.oecd.org/moip/case-studies/36
Circular economy
Brazil
FNDCT Structuring and Mobilizing Programs https://stip.oecd.org/moip/case-studies/12
Innovation Program for Sustainable-Based Industrialization – More Innovation Brazil
Integrated Sustainable Development Program for the Amazon Region – Pró-Amazônia
Nova Indústria Brasil
Sustainable and digital agro-industrial chains for food, nutrition and energy security
Sustainable infrastructure, sanitation, housing and mobility for productive integration and well-being in cities
Bioeconomy, decarbonization and energy transition and security to secure resources for future generations
Canada
National Research Council Challenge programme https://stip.oecd.org/moip/case-studies/26
Materials for Clean Fuels Challenge
Low Carbon Built Environment Challenge
Impact Canada https://stip.oecd.org/moip/case-studies/37
Crush-It! Challenge (challenge prize) - how energy is used for crushing and grinding rocks in the mining industry
Charging the Future Challenge (challenge prize) - unlock the potential in battery technologies to optimize

energy density, weight, range, life and costs
Indigenous Off-diesel Initiative (indigenous initiative) - support remote Indigenous communities in developing and implementing ambitious plans to reduce diesel use for heat and power
Power Forward Initiative (challenge prize) - challenging Canadian and U.K. companies to design better power grids, connecting our nations to clean, user-friendly grids and helping to prevent power outages
The Sky's the Limit Challenge (challenge prize) - Develop new ways to produce biojet fuels
Novel Technologies (challenge prize) Technologies that Extend the Life of Food
Novel Technologies (challenge prize) Technologies that Transform Food Waste
Business Models (challenge prize) Business models that prevent food waste
Business Models (challenge prize) Business models that divert food waste, food by-products and/or surplus food
Agricultural Methane Reduction Challenge (challenge prize) - Accelerating innovative solutions to reduce methane emissions from the cattle sector
Hull Design Efficiency Challenge (challenge prize) - challenging boat builders to develop an innovative hull that maximizes energy efficiency, lowers operational costs and reduces greenhouse gas emissions

Chile

Green Hydrogen

Green H2

Colombia

Bioeconomy mission

Bioeconomy mission

Czech Republic

RIS3 Smart Specialisation Strategy https://stip.oecd.org/moip/case-studies/38

Improving the material, energy and emissions efficiency of the economy

Denmark

Green missions/Innomissions https://stip.oecd.org/moip/case-studies/27

Carbon Capture and Storage or Utilisation

Climate and Environment-friendly Agriculture and Food Production

Green Fuels for Transportation and Industry (Power-to-X, etc.)

Recycling and Reduction of Plastic Waste

European Union

Horizon Europe's missions https://stip.oecd.org/moip/case-studies/13

Adaptation to Climate Change including Societal Transformation (ACC)

Climate-neutral and Smart Cities

Healthy Oceans, Seas, Coastal and Inland Waters

Soil Health and Food

Finland

Business Finland Missions https://stip.oecd.org/moip/case-studies/39

Zero Carbon Future
Circular transition for Zero Waste

Flagship programmes

Atmosphere and Climate Competence Center Flagship Programme

FinnCERES Flagship Programme for the Materials Bioeconomy

Growth engines

Accelerating the Growth of the Carbon Capture Market Growth Engine (Compensate platform company)

From a Socio-sized Demo of Renewable Energy Production to an International Total Solution Provider Growth Engine (Flexens platform company)

Green Electrification (GreenE2)

GreenE2 Growth Engine (CLIC Innovation orchestrator)

Team Renewable Arctic Finland (Gaia consulting orchestrator)

France

France 2030 - Stratégies nationales d'accélération https://stip.oecd.org/moip/case-studies/40

Bio-based Products and Sustainable Fuels

Carbon-neutral Hydrogen
Digitising and Decarbonising Mobility
Industry Decarbonisation
Solutions for Sustainable Cities and Innovative Buildings
Sustainable and Healthy Food
Sustainable Farming Systems and Farm Equipment contributing to the Ecological Transition
Germany
Hightech Strategy 2025 https://stip.oecd.org/moip/case-studies/1
Achieve Substantial Greenhouse Gas Neutrality in Industry
Build Up a Battery Cell Production in Germany
Create sustainable Circular Economies
Develop Safe, Networked and Clean Mobility
Future Strategy https://stip.oecd.org/moip/case-studies/28
Industry/Mobility Climate/Biodiversity/Nutrition Space/Oceans
Ireland
Research Ireland's Challenge Programmes https://stip.oecd.org/moip/case-studies/29
National Challenge Fund, 2050 Challenge
AI for Societal Good Challenge (Former SFI Future Innovator Prize)
National Challenge Fund, Future Food System Challenge
Food Challenge (Former SFI Future Innovator Prize) Plastics Challenge (Former SFI Future Innovator Prize)
Zero Emissions Challenge (Former SFI Future Innovator Prize) National Challenge Fund, Healthy Environment for All Challenge National Challenge Fund, Energy Innovation Challenge National Challenge Fund, Sustainable Communities Challenge Research Ireland-Irish Aid Sustainable Development Goals Challenge
Japan
Cross-ministerial Strategic Innovation Promotion Program – Phase 3 (SIP3) https://stip.oecd.org/moip/case-studies/15
Building a Resilient and Nourishing Food Supply Chain Management for a Sustainable Future Creating a National Platform for Innovative Ocean development Creating a Smart Energy Management Systems Development of Circular Economy System Creating a Materials Innovation Ecosystem for Industrialization
Moonshot Research and Development Program https://stip.oecd.org/moip/case-studies/16
Moonshot Goal 4: Realization of sustainable resource circulation to recover the global environment by 2050
Moonshot Goal 5: Creation of the industry that enables sustainable global food supply by exploiting unused biological resources by 2050
Korea
Korean Advanced Research Programme Accelerator (KARPA)
Plasma-based CO_2 Free Waste Organic Material as a Basic Raw Material
The Alchemist https://stip.oecd.org/moip/case-studies/30
Artificial Eco-food
Low-cost CO_2-free Hydrogen Production Facilities (former mission) Sustainable Beyond Plastics Urban Carbon Dioxide Capture and Utilization Technology Biomimetic carbon resource recycling
Comprehensive Plan to Solve Social Problems Based on Science and Technology 2023-27 https://stip.oecd.org/moip/case-studies/45
Reducing household waste
National strategic technology policyhttps://stip.oecd.org/moip/case-studies/46

Next-generation batteries Advanced mobility Next-generation nuclear energy Hydrogen
Lithuania
Mission-oriented science and innovation programmes https://stip.oecd.org/moip/case-studies/49
Smart and Climate-neutral Lithuania
Netherlands
Mission-driven Top Sectors and Innovation Policy https://stip.oecd.org/moip/case-studies/3
A Carbon-free Built Environment by 2050
A Net Climate-neutral Agriculture and Nature System in 2050
A Sustainable and Completely Circular Economy by 2050, with Resource Use Halved by 2030
An Entirely Carbon-free Electricity System by 2050
Carbon-neutral Industry with Reuse of Raw Materials and Products by 2050
Zero-emission Mobility of People and Goods by 2050
Norway
CLIMIT https://stip.oecd.org/moip/case-studies/4
CLIMIT
Green Platform Initiative
Green Platform Initiative
Norwegian national missions https://stip.oecd.org/moip/case-studies/31
Sustainable Feed
Pilot E https://stip.oecd.org/moip/case-studies/2
Pilot E
Pilot-T
New Solutions in the Interface between Transport and ICT
Spain
Catalonia - RISCAT3 https://stip.oecd.org/moip/case-studies/41 Shared Agenda of Terres de Lleida Pirineu i Aran Shared Agenda of Bages-Manresa **Science and innovation missions**
Promote a Large, Sustainable and Healthy Agri-Food Sector
Promote Sustainable and Intelligent Intermodal Transport
Promote the Substitution, Recovery and Valuation of Mineral Resources and Strategic Materials for the Ecological Transition
Promote a More Sustainable Agri-Food Sector Adapted to the New Conditions Associated with Climate Change Through the Relevant Use of Advanced Biotechnological Tools
Promote Safe, Efficient and Clean Energy for the 21st Century
Promote the Circular Economy Through New Technologies for Recycling and Recovery of Polymeric Compound Waste in Spain
Strengthen Technological Capabilities for Secure and Sustainable Energy Autonomy (Fusion, Hydrogen and Renewables)
Strengthen Technological Capacities for Safe and Sustainable Energy Autonomy (Fusion, Hydrogen and Renewables)
Sustainable and Intelligent Mobility
Promote Spanish Agriculture in the 21st Century: Sustainable, Intelligent, Efficient in the Consumption of Water Resources and Agricultural Inputs, and Adapted to Climate Change
Sweden
Challenge Driven Innovation Initiative https://stip.oecd.org/moip/case-studies/10
Business model innovation for closed-loop furniture flows (reuse of furniture to reduce climate impact)
New technology for carbon dioxide-free asphalt (Swedish Magnetite Microwave Asphalt Road Technology)
Swedish Innovation Platform for Textile Sorting

Innovation partnership programmes
Climate-neutral Industry Innovation Partnership Programme
Skills Supply and Lifelong Learning Innovation Partnership Programme
Strategic innovation programmes https://stip.oecd.org/moip/case-studies/11
Viable Cities
Vinnova's pilot missions https://stip.oecd.org/moip/case-studies/43
Healthy Sustainable Food: A New Recipe for School Meals
Healthy Sustainable Mobility
Impact Innovation https://stip.oecd.org/moip/case-studies/42 Metals&Minerals – sustainable and resilient metal and mineral supply Water Wise Societies – sustainable water for all by 2050 SustainGov – reform the public sector to ensure society's sustainability transition ShiftSweden – transform Sweden into attractive and accessible living environments for everyone
United Kingdom
Industrial Strategy Challenge Fund https://stip.oecd.org/moip/case-studies/12
Driving the Electric Revolution challenge
Faraday Battery challenge
Future Flight challenge
Industrial Decarbonisation
Prospering from the Energy Revolution challenge
Smart Sustainable Plastic Packaging challenge
Transforming Construction challenge
Transforming Food Production challenge
Transforming Foundation Industries challenge
UKRI Technology Missions Fund Engineering biology (inc. environmental solutions)
United-States
Department of Energy Grand Challenge
Energy Storage Grand Challenge
Sustainable Aviation Fuel Grand Challenge
Energy Earthshots™ https://stip.oecd.org/moip/case-studies/32
Clean Fuels & Products Shot
Carbon Negative Shot
Enhanced Geothermal Shot
Floating Offshore Wind Shot
Hydrogen Shot
Industrial Heat Shot
Long Duration Storage Shot Affordable Home Energy Shot

Annex C. Examples of net zero mission targets

Table C.1. Examples of net zero mission targets related to greenhouse gas emissions reductions

Net zero mission targets related to greenhouse gas emissions reductions
Austrian Transition missions (Austria)
Mission Climate Neutral City
Cities as pioneers of climate neutrality – 10 large cities and 50-70 smaller cities by 2030
Mission Energy Transition
Sustainable reduction of energy and resource consumption and comprehensive use of renewable energy sources by 2030
Mission Mobility Transition
Sustainable, climate-neutral and inclusive mobility and transport system by 2040
Mission Circular Economy
Resource efficiency and transformation to a sustainable and circular society by 2030
Austrian "EU" missions
Austrian EU Waters Mission (see Austrian transition missions) Climate-neutral City Mission (see Horizon Europe missions)
CSIRO's missions (Australia)
Hydrogen Industry Mission
To avoid greenhouse gas emissions equivalent to a third of Australia's current fossil fuel emissions by 2050
Towards Net Zero
Help Australia's hardest to abate sectors – including steel, sustainable aviation fuel and agriculture – halve their emissions by 2035
Energy Earthshots™ (United States)
Clean Fuels & Products Shot™
Decarbonise the fuel and chemical industry through alternative sources of carbon to advance cost-effective technologies with a minimum of 85% lower greenhouse gas emissions by 2035
Carbon Negative Shot™
Remove CO_2 from the atmosphere and durably store it at meaningful scales for less than USD 100/net metric tonne carbon dioxide equivalent (CO_2-eq) within a decade
Industrial Heat Shot™
Develop cost-competitive industrial heat decarbonisation technologies with at least 85% lower greenhouse gas emissions by 2035
Hydrogen Shot™
Accelerate innovations and spur demand of clean hydrogen by reducing the cost by 80%, to USD 1 per kilogramme of clean hydrogen within one decade
Long Duration Storage Shot™
Achieve affordable grid storage for clean power – anytime, anywhere – by reducing the cost of grid-scale energy storage by 90% for systems that deliver 10+ hours of duration within a decade
Enhanced Geothermal Shot™
Dramatically reduce the cost of enhanced geothermal systems by 90%, to USD 45 per megawatt hour by 2035
Floating Offshore Wind Shot™
Driving down costs to USD 45 per megawatt hour by 2035 to spur US leadership in floating offshore wind technology, accelerate decarbonisation and deliver benefits for coastal communities
Affordable Home Energy Shot™
Reduce the upfront cost of upgrading a home by at least 50% while reducing energy bills by 20% within a decade

Green missions/Innomissions (Denmark)
Carbon capture and storage or utilisation
To (potentially) capture, store or use in the order of 4-9 million tons., from Danish CO2 emissions (which overlap with the potential of power-to-X, as carbon can be both stored and used for example two-X products) between 2030 and 2040
Climate and environment-friendly agriculture and food production
To make the agricultural and food sectors climate-neutral by 2050
Green fuels for transportation and industry (power-to-X, etc.)
To contribute to the target of a 70% reduction of greenhouse gas emissions in Denmark by 2030 and net zero emissions by 2050
Recycling and reduction of plastic waste
To remove 80% of plastic waste from incineration in 2030, which will lead to a reduction of CO2-eq from waste incineration of approximately 0.15 million tons (Mt) CO2-eq in 2030
Hightech Strategy 2025 (Germany)
Achieve Substantial Greenhouse Gas Neutrality in Industry
To achieve net greenhouse gas neutrality by 2045, which entails the achievement of sectoral targets for industry by 2030 to reduce CO_2 emissions by 49-51% compared with 1990 emissions
Horizon Europe's missions (European Union)
Climate-neutral and Smart Cities
100 climate-neutral cities by 2030
Healthy Oceans, Seas, Coastal and Inland Waters
To reduce CO_2 emissions from the shipping sector operating in the European Union by 45% by 2030
Industrial Strategy Challenge Fund (United Kingdom)
Industrial Decarbonisation
Develop at least one low-carbon industrial cluster by 2030, and the world's first net zero carbon industrial cluster by 2040
Transforming Construction Challenge
Lifetime emissions slashed by half
Transforming Food Production Challenge
Help businesses, researchers and industry to transform food production, meet the growing demand and move towards net zero emissions by 2040
Mission Driven Top-Sector Policy (Netherlands)
A Carbon-free Built Environment by 2050
Achieve a CO_2-free built environment in 2050, requiring a 3.4 Mt CO_2 reduction in 2030
A Net Climate-neutral Agriculture and Nature System in 2050
"By 2030, an additional reduction of at least 1 Mt CO_2-eq for methane, 1 Mt CO_2-eq for energy consumption in glasshouse horticulture and 1.5 Mt CO_2-eq through smarter land use will have been achieved"
An Entirely Carbon-free Electricity System by 2050
To achieve a completely CO_2-free electricity system in 2050, reducing CO_2 emissions by at least 20.2 Mt by 2030
Carbon-neutral Industry With Reuse of Raw Materials and Products by 2050
To achieve a climate-neutral industry with reuse of raw materials and products in 2050, with an (interim) objective of a 50% reduction in the use of primary raw materials (minerals, fossil and metals) by 2030 amounting to an intermediate station with an indicative CO_2 reduction target of 14.3 Mt
Zero-emission Mobility of People and Goods by 2050
To achieve zero-emission mobility for people and goods in 2050. By 2030, a maximum CO_2 emission from mobility of 25 Mt, corresponding to a reduction of approximately 7 Mt extra compared to current emissions.
National Research Council Challenge programme (Canada)
Materials for Clean Fuels Challenge
Reduce 716 Mt of carbon dioxide emissions per year to reach the goal of net zero emissions by 2050
France 2030 Stratégies nationales d'accélération (France)
Carbon-neutral Hydrogen
Develop clean mobility solutions, particularly for heavy vehicles, which will enable saving more than 6 Mt CO_2 by 2030 (equivalent to the annual CO_2 emissions of the city of Paris)

Annex D. Results of five mission-oriented innovation policy evaluations against three types of expected systemic effects

Table D.1. Mission-driven Top Sectors and Innovation Policy

Focusing	Alignment	Integration
• The missions themselves are relatively uncontested societal goals and serve as a reference point for all mission actors. • Confusion due to the high number of missions sometimes being interrelated. • The strategic agendas (MMIPs) are structured according to coherent solution paths also addressing commercialisation and societal acceptance but are criticised for lacking selectivity. The influence of the MMIPs on the activities remain difficult to assess. The sectoral (technology/supply-push) directions still appear to be very strong.	• The mission teams are not always operational and some of them can struggle to assert their mandate relative to sectoral bodies. • The sectoral ministries are increasingly committed to incorporate innovation into their interventions and co-ordinate them with other policies. There is still significant variation in the level of commitment and in general these ministries are primarily partners and facilitators in the mission, without exerting leadership. The missions remain more technology-push than demand-pull. • The governance structure is too complex, with too many advising and guiding bodies, and overlaps between the mission- and sector-specific teams.	• The missions mainly co-ordinate existing instruments, but the mission approach led the leading ministry to implement many additional policy initiatives for ensuring the actual uptake of promising innovations. • One (unique) new integrated instrument in the Carbon-free Built Environment Mission stretched across the whole innovation chain (including high TRLs). It was assessed positively for avoiding discrepancies between instruments within the mission portfolio. • Financial commitments announced by public and private actors in missions are higher than in previous periods. However, it is unclear how much of these will materialise and the extent to which they are "new money".

Source: Adapted from Janssen (2020[1]).

Table D.2. Pilot-E

Focusing	Alignment	Integration
• The mission orientation is ensured by the emphasis put during project selection on the relationship between the suppliers and the potential (pilot) buyers and users.	• There is strong alignment in the MOIP since the three agencies jointly select the annual themes and assess the project applications. • The joined-up approach of the three agencies resulted in	• The MOIP offers a relevant solution to better integrate the different support measures along the innovation chain, which increase the likelihood that new solutions reach the market faster,

• However, in most cases the users are not sufficiently involved and several projects stopped before the deployment stage due to the lack of a user.	more ambitious and larger consortia being funded and more predictable funding for the projects at different stages of development. • The additional co-ordination costs of Pilot-E is estimated at 15%.	• The collaboration between the three agencies is effective and results in synergies between their respective interventions. • However, the monitoring of projects still relies on each agency's system (e.g. several reporting channels), which creates complexity and transaction costs for beneficiaries.

Source: Adapted from Menon Economics (2020[2]).

Table D.3. UKRI Challenge Funds

Focusing	Alignment	Integration
• The 24 challenges (missions) are clearly linked to the 4 grand challenges set out in the national Industrial Strategy. • The multi-stage process for selecting the challenges has been too long (72 weeks from ideas Challenges) and resulted in delays that had detrimental effects on partners motivations. • The increasing number of challenges supported by the fund, each with its own objectives, and range of different objectives at fund level risk diluting priorities. • Each challenge has developed benefit maps that include what is intended to be delivered as well as how the different projects supported by the challenge will contribute to these challenge objectives.	• No specific attention to the co-ordination aspects in the audit (focused on management issues). • The fund objectives focus on who receives support from the fund, such as business and academic bodies, rather than on the impacts that projects may deliver (set at a challenge level).	• UKRI has faced difficulty recruiting staff to help manage the MOIP (up to 60% under capacity in the most recent years). • It proved particularly difficult to hire the challenge directors who co-ordinate the whole portfolio of activities, a key position that demands a rare mix of science and industry experience.

Source: Adapted from National Audit Office, United Kingdom (2021[3]).

Table D.4. Strategic Innovation Programmes

Focusing	Alignment	Integration
• Strategic innovation programmes (SIPs) are required to document their theory of change in the form of a logic diagram and to keep this up to date. This has been unevenly used and useful among the different SIPs. • The agendas of the SIPs were informed by significant strategic intelligence through market	• The SIPs have had a broader scope composed of diverse groups of actors, value chains and branches of industry. • The SIPs provided a platform for strategic dialogue among system actors.	• The innovations produced have been limited and incremental rather than radical or system-changing in nature. • Most of the effects of the SIPs have been at the level of individual projects rather than at the mission level. • Increased integration of research, innovation and higher education.

studies and state-of-the-art reviews. This foundational and wide-scoping work provided the opportunity to take a more systemic perspective. • The initiative has led to a stronger integration of sustainability goals in the SIPs' agendas (although it is less clear what effects it had in activities). • The initiative allowed SIPs to have a longer term horizon (12-year funding horizon).		• The fragmented nature of the SIP project portfolios and the often-short-term character of the project ambitions limit the SIPs' ability to effect systemic change.

Source: Adapted from Technopolis (2023[4]).

Table D.5. Horizon Europe missions

Focusing	Alignment	Integration
• Missions are timely and inspirational initiatives that provide new impetus to important European Union (EU) policy priorities and help direct EU, national, regional and local policy efforts towards shared goals. • The mission development process enabled the co-creation of missions by leading experts and a wide range of stakeholders • EU missions have managed to gather large stakeholder communities, including by building and engaging communities at the regional and local levels. • Lack of high-level political discussions on progress and for re-orientation where needed.	• The mission governance is breaking organisational silos and bringing different organisations closer together in pursuit of the shared, timebound goals. • Dedicated cross-sectoral steering and co-ordination bodies enabled new forms of collaboration across European Commission services and levels of government. • Several member states such as Austria established interministerial taskforces and national mirror groups to better liaise with the European Commission on national implementation. • Many stakeholders perceive the governance system as being cumbersome, complex and lacking transparency. • No coherent, consistent monitoring system at initiative and individual mission levels.	• All missions have managed to gain some level of interest and commitments from sources of funding beyond Horizon Europe, including the private sector. • However, missions benefit from rather limited leverage so far of funding beyond Horizon Europe, and synergies with other EU instruments are too modest. • The portfolio of instruments mobilised is too narrow. • The involvement of the private sector is low.

Source: Adapted from Angelis et al. (2023[5]).

References

Janssen, M. (2020), *Post-commencement Analysis of the Dutch 'Mission-oriented Topsector and Innovation Policy' Strategy*, Utrecht University, Utrecht, Netherlands, https://www.uu.nl/sites/default/files/Post-commencement%20analysis%20of%20the%20Dutch%20Mission-oriented%20Topsector%20and%20Innovation%20Policy.pdf. [1]

Menon Economics (2020), *Evaluation of Pilot-E*, Menon Publication 147 [in Norwegian], Menon Economics, https://www.menon.no/wp-content/uploads/2020-147-Evaluering-av-PILOT-E.pdf. [2]

National Audit Office, United Kingdom (2021), *UK Research and Innovation's Management of the Industrial Strategy Challenge Fund*, National Audit Office, London, https://www.nao.org.uk/wp-content/uploads/2021/02/UK-Research-and-Innovations-management-of-the-Industrial-Strategy-Challenge-Fund.pdf. [3]

Reid, A. (ed.) (2023), *Study Supporting the Assessment of EU Missions and the Review of Mission Areas: Mission Areas Review Report*, Publications Office of the European Union, https://data.europa.eu/doi/10.2777/61143. [5]

Technopolis (2023), *Meta-evaluation of the Swedish Strategic Innovation Programmes*, Technopolis, https://www.vinnova.se/globalassets/publikationer/2024/meta-evaluation-of-sip---long-summary.pdf. [4]

Annex E. List of interviewees

This tables presents the list of persons interviewed in the context of the 17 net zero case studies performed in this study. Forty interviews were performed, representing a total pool of 63 interviewees across 14 countries and the European Commission.

Table E.1. List of interviewees

#	Interviewee(s)	Country	Name of the mission MOIP initiative
1	Patrick Hartley Leader CSIRO Hydrogen Industry Mission at CSIRO	Australia	Hydrogen Industry mission CSIRO's missions
2	Michael Battaglia Mission Lead, Towards Net Zero Mission CSIRO Alex Cooke Director Strategic Delivery CSIRO		Towards Net Zero Mission CSIRO's missions
3	Alex Cooke General Manager, Missions CSIRO Amelia Olsen-Boyd Executive Manager, Mission Innovation and Strategy CSIRO		CSIRO's missions
4	Hans-Günther Schwarz Strategic Programme Coordinator Federal Ministry for Climate Action, Environment, Energy, Mobility, Innovation and Technology DG III – Innovation, Unit III/3 – Energy and Environmental Technologies Anna Wang Federal Ministry for Climate Action, Environment, Energy, Mobility, Innovation and Technology DG III – Innovation, Unit III/3 – Energy and Environmental Technologies	Austria	Climate-neutral City Mission Austrian Transition Missions Austrian EU missions
5	Walter Wasner Federal Ministry for Climate Action, Environment, Energy, Mobility, Innovation and Technology DG III – Innovation and Technology, Unit III/4 – Mobility Technologies Gudrun Haindlmaier Scientist, Innovation Systems and Policy Unit Austrian Institute of Technology Gasser Maximilian Innovation Systems and Policy Unit Austrian Institute of Technology		
6	Susanne Meyer Federal Ministry for Climate Action, Environment, Energy, Mobility, Innovation and Technology		Austrian Circular Economy Mission Austrian Transition Missions

	DG III – Innovation and Technology Rene Albert Mission Coordinator Circular Economy Federal Ministry for Climate Action, Environment, Energy, Mobility, Innovation and Technology DG III – Innovation and Technology, Unit III/4 – Mobility Technologies		
7	James McKinnell Strategic Advisor National Research Council Canada	Canada	Materials for Clean Fuels challenge National Research Council Challenge programme
8	Phil De Luna Expert, Sustainability McKinsey & Company and former Program Director for Materials for Clean Fuels National Research Council Canada		
9	Jakob Dahl Wedel Program Officer Innovationsfonden Karina Marie Søgaard Senior Executive Officer Department of Chemistry, Technical University of Denmark Bo Frølund Scientific Officer Innovationsfonden	Denmark	Carbon Capture and Storage or Utilisation INNOmission
10	Karina Marie Søgaard Senior Executive Officer Department of Chemistry, Technical University of Denmark		
11	Paul Tuinder Legal and Policy Advisor Cities Mission Secretariat DG RTD European Commission	European Union	Climate-neutral and Smart Cities Horizon Europe's missions
12	Leo Huberts Policy Officer DG MOVE European Commission		
13	Thomas Osdoba Programme Director NetZeroCities		
14	Rosenow Head of Unit Research and Innovation DG Agriculture and Rural Development European Commission		
15	Julien Guerrier Formely Director, Common Policy Center DG RTD European Commission		Horizon Europe Missions
16	Markku Kulmala Head of ACCC Flagship and Director for Institute for Atmosphere and Earth System Research University of Helsinki) Anneli Pauli Professor of Practice (Global Grand Challenges) University of Helsinki Ari Laaksonen Professor Finnish Meteorological Institute Miikka Dal Maso Professor	Finland	Atmosphere and Climate Competence Center Flagship Programme Flagship Programs

	Faculty of Engineering and Natural Sciences Tampere University Petteri Kauppinen Senior Ministerial Adviser Ministry of Education, Science and Culture Sami Paatero Policy Advisor to ACCC & CEO, Climate Analytics Finland Ltd.		
17	Sami Paatero Policy Advisor to ACCC & CEO, Climate Analytics Finland Ltd		
18	Annu Kotiranta Senior Advisor Business Finland		Green E2 – CLIC Innovation Growth Engines
19	Tero Ijäs Ecosystem Lead Business Finland		
20	Pia Salokoski Head of Co-Innovation CLIC Innovation Oy		
21	Christopher Palmberg Senior Director Strategic Insight Business Finland		Growth Engines
22	Hoang Bui Secrétaire du CNH, Coordinator of the Stratégie Nationale d'Accélération Hydrogène décarboné et Stratégie Nationale d'Accélération Décarbonation de l'Industrie Secrétariat général pour l'investissement	France	Stratégie Nationale d'Accélération Hydrogène décarboné Stratégies Nationales d'Accélération
23	Lionel Prevors Chef de projet H2 DG, Energy and Climate General Directorate Ministry of Ecology, Sustainable Development, Transport and Building		
24	Fabien Delafalize Project Manager R&D Steering & Coordinator of the Strategy for Advanced Energy System Technologies Energy and Climate General Directorate Ministry of Ecology, Sustainable Development, Transport and Building Marine Plassier Chargée de mission Energy and Climate General Directorate		Stratégie Nationale d'Accélération Décarbonation de l'Industrie Stratégies Nationales d'Accélération
25	Géraldine Leveau Secrétaire Générale Adjointe Secrétariat général pour l'investissement William Vickery Conseiller au Cabinet Secrétariat général pour l'investissement Marc-Antoine Lacroix Directeur de l'Évaluation, Chef Économiste Secrétariat général pour l'investissement		Stratégies Nationales d'Accélération
26	Frédéric Ravel Directeur Scientifique, secteur énergie, développement durable, chimie et procédés Direction générale de la recherche et de l'innovation Ministère de l'Enseignement supérieur, de la Recherche et de l'Innovation		Stratégies Nationales d'Accélération
27	Darragh O'Neill Scientific Programme Manager Research Ireland	Ireland	Zero Emissions Challenge Science Foundation Ireland's Innovative Prizes

28	Maria Pilar Gonzalez Head of Department Centre for the Development of Industrial Technology Carlos Joaquín Durán Guinot CDTI	Spain	Centre for the Development of Industrial Technology missions
29	Kenji Yamaji President, Research Institute of Innovative Technology for the Earth Joe Yuzuru Masuda Technical Researcher Frontier and Moonshot Technology Department Moonshot Research and Development Program Office New Energy and Industrial Technology Development Organization Yoshida Tomonao Director Frontier and Moonshot Technology Department Murata Jo Chief Officer Frontier and Moonshot Technology Department	Japan	Moonshot Goal 4: Realization of sustainable resource circulation to recover the global environment by 2050 Moonshot Research and Development Program
30	Mark de Bode Ministry of Economic Affairs and Climate Policy	The Netherlands	
31	Guus Mulder Program Manager Top Consortium for Knowledge and Innovation Urban Energy		A Net Climate-neutral Agriculture and Nature System in 2050 Mission-driven Top Sectors and Innovation Policy A Carbon-free Built Environment by 2050 Mission-driven Top Sectors and Innovation Policy
32	Joram Snijders Senior policy officer, Ministry of the Interior and Kingdom Relations		
33	Trond Moengen Head of Energy and Society DigitalNorway	Norway	Green Shipping Pilot E
34	Maja Nellström Project Manager Swedish Environmental Research Institute Sophie Grahn Lydig Project Manager Swedish Environmental Research Institute	Sweden	Swedish Innovation Platform for Textile Sorting (SIPTex) Challenge Driven Innovation Initiative
35	Jens Von Axelson Programme Manager Vinnova Anna Ottenhall Programme Manager Vinnova		
36	Prof. Olga Kordas Director Viable Cities		Viable Cities Strategic Innovation Programmes
37	Alexander Alvsilver Senior Programme Manager Vinnova Lennart Stenberg Senior Advisor Vinnova Joanna Franzén Area Manager Sustainable Food Systems Vinnova		Healthy sustainable food: Ensuring that every student in Sweden eats healthy, sustainable, and tasty school food Vinnova's pilot missions
38	Viveca Bergstrand Ministry for Enterprise, Energy and Communications Marcus Hellqvist Deputy Director, Enterprise and Innovation Division Ministry for Enterprise, Energy and Communications		Climate-neutral Industry Innovation Partnership
39	Bryony Livesey Challenge Director Industrial Decarbonisation	United Kingdom	Industrial Decarbonisation Industrial Strategy Challenge Fund

	Challenge UK Research and Innovation		
40	Dr. Sunita Satyapal Director, Hydrogen and Fuel Cell Technologies Office, and the Department of Energy Hydrogen Program Coordinator US Department of Energy Dr. Jennifer Arrigo Director, Science and Energy Crosscuts Office of the Under Secretary for Science and Innovation US Department of Energy Devinn Lambert Deputy Director, Science and Energy Crosscuts Office of the Under Secretary for Science and Innovation US Department of Energy	United States	Hydrogen Shot Energy Earthshots™

Annex F. Composition of the OECD MOIP Steering Group

This report and all CSTP MOIP work since 2019 benefited from the support of a project steering group composed of experienced mission policy makers and experts. The composition of this group as of October 2024 is presented in Table F1.

Table F.1. Composition of the OECD MOIP Steering Group

Australia	**Amelia Olsen-Boyd**, Executive Manager, Mission Innovation and Strategy, CSIRO
Austria	**Brigitte Weiss**, Sector EU Coordination in Innovation Policy, Austrian Federal Ministry of Climate Action, Environment, Energy, Mobility, Innovation and Technology **Christian Naczinsky**, Head of the Department for EU and OECD Research Policy, Austrian Ministry of Education, Science and Research, Directorate General for Scientific Research and International Affairs
Czechia	**Tomáš Holinka**, Head of Smart Specialization Strategy (S3) Unit, Ministry of Industry and Trade of the Czech Republic **Lenka Parikova**, Ministry of Industry and Trade of the Czech Republic
Finland	**Kirsti Vilén**, Ministerial Adviser, Ministry of Economic Affairs and Employment, Skills, Innovations and Renewal, Innovations and Enterprise Department **Christopher Palmberg**, Senior Director, Strategic Insight, Business Finland
France	**Ralf Engel**, Chef du Département des Politiques et Actions Transverses, Service de la Stratégie de la Recherche et de l'Innovation, Ministère de l'Enseignement Supérieur et de la Recherche
Germany	**Professor Jakob Edler**, Executive Director, Fraunhofer Institute for Systems and Innovation Research ISI, and Professor of Innovation Policy and Strategy, Manchester Institute of Innovation Research **Ralf Lindner**, Head of the Competence Center Politics and Society, Fraunhofer Institute for Systems and Innovation Research ISI
Japan	**Tateo Arimoto**, Principal Fellow, Japan Science and Technology Agency, Center for Research and Development Strategy **Kazuhito Oyamada**, Japan Science and Technology Agency, Center for Research and Development Strategy
Korea	**Byeongwon Park**, Director of Center for Strategic Foresight, Science and Technology Policy Institute
Netherlands	**Marjolein van Splunder,** Senior Policy Advisor Energy Innovation, Ministry of Economic Affairs and Climate **Lara Engelfriet**, Senior Policy Advisor Green Chemistry & Circularity, Ministry of Economic Affairs and Climate
Norway	**Philip Lorentzen**, Special Adviser, Research Council of Norway (RCN)
Sweden	**Goran Marklund**, Deputy Director General and Head of Strategic Intelligence, Vinnova
European Union	**Marion Jamard**, Policy Officer, European Commission, DG Research and Innovation **Neville Reeve**, Former Senior Policy Analyst, European Commission, DG Research and Innovation

Annex G. List of Net zero mission case studies

This report's analyses were mainly based on 17 net zero mission case studies. This annex presents an overview of each mission and the MOIP initiatives to which they belong.

Table G.1. List of Net zero mission case studies

	Basic information
CSIRO Team Australia Missions (Australia)	
CSIROH2-AU	The **Commonwealth Scientific and Industrial Research Organisation (CSIRO) Missions programme initiative** was launched in 2020 as a way to focus collective responses to key national challenges, identified through trend modelling and forecasting, that would allow Australia to better coordinate research and translation activities across the national innovation system, anticipate industry trends, be alert to where future issues could arise, position Australia to leverage opportunities to create new industries and jobs, capitalise on existing global advantages, and foster major science and technology breakthroughs. The missions are developed/ co-created in partnership with industry, research organisations, government and communities and aim to accelerate post COVID 19 recovery, create new jobs, stimulate the economy, and build long-term resilience. While the missions are initiated by CSIRO, a leading research organisation in Australia, to increase the strategic integration of its various centers, they also aim to bring together towards common goals all the relevant actors within and outside CSIRO, in line with policy priorities. Each mission defines its own agenda based on interactions between the different partners. The activities expand beyond research. **The Towards Net Zero Mission** looks to build the innovation system coherence, capability and directionality to allow Australia's hard to abate sectors to reduce emissions by 50% by 2035 and in doing so generate environmental, societal and regional benefits. The mission focuses on three core activities: firstly roadmapping and system orientation to guide investment action and drive coordinated action; secondly institutional strengthening to build capacity for coherence and inclusivity and to bring knowledge of the current and future technology landscape into funding and policy decision making; and thirdly building coalitions to build demonstrator systems. At an overarching level the Mission is co-creating with system actors a net zero transition monitoring, evaluation and learning framework to enhance system reflexivity. Because the Mission is convened in CSIRO it is able to send strong signals back into the foundational science parts of the organisation (and into the wider innovation system) on the research direction saliency and on future capability needs that are being surfaced through mission core activities. Having built national transition roadmaps for the low emissions steel, sustainable aviation fuel and agriculture sectors the mission is now scoping demonstrator systems such as a green steel hub, working with finance to develop $100M concessional loan products for net zero farm financing, and designing SAF feedstock demonstrator systems. The Mission is supported by an estimated $AUD88m in CSIRO investment and $310m in investment from national innovation system partners, including government, industry and the research sector. **The Hydrogen Industry Mission** is supported by $100 million in investment from from CSIRO, with contributions of $110 million from industry partners and the Australian Government. The mission is helping to build Australia's clean hydrogen industry by scaling demand and driving down hydrogen costs to deliver a secure and resilient energy system and support our transition to a low emissions future. Additionally, it also intends to create more than 8000 jobs and generate $11 billion a year in GDP and help to position Australia to lead the world in exporting hydrogen by 2030. Among the supported activities are a Hydrogen Knowledge Centre, a national resource for industry, government, and the research community which highlights Australia's hydrogen projects and provides modelling tools and educational resources. In partnership with National Energy Resources Australia, there is also the Hydrogen Technology Cluster Australia, to accelerate the hydrogen supply chain development by enabling connection, collaboration, and alignment of action; HyCapability, a hydrogen capability finder to connect Australian hydrogen businesses with a domestic and global market; and HyResource, a repository of core information around projects, policies and key organisations involved in the research, development and deployment of clean hydrogen as a low-emissions energy source.
Austrian Transition Missions (Austria)	
NM-COT	**Mission Climate-neutral City** By creating innovation spaces, the mission "Climate-neutral city" supports Austrian cities in accelerating the necessary transformation for a climate-neutral future. 10 large pionieer cities (>50.000 inhabitants) and 50-70 small pionieer cities (10.000-50.000 inhabitants) will be go large steps towards climate neutrality by 2030. Austria has an ambitious goal: the country is to become climate-neutral by 2040 - this requires fundamental changes in framework conditions, economy and society. Cities play a central role here. The Austrian Ministry for Climate Action will conclude partnership contracts with the

	10 large pionieer cities. As part of the "Climate-neutral city" mission, pioneer cities show exemplarily how strategies and measures must be targeted to implement climate neutrality in cities and municipalities. The mission also fosters learning environments for cities and promotes the development of innovative solutions, which can also be used and further developed by other cities and municipalities. The focus is on the demonstration of climate-neutral districts and holistic solutions for the energy and mobility transition as well as the circular economy for the realization of a future climate-neutral city. The Mission was established in 2021. The Austrian Ministry for Climate Action allocates 2023-2026 (RTI PAKT PERIOD) 20 Million Euro per year towards the mission for climate neutral city. **Mission Energy transition** In terms of a mission-oriented innovation policy, the energy transition is anchored in the Austrian Ministry for Climate Action as an RTI focus. The interdisciplinary approach includes all RTI topics (space applications, mobility system, production, digital technologies) and provides an impact-oriented mix of instruments for implementation. The follow three impact pathways are set: Successful energy transition in Austria The energy transition requires major changes in the energy system, but also all around and within the economic system. We therefore need interdisciplinary and intersectoral developments of technology-based solutions to transform the Austrian energy and economic system towards climate neutrality. The RTI missions and innovation goals formulated in the implementation plan for the energy research initiative in the national energy and climate plan (NEKP) serve as guidelines. Successful Austrian players in global value creation cycles With the FTI focus on energy transition, the innovative power and competence of Austrian actors for contributions to the energy transition is being expanded and their contributions integrated into international value chains. Future competence in the RTI system In addition, the development of strategic competence for future developments in the field of energy innovation in research, business and administration is being promoted. We are thus making a significant contribution to Europe's technological sovereignty. The Mission was established in 2021. The Austrian Ministry for Climate Action allocates 2024-2026 (RTI PAKT PERIOD) 30 Million Euro per year towards the mission Energy Transition. **Mission Mobility Transition** The Austrian Ministry for Climate Action, Environment, Energy, Mobility, Innovation and Technology (BMK) supports the transformation towards a sustainable, climate-neutral and inclusive mobility and transport system. The cross-cutting topic of mobility affects a wide range of areas of life and politics, such as spatial planning, health, infrastructure, propulsion technologies, behavioural sciences and logistics. To mobilize actors from such diverse fields for mission-oriented innovation policies, the search for solutions to concrete problems in concrete spatial or systemic contexts must be in the foreground. The mobility transition not only ensures quality of life and supply in changing economic and ecological conditions, it also increases competitiveness, employment and international demand for Austrian innovations. The strategic framework for this is provided by the Research, Technology and Innovation (RTI) Mobility Strategy with impact-based measures such as the targeted allocation of RTI funding, forging alliances and implementation partnerships, the facilitation of exploration spaces as well as, European and international positioning. This results in the necessary technological, social and organizational innovations in the field of urban and regional mobility, digitization and technology development for a sustainable transformation of the mobility system. The Mission was established in 2021. The Austrian Ministry for Climate Action allocates 2024-2026 (RTI PAKT PERIOD) 30 Million Euro per year towards the mission Mobility Transition. **Mission Circular Economy** With the mission "Austria on the way to a sustainable and circular society", the Austrian Ministry for Climate Action, Environment, Energy, Mobility, Innovation and Technology (BMK) is pursuing the goal of anchoring the circular economy across all disciplines. This approach incorporates all RTI topics and provides an impact-oriented mix of instruments for implementing circular economy. Circular economy requires system changes around and within the economic system. In the past, innovations often took place in 'silos' and were optimized for a specific aspect of the product or material. While these innovations brought improvements in one area, they often weakened value creation in other, usually downstream stages of the value chain. For this reason, there is a need for systemic innovations that create value for both the actor(s) and the system as a whole. The fundamental transformation of the economic system to a circular economy can only succeed through systemic and holistic research and development. This requires developing radically new solutions and successfully establishing them on the market. The future circular use of resources will consist of interconnected subsystems, which requires the interaction of a multitude of technologies, innovations and actors. The Mission was established in 2021. The Austrian Ministry for Climate Action allocates 2024-2026 (RTI PAKT PERIOD) 30 Million Euro per year towards the mission Circular Economy.
National Research Council Challenge (Canada)	
MCF-CA	**The Materials for Clean Fuels Challenge Program** is part of the Collaborative Science, Technology and Innovation Program (CSTIP) of the National Research Council Canada (NRC). Announced in 2019, CSTIP supports innovation across 'superclusters' (areas of intense business activity made up of companies, academic institutions and not-for-profit

	organisations that boost innovation and growth in a particular industry) and mission-oriented Challenges targeting beneficial disruptive technologies. The Challenges aim to generate partnerships among private and public sectors, academic and other research organisations in Canada and abroad to advance transformative, high-risk, high-reward research that address Canadian priorities. It brings together researchers and facilities from across the NRC's 14 research centres, with academic and industrial partners, and are coordinated through program-specific management boards, executives, with support from relevant external Advisory Boards. The Program has CAD 150 million, with CAD 30 million per year ongoing to fund NRC researchers and their innovative partners from higher education institutions and businesses on multi-party R&D programmes. An additional CAD 15 million in funding will address R&D needs in the fight against COVID-19. Under the jurisdiction of a Program Team and the guidance of an Advisory Committee comprised of 'clean technology' professionals, **the Materials for Clean Fuels Challenge program** aims to develop transformative technologies for the sustainable transition of Canada's energy and chemical industries to a low-carbon economy through materials innovation. Canada's commitment to the Paris Agreement includes a national target of reducing 716 megatons of carbon dioxide emissions per year to reach its goal of net-zero emissions by 2050. The mission focuses on developing and demonstrating climate change mitigation technologies related to transportation and energy generation for use in industry and the transport sector. The program has three areas, related to carbon dioxide conversion into renewable fuels and chemical feed stocks such as syngas and ethylene; industrial-scale hydrogen conversion, to support new technologies that can produce hydrogen for industrial use; AI-accelerated materials discovery incorporating diverse areas such as robotics, artificial intelligence, and high-throughput experimentation to accelerate the discovery of new catalyst materials. It is supported by new infrastructure development by the NRC, specifically a new national facility to accelerate materials discovery and dedicated computing facilities and in operando catalyst equipment.
Innomission (Denmark)	
GM-CCSU	The political decision to launch four 'green missions' was made in 2020 as part of the Green Research Strategy. They focus on capture and storage or use of CO_2, green fuels for transport and industry (Power-to-X, etc.), climate and environment friendly agriculture and food production, and circular economy. Through these missions, Denmark aims to invest in mission-driven green research and innovation partnerships that can contribute to two overarching goals: 1. 70% reduction in greenhouse gas emissions in Denmark by 2030 and net zero emissions in 2050 and to strengthen the environment and nature; 2. increased competitiveness for Danish business and industry. Since then, the Danish government has set even more ambitious goals: Net-zero by 2045 and net-negative (110%) in 2050. The Missions focus on the thematic areas of high priority, ascertained through an assessment of where new solutions are needed to reduce greenhouse gas emissions and to best exploit opportunities for Danish research and business. Each mission operate in two steps: 1. a call for 'Innomission-roadmaps' where all relevant actors are invited to develop a sociotechnical back-track roadmap from 2050, which describes challenges and shortcomings within the mission, positions of strength and potential and outlines key activities and relevant work stream themes for future partnerships; 2. Following a selection of the roadmaps proposed in step 1, a call for partnerships to implement the roadmaps. The INNOmission partnerships started in the middle of 2022. The **Mission for Carbon Capture and Storage and Utilisation** aims to develop and demonstrate sustainable solutions and value chains to benefit socio-economic development and the environment. In line with a broader goal to reduce Denmark's greenhouse gas emissions by 70 percent by 2030, this mission, in 2030-40, harness the potential to capture, store, or use the order of 4-9 mill. t. from Danish CO_2 emissions, make CO_2 capture cheaper, to better support the development of cost-effective, safe and environmentally responsible infrastructure for the transport and storage of CO_2, and leverage Danish research environments to build a base where Danish businesses are able to store CO_2 from other countries and position themselves well to exploit this growing market. The mission seeks on the following potential future applications, such as the capture CO_2 from point sources or the atmosphere; application of CO_2 to climate-neutral products; storage of CO_2; materials for transport and industry; intelligent solutions for integration of RE in relation to CCUS; cost-effective renewable energy technologies for CCUS. Activities to generate these possible future applications is devised through the advent of a roadmap, whereby diverse partners come together to collaborate and mutually agree on a course of action. It is a way of coordinating missions that balances directionality (as distinct from historical bottom-up approaches to innovation) with collaboration.
Horizon Europe Missions (European Union)	
EU-CNSC	**The European Union's Horizon Europe's Missions** make EUR 1.9 billion available for the period 2021-23 to implement five missions on the following themes: adaptation to climate change including societal transformation, cancer, climate-neutral and smart cities, healthy oceans, seas, coastal and inland waters, and soil health and food. This mission-oriented turn came about through the design of the latest Framework Programme Horizon Europe, shifting away from individual calls and moving toward large-scale research and innovation missions which encompass an entire portfolio of activities. These missions have been chosen because they require a systemic, cross-disciplinary, cross-sectoral and cross-policy approach to research and innovation. With a budget of EUR 360 million for the period of 2021-2023, the **Climate-Neutral and Smart Cities Mission** has the objective of delivering at least 100 European climate-neutral and smart cities by 2030 and ensuring that these cities also act as experimentation and innovation hubs for others to follow, to enable all European cities to become climate-neutral by 2050. Each EU Mission has its own respective Mission Board, comprising up to 15 experts coming from diverse fields like innovation, business, science, farming, civil society, communications and media. The Board is responsible for advising the Commission on the design and implementation of the Mission. In accordance with the Implementation Plan seven Specific Objectives have been identified: to develop and support a 'demand-driven' and city-focused process to aid preparation of

	Climate City Contracts; support Research and Innovation pilots and demonstrators within the Mission Platform to scale-up and replicate solutions developed in past R&I programmes; develop synergies and complementarities and facilitate mutual support with existing Commission initiatives; provide access to city administrations and their local businesses to EU-wide skills and expertise and help cities connect in international networks; help cities develop the administrative, financial; and policy capacity through innovative governance; establish a system of measuring and monitoring the progress towards climate neutrality for cities; increase the level of assistance from national, regional and local authorities as well as from NPBs, municipal banks and private sector investment, through regulatory, funding and financing levers to help cities implement the mission.
Flagship Programs (Finland)	
FP-FI	Launched in 2018, the Finland's **Flagship Program** initiative aims to create solutions to societal challenges, develop new business opportunities, and contribute to sustainable growth. The Programs have a long-term plan for eight years, developed in collaboration with business, industry and society. Programs are comprised of a series of calls to implement the plan. The budget for 10 Flagships from the first and second calls have a budget of EUR 500 million (funded by the host organisations including seven universities, five research institutes, Helsinki Hospital and the Finnish Red Cross Blood Service). This budget was supplemented in 2020 with an extra EUR 25 million to fund new Flagships. The **Atmosphere and Climate Competence Center (ACCC) Flagship** constituted by the University of Helsinki, Tampere University, University of Eastern Finland and the Finnish Meteorological Institute. It addresses climate change and deteriorating air quality. Its objectives are to provide state-of-the-art scientific knowledge on these two themes, establish a platform (ACCC Service Portal) to collect big data from comprehensive observations and multi-scale models to be delivered to various stakeholders, co-create science-based solutions for guiding the world toward climate neutrality, and establish international and interactive atmospheric research-business innovation ecosystem in Finland. It coordinates its work via two Research Programs (focused on quantifying and activating the potential of land-based climate change mitigation and quantifying the air quality climate interactions), one Impact Program (that connects and tests the economic and social impact of the research results generated through the research programs) and 13 Impact Tasks that will maximise the interaction between the research communities, businesses, policy, and societal sectors.
Growth Engines (Finland)	
GE-FI	Launched in 2018, Finland's **Growth Engines initiative** aims to disrupt global markets and create new growth sectors by supporting the development and maintenance of innovation ecosystems. These ecosystems aim to generate over 1-billion-euro new business, exports and investments in Finland through the activation of growth-oriented businesses from different industries, research organisations, public actors and end customers, attracting innovation activities of foreign companies to Finland, and inaugurating new Public-Private Partnerships. Growth Engines are typically funded in two-year periods, for a maximum of ten years. The **GreenE2 Growth Engine** looks to develop a new broad-based innovation ecosystem to serve as the foundation for substantial new business in the field of Power-to-X, for the utilization of hydrogen and carbon dioxide and the reform of value chains regarding green electrification using hydrogen. Foreseen applications include green hydrogen in the hydrogen production industries and green technologies and e-products such as new forms of chemicals and fuels. It is coordinated by a funded platform company, CLIC Innovation, which is a public partnership that orchestrates large companies, research organisations, public institutions, small and medium-sized enterprises with Business Finland's support to focus on areas such as RDI projects, influencing the regulatory landscape, identifying areas for current and future education needs, development of international cooperation, new markets, and market shaping. The mission uses various policy instruments to aid implementation, including those which support social innovation, such as the 'Citizen Science Initiative', which enables the general public to contribute to problem definition, data collection and analysis in climate science and the 'Climate University', a network of 11 universities in Finland coordinated by University of Helsinki, developing climate change and sustainability education in higher education to educate people to bring climate change awareness and sustainability into their working lives.
France 2030 Stratégies Nationales d'Accélération (France)	
StratAc1-FR	**Acceleration strategies (Ass)** are a new instrument of the so-called 'directed logic' of the Investments for the Future programme (PIA) – launched by the French government in 2010 and now integrated in the French recovery plan (France 2030). One of the key objectives of Ass is to provide support to specific technology areas via integrated support across all stages of the innovation chain, from exploratory research to market deployment. Each strategy has its own structure of governance, with a dedicated interministerial coordinator. **The carbon-free hydrogen AS** has set targets for 2030, including the installation of a carbon-free hydrogen production capacity of 6.5 GW by electrolysis, the saving of more than 6 Mt of CO_2 and the creation of 50,000 to 150,000 direct and indirect jobs in France. The task of the coordinator is to lead the interministerial coordination and monitoring of all the actions implemented using a rather broad collectively developed roadmap as guideline. The Carbon free Hydrogen AS has a budget of EUR 3.4 billion during the period 2020-2023, and EUR 7 billion are planned until 2030. The Strategy covers all aspects related to the establishment of a hydrogen value chain from research to production, pipelines and markets. The Acceleration Strategy also aims to develop key technologies and components through pilot projects for different types of usages and markets.
StratAc2-FR	**The Industry Decarbonisation Acceleration strategy (AS)** is one of the more than 20 Ass launched by the French government (see above the carbon-free hydrogen AS). Based on a strategy co-developed with the different actors (various public authorities, research, industry, etc.), the AS aims to ensure the emergence of a competitive French offer of industrial decarbonisation solutions. The AS, for instance, supports breakthrough and incremental innovation; initiates large-scale

	demonstration of decarbonisation solutions; the industrialisation of equipment in France and their distribution on the market; promotes low carbon industry products public procurement and eliminate regulatory obstacles to decarbonisation; creates and strengthens the training offer relevant to the challenges of industry decarbonisation
Research Ireland's Challenge Programmes (Ireland)	
SFIIP-IR	Research Ireland launched the **Challenge Programmes**, a Challenge Funding Programme in 2018 to support the development of novel, potentially disruptive, technologies to address significant societal challenges and to amplify the country's innovation capabilities to create sustainable, equitable and innovation-led growth. The Programme's challenge-based funding approach allows it to be wholly focused on solutions, providing the necessary scale to advance solutions to societal and economic challenges including Irish and European national missions, the UN Sustainable Development Goals, and specific technological and cross cutting challenges. The initial streams of funding focused on challenges related to zero emissions, AI for societal good, plastics, food and the SDGs. **The Zero Emissions Challenge** had a budget of €5.7M and supported the advent of disruptive solutions that accelerate progress towards net-zero greenhouse gas emissions in Ireland by 2050. The mission is implemented through a stage-gated competitive challenge to identify and develop a field ready prototype. The challenge process is comprised of a concept phases, wherein teams develop the feasibility and viability case for their concept, a seed phase wherein five the top concepts are funded to undertake further stakeholder engagement and collaborative co-development towards a field-ready prototype, then finally a prize, where the winning team will finalise and implement their plan for solution deployment with a view to demonstrating the solution within two years. The implementation of the mission prioritises the generation of many multiple, possible solutions to a problem in a bottom-up way and puts a heavy emphasis on the social dimension of the mission, encouraging interaction between mission teams and their respective stakeholders and beneficiaries. The winner of this particular challenge prize was 'Farm Zero C', a climate-neutral farm (to be demonstrated in Shinagh Farm in Cork) to achieve net-zero emissions by 2027 with the plan being to extend the strategy to a further 5000 farms within five years. In partnership with dairy producer Carbery Group, Farm Zero C will test using renewable energy that reduces greenhouse gas emissions, planting different types of grasses and clovers on pastures and supporting hedgerows to boost biodiversity and soil health, changing livestock feed can affect how much methane gas they produce, and how a mobile app will help wider deployment by integrating farm and satellite data, habitat mapping and natural capital accounting, to provide users with information on the carbon footprint of their activities and to develop strategies to reduce these. More recently, and building on earlier approaches, Research Ireland has implemented a large-scale initiative -**The National Challenge Fund** – which is a €65M research fund that provides ambitious researchers with the chance to make a difference by developing solutions to key challenges in the areas of Green Transition and Digital Transformation. The National Challenge Fund was established under the Irish Government's National Recovery and Resilience Plan (NRRP)funded by the EU's Recovery and Resilience Facility. The fund comprises eight individual challenges and will fund more than 95 research teams with initial awards of up to €250k for 18 months, with teams competing for eight prize awards of up to €2M. Green Transition challenges include 2050 Challenge, Energy Innovation Challenge, Healthy Environment for All Challenge, Sustainable Communities Challenge and Future Food Systems. Digital Transformation challenges include the Future Digital Challenge, Digital for Resilience Challenge and the OurTech Challenge.
Moonshot Research and Development Program (Japan)	
MRDP-J	**The Moonshot Research and Development of Program** supports high risk, high impact R&D projects. It has three Target Areas which relate to: harnessing diversity through techno-social transformation to create an innovative and sustainable society, recovery for global environment and growth of civilisation, exploring frontiers with science and technology. In turn, these are supported by visions and goals. It is overseen by the Council for Science, Technology and Innovation, covering the whole program except for Moonshots related to health which are supervised by the Headquarters for Healthcare Policy. Both headquarters are supported by the Strategy Council which comprises industry leaders, relevant ministries, academics and the executive members of the Council for Science, Technology and Innovation. As of 2018, the program has a five year fund of Yen 100 billion to which a further 15 billion was added in 2019. The mission on the **Realisation of Sustainable Resource Circulation to Recover the Global Environment by 2050** aims to develop solutions to global warming and environmental pollution problem through the realisation of sustainable resource circulation for the global environment. It is overseen by the Moonshot Programme, New Energy and Industrial Technology Development Organisation which implements challenging R&D to accomplish Moonshot Goal 4 and realises the R&D concept formulated by the Ministry of Economy, Trade and Industry (METI). The mission's targets include having prototypes/ pilots for circulation technology for GHG and technology in which environmental harmful substances are converted into valuable or harmless materials. By 2040, to have several small markets for the resources circulation technology and global commercial plans and products for circulation technology. In terms of the portfolio management for the implementation, the Program Director constructs a program portfolio by combining multiple projects in consideration of their level of ambition, feasibility, and potential for impact, and also manages and supports the overall program. In the portfolio, there exists four types of projects together which are aimed to achieve the final goal. This allows the program to select projects according to their level of progress, moving progressive to 'spin out' one research result to the next stage, at a time.
Mission-driven Top Sectors and Innovation Policy (The Netherlands)	
MDTPS-NE	Introduced in 2011, the **Dutch Top Sectors Policy** covers research, higher education and innovation through a new form of public-private collaboration. It is structured around nine sectoral areas integral to the Dutch economy: agriculture, horticulture, logistics, high tech systems and materials, life sciences and health, chemicals, creative industry, energy, water. It sets ambitious goals to challenge entrepreneurs and scientists to develop pioneering solutions and contribute to the

	competitiveness of the Netherlands. A Steering Committee takes carriage of the overall horizontal and vertical coordination and monitoring of the whole Top Sector policy, with each Top Sector managed by its own respective Top Team and Advisory Board, supported by their relevant Consortium for Knowledge and Innovation Boards, which develop and implement their strategic agenda. In 2018, it was reformed to become the Mission-driven Top Sectors and Innovation Policy structured along several societal challenges and 25 missions to which the Top Sectors must jointly contribute. **The Carbon free Built Environment by 2050** mission seeks to reduce dependence on natural gas and increase development and uptake of sustainable resources in local energy consumption. It targets achieving a CO2 free built environment in 2050, requiring a 3.4 Mton CO 2 reduction in 2030, disconnecting 30,000-50,000 existing houses per year from the natural gas infrastructure by 2021, and 200,000 existing houses per year before 2030; making 1.5 million houses and 15% of utility buildings and societal real estate natural gas free by 2030, as well as making at least 20% of local energy consumption (incl. EV) within the built environment from sustainable energy production. As with other Top Sector missions, it has a Top Team and Advisory Board and, notably, the Ministry of Interior (BZK) is actively engaging with the Mission Team since this ministry has committed itself to the goals such as making large amounts of natural gas-free and sustainable houses already within a few years. To implement this mission, a new policy instrument named 'Mission-oriented research, development and innovation (MOOI)'. Was developed. It requires the multidisciplinary consortia of at least three organisations (including small and medium-sized enterprises and stakeholders concerned with/affected by the usage of the solution) to submit plans proposing integrated solutions rather than individual technologies for tackling the mission. Through integrating the policy mix in this area, the mission aims to develop technologies that can transform the construction sector.
Pilot E (Norway)	
PE-NO	Launched in 2016, the **Pilot E** initiative brings together Norwegian research and innovation support agencies (the Research Council, Innovation Norway, and Enova). This new form of cooperation and coordination aims to fast track the development, testing, and deployment of new solutions that are able to produce tangible results in a given timeframe, while still allowing for the exploration of different options to contribute to emission reductions both in Norway and internationally, address challenges of national relevance through different 'calls for proposal'. A Steering Board gathers representatives of the three agencies and the Pilot-E programme working group to decide on the overall plan for the scheme, the theme, and content of the calls. OECD has grouped a number of individual Pilot E calls under the title of **'Green Shipping'** due to their thematic similarity, thereby effectively terming them a mission. This mission seeks to reduce emissions from domestic shipping by promoting the development of low- and zero-emission solutions for all vessel categories, for example by making a third of car ferries use electric propulsion systems, in a way that will positively contribute to the target of reducing Norway's emissions by 80–95 % compared with 1990. Cumulatively, the calls that comprise this mission Integrate their relevant innovation and value chains to create solutions for the maritime transport sector.
Challenge Driven Innovation Initiative (Sweden)	
CDII-SW	Sweden's **Challenge Driven Innovation**, initially launched in 2011, supports research and innovation in areas relevant to four key societal challenges. The focus was initially on four key challenges: the future of healthcare, sustainable attractive cities, information society 3.0, and competitive production. The initiative was born out of the Lund Declaration, stating that European research policy and STI activities should move toward addressing societal challenges (and away from rigid thematic approaches) better engage global, public and private stakeholders, and (as a process) be 'owned' by the European Union, but involving the alignment of national initiatives. The Challenge Driven Innovation program was a way for Sweden to decrease fragmentation in operational focus and resourcing and better embrace user/ demand driven innovation initiatives, while also developing solutions that are internationally marketable, drive foreign investment, and ultimately contribute to green and socially sustainable growth. Research and innovation projects were funded through a stage-gated implementation approach, Step 1 – Initiation, focusing on developing the idea, Step 2 – Collaboration between actors, testing the innovative solutions and Step 3 – Implementation, focusing on implementing the results in a larger scale. When the UNs adopted the sustainability development goals in 2015 the focus for Challenge Driven Innovation was broadened to include all 17 sustainability development goals of Agenda 2030. As part of the initiative's focus on competitive production, the **Innovation Platform for Textile Sorting (Siptex)** established a fully automated industrial scale textile sorting facility to produce quality assured recycling products for fibre-to-fibre recycling. Automated sorting is currently the missing link between collection of textiles and high-quality textile recycling, and Siptex aimed to bridge that gap. The Siptex facility works by using near-infrared (NIR) and visual spectroscopy (VIS) to sort textile waste by fibre type and colour. The Siptex project had six impact goals. These are increased circularity in the textile value chain, contribution to availability of raw materials for textile production, established capacities for automated textile sorting in Europe, functioning markets for recyclable textiles, established 'eco system' of actors along the textile value chain, and implemented policies for more circular textile flows and strategies for safe use of recycled textile fibres. Through the establishment and operation of the SipTex facility, testing and evaluation of automated sorting of textile waste on an industrial scale was made possible. Knowledge and new insights were gained about opportunities and challenges linked to automated textile sorting. This contributed to the creation of a product range of Siptex sorted textiles of specific fiber content that was developed based on market demand. Knowledge was also gained about the importance of well-functioning textile collection and manual sorting to enable subsequent automatic sorting. The last batch of Step 3 projects in the program Challenge Driven Innovation were funded in the end of 2023 and they will finish in 2026.
Strategic Innovation Programmes (Sweden)	

SIPS-SW	The Swedish **Strategic Innovation Programs** (SIPs) bring together various actors aim to create conditions for sustainable solutions to global societal challenges and international competitiveness. Functionally, SIPs are the implementation of various Strategic Innovation Agendas (SIAs). The SIA initiative ran from 2012 to 2016 and brought together various actors and partners to co-develop common visions and innovation agendas to guide the sustainable growth of emerging cross-sectoral areas. This strategic orientation foregrounded the need to meet societal challenges, create growth, and strengthen Sweden's competitiveness in these areas. To meet these high-level goals, SIPs bring leading actors from business, academia, and the public sector define areas where they see a need for a Swedish pool of forces and provide joint efforts. The initiative gives companies, public activities, as well as universities, colleges and institutes an increased opportunity to collaborate in the implementation of various initiatives. This type of program has allowed Sweden to increase stakeholder networks as well as the participation of unique actors, enhance system level knowledge, and better concentrate and mobilise actors. Starting in 2017, the **Viable Cities SIP** aims to achieve climate-neutral cities by 2030, with a good life for all within planetary boundaries. With a budget of approximately SEK 1 billion to invest in research and innovation over 12 years, nine cities and their partners were selected to act as pioneers in accelerating climate transition in cities. These cities will act as holistic system demonstrators to enable transformative systems change to climate-neutral and sustainable cities using infrastructure that supports new forms of governance and management, citizen engagement, forms of coordination in financing climate investments in cities, policy development and decision-making processes, knowledge support and digital tools, and ways to develop, implement, spread and scale-up new solutions with a focus on impact. Implementation is phased, with a focus on internationalisation to strengthen innovation power and growth opportunities, entrepreneurship to strengthening innovation ecosystems, a 'liquid roadmap' to examine the future direction of the program, and building a learning community. Then, there is the focus on building demonstrators, creating a lab to explore how to create better mission infrastructure and governance, and national cooperation and local mobilisation and financing models. Ultimately, the mission seeks to engender sociotechnological and socio-ecological systems of cities in line with the 2030 Agenda and the Paris Agreement.
Vinnova's pilot missions (Sweden)	
VPM-SW	Arising out of commitments to make Sweden the first fossil-free welfare countries of the world, achieve the UN's Sustainable Development Goals, and participate in EU missions programs, **Sweden's Pilot Missions** uses a mission-oriented innovation process strongly influenced by design thinking across two core themes: Healthy Sustainable Mobility and Healthy Sustainable Food. The objective of the initiative is to drive systems change in key strategic areas, identify and exploit economic development opportunities, and achieve clear societal outcomes. The **Healthy and Sustainable Food mission** was launched in 2020, bringing together Swedish municipalities, school staff, suppliers, food producers and students work together to improve the quality and experience in the system around the school meal (a lever in the broader food system). The development and implementation of the pilot missions is undertaken through a sequence of activities, as a modified form of a classic design approach. Each stage is co-designed with system actors, from public, private and civic sectors, supported by academic and design expertise, and with increasing citizen participation as the process progresses. All of these actors work together simultaneously where possible, and thus the process forms new networks for action along the way. A joint collaboration was formalised, led by the Swedish food agency and included seven other national agencies. Within the mission of "Every child in Sweden eats healthy, sustainable and tasty school food" a portfolio of interventions was formed. For example, innovation management course for the leadership team of the participating organisations, collaboration platform for frontrunning schools, smart policy development projects, and prototypes with potential of system change. The prototype design included stages such as theme selection and framing, prototype development, and the development of system demonstrators. An open invitation was designed for municipalities to join the mission. Four municipalities were selected (Munkedal, Hofors, Vallentuna and Karlstad) and they functioned as development environments to create the sustainable school meal system of the future to test prototypes. The experience from the work can then be used to give all municipalities in Sweden the opportunity, with school meals as a tool, to approach the global sustainability goals and the goals in other sustainability and food strategies.
Industrial Strategy Challenge Fund (United Kingdom)	
ISCF-UK	**The Industrial Strategy Challenge Fund** is a long-term plan to raise productivity and earning power in the UK by harnessing the opportunities of technological change. With a total budget of £4.7 billion over four years, and arising out of the 2017 UK Industrial Strategy, it has four grand challenges focusing on clean growth, ageing society, future of mobility, and artificial intelligence and data economy. Challenges have concomitant missions. The challenge of clean growth has a mission on **Industrial Decarbonisation** which looks to establish the world's first net zero carbon industrial cluster by 2040 (and at least one low-carbon cluster by 2030). The mission focuses on decarbonising six of the most heavily industrialised regions to reduce the carbon footprint of heavy and energy intensive industries in the UK (such as iron and steel, cement, refining and chemicals) and create competitive alternatives that will drive clean growth. The mission has the targets of reducing emissions in 1 cluster to net zero by 2040 (and, in the interim, in four industrial clusters by 2030, that will effectively capture 20-30 MtCO2 across the economy, including 6 MtCO2 of industrial emissions, per year by this interim date). It also seeks to ensure that multiple industrial facilities will already have reduced their emissions, by the greatest possible extent, position UK clusters as top areas for global inward investment and driving demand for low carbon products and technologies by harnessing the power of markets, the public sector, universities and local communities, support up to 54 000 jobs in 2030 in industry, and start to mobilise additional public and private investment of at least £14 billion in industry. The implementation of the mission involved diverse activities across three work streams: deployment (developing engineering studies to decarbonise an industrial cluster, with plans considered through a

	competitive round), cluster plans (successful studies progress to cluster plans that intend to act as a roadmap for the region in question), and the creation of an industrial decarbonisation research and innovation centre (the advent of a virtual multidisciplinary research and innovation centre, which will function as the national focal point and international gateway for UK industrial decarbonisation research and innovation).
Energy Earthshot Initiative (United States)	
EE-US	**Energy Earthshots**[1] seeks to accelerate breakthroughs of more abundant, affordable, and reliable clean energy solutions within the decade to reach 2050 net-zero carbon goals and create the jobs of the new clean energy economy. As an initiative, it drives integrated program development across the U.S. Department of Energy's science and applied energy offices and ARPA-E and corrals the RD&D community to lead science and technology innovation to rapidly advance solutions. As the first mission of this initiative, the **Hydrogen Earth Shot** (Hydrogen Shot™) launched in 2021, aims to accelerate innovations, reduce cost, and spur demand of clean hydrogen. Specifically, it targets reducing the cost of clean hydrogen by 80% to $1 per 1 kilogram in 1 decade ("1 1 1") and the budget contributing to this initiative across DOE in 2022 was approximately USD $250 million. In addition, the Bipartisan Infrastructure Law in the U.S., provided a total of $200 million per year through 5 years (a total of $1 billion), specifically for research, development, manufacturing, and demonstration related to electrolyzers, which would also contribute to Hydrogen Shot. Through coordination across basic science and applied research, development, and demonstration, the mission aims to develop and demonstrate technologies that can help lower the cost of hydrogen, reduce carbon emissions and local air pollution, create good-paying jobs, and provide benefits to disadvantaged communities. These and other hydrogen activities are coordinated within the U.S. Department of Energy Hydrogen Program by the Hydrogen and Fuel Cell Technologies Office (HFTO) within the Office of Energy Efficiency and Renewable Energy. HFTO conducts research, development, and demonstration activities in hydrogen production, delivery, infrastructure, storage, fuel cells, and multiple end-uses across transportation, industrial, and stationary power applications. The program also includes activities in technology validation, manufacturing, analysis, systems development and integration, safety, codes and standards, education, and workforce development. While HFTO focuses on hydrogen production via renewable energy pathways, other offices within the Department of Energy include focus areas on fossil energy with carbon capture and nuclear energy, coordinated through the Hydrogen Program.[2]

Endnotes

[1] www.energy.gov/energy-earthshots-initiative.

[2] www.hydrogen.energy.gov/docs/hydrogenprogramlibraries/pdfs/hydrogen-program-plan-2020.pdf.

www.ingramcontent.com/pod-product-compliance
Lightning Source LLC
Chambersburg PA
CBHW061218240926
51846CB00006B/1273